AF713273

8087/80287/80387 For the IBM PC & Compatibles

Applications and Programming With Intel's Math Coprocessors

Third Edition

Richard Startz

Brady
New York

Copyright © 1983, 1985, 1988 by Brady Books
a division of Simon & Schuster, Inc.
All rights reserved
including the right of reproduction
in whole or in part in any form.

B R A D Y

Simon & Schuster, Inc.
Gulf + Western Building
One Gulf + Western Plaza
New York, NY 10023

Distributed by Prentice Hall Trade

Manufactured in the United States of America

1 2 3 4 5 6 7 8 9 10

Library of Congress Cataloging-in-Publication Data

Startz, Richard, 1952-
8087/80287/80387 for the IBM PC and compatibles : applications and programming with Intel's math coprocessors / Richard Startz.
p. cm.
Includes index.
1. Intel 8087 (Microprocessor)—Programming. 2. Intel 80287 (Microprocessor)—Programming. 3. Intel 80387 (Microprocessor)—Programming. 4. IBM Personal Computer—Programming. I. Title.
QA76.8.I2923S79 1988
005.265—dc 19 88-3936
CIP

ISBN 0-13-246604-X

Other Books by Richard Startz

Working With 1-2-3
Study Guide to Accompany Macroeconomics

CONTENTS

About the Diskette

The diskette, which is available as an option with the book, contains the source code for all the programs listed in The Cookbook. Complete descriptions of the routines appear in the text of the book. The assembler routines can be assembled using Microsoft's Macro Assembler (Version 4.0 and 5.0). The routines are compatible with the following high-level languages: Microsoft QuickBASIC (Version 4.0), FORTRAN (Version 4.0), and C (Version 4.0) and Borland's Turbo Pascal (Version 3.0 and 4.0).

Preface to the Third Edition

The ability of personal computers to crunch numbers continues to grow. Two things have happened since I wrote the second edition. First, Intel has introduced the 387 chip. Second, compilers that really make a math coprocessor scream are now available for several languages. As a consequence of these developments, I've added material on the 387 throughout the book and I've rewritten all the routines so that they can interface with a variety of languages. (Use of interpreted BASIC has pretty much disappeared from this edition.)

A number of people lent a helping hand in putting together this edition. Terry Anderson got the ball rolling as editor at Brady before taking off for Harvard Business School. Intel and Microsoft made hardware and software available and also helped out with technical advice. Marvin Bryan, Ed Conrow, Stephen Randy Davis, and James Hager provided valuable and kind reviews for this revision. Aptech Systems, Inc. (makers of the mathematical programming language Gauss) ran some of the benchmarks for me and helped with 387 debugging. Friends at the University of Washington provided access to a variety of machines for other benchmarks. On a number of occasions, inhabitants of the Microsoft SIG on CompuServe provided much needed aid and comfort. Finally, Meagan Calogeras at Brady did a wonderful job getting things unstuck (over and over again). My thanks to all these folk.

Dick Startz
Seattle, Washington

Preface to the Second Edition

Do you know the two elements required for a publisher to request a new edition of a book? They are:

1. There has to be something new to say.
2. Quite a few people have to have bought the first edition.

Something New

Nearly two years have passed since I finished the manuscript for the first edition of *8087 Applications and Programming*. In that time, use of the 8087 has boomed, and the introduction of powerful new personal computers based on Intel's 286 and 287 chips, notably the IBM AT, has greatly expanded the range of computing available on a desktop.

This new edition of 8087 *Applications and Programming* covers all the news about the 287 coprocessor. The good news for 8087 users is that the 8087 and 287 are about 99.44 percent compatible. (This edition covers the remaining 0.56 percent difference, too.)

For Old Friends

In addition to new material, I've fixed several bugs and typos in the text in program listings. (There were only about half a dozen errors in the first edition, which, to be perfectly honest, left me feeling pretty smug.) Almost all the corrections are due to alert readers. To these friends and helpers around the country, many, many thanks.

Dick Startz
Seattle, Washington

Trademarks

The following trademarks are used in this book:

- IBM, IBM Personal Computer, IBM PC, IBM AT, PS/2 and PC-DOS are trademarks of International Business Machines Corporation
- 8086, 8087, 8088, 186, 188, 286, 287, 386, 387, Numeric Data Processor, and iAPX are trademarks of Intel Corporation. The 8087 and 8088 instruction mnemonics are copyrighted by Intel.
- Microsoft, QuickBASIC, and MS-DOS are trademarks of Microsoft Corporation
- Apple II+ is a trademark of Apple Computer.
- DEC-2060 and VAX are trademarks of Digital Equipment Corporation.
- IMSL is a trademark of IMSL Inc.
- Turbo Pascal is a trademark of Borland International.

Limits of Liability and Disclaimer of Warranty

The author and publisher of this book have used their best efforts in preparing this book and the programs contained in it. These efforts include the development, research, and testing of the theories and programs to determine their effectiveness. The author and publisher make no warranty of any kind, expressed or implied, with regard to these programs or the documentation contained in this book. The author and publisher shall not be liable in any event for incidental or consequential damages in connection with, or arising out of, the furnishing, performance, or use of these programs.

Acknowledgments From the First Edition

I've decided that the only reason a book ever reaches print is that about the time the author runs out of steam someone else comes along and gives the project a boost. At least that's certainly been true for this book.

The people at the Brady Communications Company, editors and staff, have been a pleasure to work with.

Books are reviewed for style and accuracy before going to press. I've been fortunate in having three reviewers make substantial contributions to the final product. Many thanks are due to Peter Norton, Leo Scanlon, and Andy Verhalen.

Intel has been most generous in allowing the use of copyrighted material and in supplying technical information. The authoritative source on the 8087 is Intel's *iAPX 86, 88 User's Manual*, from which I have borrowed liberally.

My wife, Shelly Lundberg, performed a final inspection of the manuscript. As always, I get my best suggestions from my best friend.

Before I let anyone else see the initial manuscript, I sent it to my sister, Barbara Startz, for editing. Barbara knows a little about computers and a great deal about writing. I haven't quite figured out how she found the time to repair my writing after 90 hours a week at her own job, but I'm awfully glad she did.

It should go without saying that all the people named above are entitled to credit for things you like in the book, but that I alone remain responsible for any remaining inaccuracy or awkwardism.

Introduction

Let me explain why I'm excited about the 8087. I've used large computers for many years as a tool for professional research. When I bought my personal computer, I found I could do many things far more conveniently than on these larger machines. But I quickly discovered that my machine wasn't fast enough for large scale numerical computing.

Having an 8087 means that now I can solve many large problems on my personal computer. While some problems still belong on big machines (and always will), my personal computing horizon has expanded tenfold.

The 8087 isn't just fast; it's very easy to use. Whether you are mostly a "program user" or mostly a "program writer," you will find that the 8087 is a remarkable device. I hope you will find *8087/80287/80387 For the IBM PC & Compatibles* an enjoyable, as well as an educational, introduction.

Who Is This Book For?

- People who want to know what the 8087 will do (especially Part I, Chapters 1 and 2).
- People who want to learn how to program the 8087 (especially Part II, Chapters 3–6 and Chapter 10 in Part III).
- People who want prepared programs for number crunching applications on their personal computer (especially Part III, Chapters 7–13).

Part I describes the capabilities of the 8087 at a fairly non-technical level. If you are considering buying an 8087 and want to know about 8087-compatible hardware and software, Part I is for you.

Parts II and III are for the more technically inclined reader. While we "begin at the beginning," some prior programming experience is helpful. You needn't be an expert by any means, but this book isn't an Introduction to Computers.

Part II (Chapters 3–6) provides an in-depth description of the 8087's instructions. We also discuss some of the fundamentals of assembly language for the 8088. We pay special attention to linking assembly language and high-level language programs.

Part III concentrates on applications. We develop many useful 8087 assembly language routines in Part III. You can use these programs as examples, to learn more about 8087 programming, or you can use the programs "cookbook" fashion. (Part III also includes, in Chapter 10, an explanation of some of the 8087's most advanced instructions.

How to Read This Book

I've taken care to write so that you can skip around from one section to the next as suits your mood. Please don't feel constrained to read from beginning to end.

Most readers will probably find Part I informative and easy reading. If you want to write 8087 assembly language programs, concentrate on Part II. (If you are an experienced 8087 programmer, you can skip Part II and move on to the applications in Part III.) If you are interested in applications, but don't care about intimate programming details, read Part III. You can always flip back to Part II if you need to check something.

Finally, you can use the programs here "cookbook" style. You don't need to know why a program was written in a certain way or how it operates internally, if you just want to get a fast answer. Go ahead and use the programs. If a program is useful enough that you want to modify it or write a similar one yourself, you can return later for the "how and why."

The Cookbook

Several chapters begin with an introductory paragraph and then a sign that says

The Cookbook

Under this sign, you will find a list of the programs appearing in the chapter, together with a brief description of the purpose of the program and the input and output required. Use the cookbook when you want to flnd a program in a hurry. We spend quite a bit of time discussing why certain things are done in certain ways. If you want to run programs, but not build your own, you don't need to read the "how and why" material. Do scan the material which describes the information you need to pass to the programs.

Strategic Number Crunching

In addition to a great deal of detail about the 8087 and about numerical programming, this book presents a strategic approach to serious computational work. Our strategy grows from two programming maxims:

- *10 percent of program code accounts for* 90 *percent of program execution time.*
- *The cost of creating a working program is proportional to the square of the length of code, regardless of the power of the programming language being used.*

Serious programmers sometimes go to great effort, mistakenly, to write "efficient programs." A far better strategy is to identify the 10 percent of the code that has 90 percent of the computational burden. Re-write the 10 percent for maximum efficiency; write the other 90 percent for maximum clarity.

The search for efficiency often leads to writing programs in assembly language. Because assembly code can be 10 times the length of equivalent BASIC or FORTRAN code, assembly language programs can be 100 times harder to debug. It (almost) never makes sense to write an entire program in assembly language. It does make sense to code the *critical routines* in assembly language. In this way, we get almost the entire advantage of assembly language speed at a small fraction of the cost of assembly language programming.

We can actually do even better by recognizing that many numerical programming problems use the same underlying subroutines. An 8087 assembly language program to add up an array is somewhat more complicated than a FOR/NEXT loop in BASIC. But we only need to write and debug the 8087 program once. Having done so, using the subroutine over and over is probably easier than writing a FOR/NEXT loop every time we need to add up an array. Computer scientists call this planned reuse of subroutines "modular programming." For an example of the convenience and power of modular 8087 subroutines, take a look at the statistical package in Chapter 12.

You can actually do *even* better. 8087 routines for many numerical computing needs appear in this book (and on the optional diskette). While we hope you decide to learn about all the capabilities of the 8087 and to write your own special subroutines, you're more than welcome to begin by lifting the subroutines bodily from these pages and putting them to use in your 8087-equipped personal computer.

Hardware and Software Requirements

The programs in this book run on computers based on the Intel 8087 Numeric Data Processor and the 8088/8086 family of Intel microprocessors. The family includes the original IBM PC and XT (8088/8087), IBM's PS/2 models 25 and 30 (8086/8087), the IBM AT and PS/2 models 50 and 60 (286/287), IBM's PS/2 model 80 (386/387)—and of course machines from many other manufacturers as well. (The relatively uncommon Intel 188 and 186 cpus, which take 8087 coprocessors, are also family members.) In the interest of brevity, we generally use "cpu" or "8088" to mean any of 8088/8086/188/186/286/386 and "coprocessor" or "8087" to mean any of 8087/287/387, distinguishing between family members only where necessary.

Example programs are in assembly language or BASIC. Almost all the assembly language programs were written and debugged using Microsoft's Macro Assembler (MASM) Version 4.0. A few of the programs require Version 5.0 of the assembler, which is highly recommended in any event. The BASIC programs all run in Microsoft's QuickBASIC, Version 4.0 or later. The programs were tested on a PC Limited 286[8]—a "clone" of the 8 megahertz IBM AT—running PC DOS 3.2. Where not otherwise qualified, all timings refer to this machine-which runs an 8 megahertz 286 cpu together with a 5.33 megahertz 287 coprocessor.

With a few exceptions, all the programs in the book should run on any member of the 8088/8087 family and can be used together with QuickBASIC, Microsoft FORTRAN, Microsoft C, and Borland's Turbo Pascal. Since BASIC remains the lingua franca of personal computing, all high-level language examples are presented in QuickBASIC.

1

Easy, Accurate, and Fast

The 8087-equipped personal computer has three nice features: it's *easy, accurate,* and *fast.* Everything you need to apply 8087 power to practical computational problems is in this book. This first chapter describes the 8087 and its use at the broadest level.

Throughout the book, we try to take a scientific and analytical approach to understanding the 8087. Wherever possible, we discuss general principles—the "why" of programming—along with the hundred-and-one technical details needed to make a computer work. To keep the discussion concrete, each general principle is illustrated with a practical application. The 8087 is powerful, yet easy to use. We hope this book will be occasionally mind-stretching—and fun as well.

How Easy Is Easy?

The 8087 has been designed to emphasize ease of use as much as raw computational power. Your first step as an 8087 user is especially easy. Just add an 8087 to a personal computer and run your programs as usual. (You will need software intended for use with the 8087.) Without any further effort, you can expect to see improvements in execution speed ranging from about 20 percent to as much as a factor of 10.

If you want the maximum advantage from the 8087's hardware power, you will need software specifically designed for the 8087. There is an extended discussion later in the chapter of what to look for—and what to look out for—when purchasing software for the 8087. Here we give a quick overview.

The most important piece of knowledge about 8087 compatible software is really a statement about hardware. The 8087 *extends* the capabilities of existing processors without interfering with the processors' usual operations. Therefore, any software designed "pre-8087" should continue to operate normally when the 8087 is present.

Such 100 percent "upward compatibility" is a great advantage, but it does have a flip side. When you add an 8087 to a system, programs using "pre-8087" software do not speed up at all. For example, you can add an 8087 to the original IBM Personal Computer in a minute or two. (I added one to my computer in order to write the programs for this book.) All your interpreted BASIC programs will run correctly, but no faster. So when we make statements about the speed advantage from adding an 8087, there is also an implicit statement made about using 8087 compatible software.

You should be aware of one potential trap in buying software for use with the 8087. It is possible, though unlikely, that you will get into trouble by mixing software designed to take advantage of the 8087 with pre-8087 software. More on this below.

Assuming you have the versions of BASIC or other programming languages intended for use with the 8087, you can run all your usual programs. Programs that do a great deal of numerical computing will race when compared to pre-8087 performance. If you are a really heavy number cruncher, you will eventually want to use a library of specially written high-speed 8087 subroutines.

Part III of this book (Chapters 7-13) includes the most important subroutines for numerical computing. All you need do is read the explanation of how to use each subroutine, enter them into the computer, and combine them with your BASIC programs. (On the diskette available with this book, the subroutines have been typed in for you.)

Part II of this book (Chapter 3-6) prepares you for the most advanced stage of 8087 use: writing your own subroutines. As you will see in the examples throughout this book, programming the 8087 in assembly language is relatively simple because of the 8087's elegant design. When you've seen the examples and instructions here, you'll have no trouble writing your own special purpose programs.

How Accurate Is Accurate?

Easily written, fast-executing programs are no great trick—if you don't care about getting the right answer. The most important attribute of the 8087 is its remarkable accuracy. The 8087 has three accuracy-enhancing features:

- Internal calculations yield 11 more bits of accuracy than BASIC double precision numbers. That's worth three extra decimal places.
- Internal calculations have an extremely wide range. The 8087 can represent numbers as large as 10^{4932} and as small as 10^{-4932}. As a result, calculations rarely overflow or underflow during intermediate steps. In fact, both the precision and range of numbers are greater than those found on most traditional mainframe computers.
- The 8087 is designed to handle a wide range of error conditions and make an automatic, and graceful, recovery. As a result, simple "paper and pencil" algorithms are much more likely to work. And when something goes wrong, the 8087 follows well-behaved rules instead of producing the wrong answer.

How Fast Is Fast?

Just how fast is an 8087-equipped PC? A good comparison can be made to either a standard mainframe computer or to a microcomputer without an 8087.

Perhaps the most remarkable statement to be made about the 8087 is that it actually makes sense to compare its speed to that of a mainframe computer costing hundreds of thousands of dollars. The 8087 is several times slower than a half million-dollar machine—but then it's more than several times cheaper.

Exact comparisons are always risky, but a few numbers can give you a feeling for the speed of the 8087. Moderate speed mainframe computers require from about one to five microseconds to multiply two numbers. A supermini might require one microsecond. A $25,000 table-top mini might require about 3 microseconds. Efficient 8088 software uses about 400 microseconds to multiply two numbers (about 900 microseconds for double precision). The 8087, which is an inexpensive add-on to a personal computer, uses 20 to 30 microseconds for the same task.

For the very first time, a microcomputer is a cost-effective alternative to number crunching on large computers. The PC with an 8087 has $^1/_4$ to $^1/_{20}$ the speed of a large computer at $^1/_{10}$ to $^1/_{100}$ of the large machine's cost. While large machines will always be more cost-effective than micros for some tasks, the 8087-equipped personal computer is the first micro to compete economically with its larger cousins.

Most PC owners care more about how the 8087 will speed up their personal computing than about comparisons to large central computer facilities. The speed advantage of adding an 8087 to a PC depends on the application and on how you use the 8087. (Having read through this book, you'll know the methods for attaining the greatest possible advantage.) The central point to understand is that the 8087 is a *Numeric Data Processor.* The 8087 only speeds up programs involving numerical computation. If you only use the PC for word processing, the 8087 is about 99 percent irrelevant. But if you crunch the occasional number, adding an 8087 is like trading a sparkler for the Fourth of July fireworks display.

Speed depends on both hardware and software. As a rule of thumb, adding a coprocessor speeds things up by a factor of 5 or 10. Going to a faster machine of a given class (e.g., 6 megahertz AT to 8 megahertz AT) speeds things up both more or less in proportion to the increase in machine speed (e.g., 33 percent). However, for number crunching it's the coprocessor that counts. So an 8 megahertz AT class machine (running its 287 at 5.33 megahertz) is only a moderately faster number cruncher than a 4.77 megahertz PC/XT class machine (which runs the 8087 at 4.77 megahertz. You can figure, very roughly, that 8087 and 287 coprocessors of a given speed give about the same performance. At a given speed, a 387 is about twice as fast as an 8087 or 287.

Real speed requires a combination of good hardware and good software. The author's first computer was an IBM PC running interpreted BASIC. Today, for about the same price as that PC, you can buy a 16 megahertz 386/387 machine runing programs written in assembly language or with an optimizing compiler. *The speed ratio is about a 1,000 to 1!*

What Equipment Do You Need to Use an 8087?

You need an 8087, of course. You can get an 8087 either as part of the original equipment of your personal computer or by adding it to an existing machine, The vast majority of 8088-family machines include a socket in which a coprocessor can be inserted. The 8087 is a single chip rather than a whole board, so adding a coprocessor does not use up a slot. (There are a few machines that lack a coprocessor socket, but for which third parties have developed a method to add coprocessors nonetheless.

If you have any experience working inside your computer, adding an 8087 is easy. You just need to pop the chip into the socket, and (depending on the model) you may need to set a switch. Installing an 8087 requires the same level of "expertise" as installing a new memory chip. As with a memory chip, you have to be careful about static electricity and you also have to be careful not to break one of the little pins on the bottom of the chip. (If you've never installed a chip, the 8087 might not be the one to start with. A small mechanical mistake can ruin a several-hundred-dollar chip.)

We generally use "8087" to refer to any of the 8087/287/387 family. Of course, when it comes to hardware you must use precisely the right member of the family. Further, you should use a chip rated for at least the speed of your machine. A machine based on the 8088, 8086, 188, or 186 requires an 8087. Traditionally, the cpu and coprocessor in these machines run at the same speed. (Table 1.1 shows the Intel part number for the coprocessor chips available circa 1987–88.) Thus an IBM PC or XT requires an "8087," while a PS/2 model 30 requires an "8087-1." Computers based on the 286 cpu require a 287 coprocessor. (The official names for the newer chips are 80286/80287 and 80386/80387, but everyone except Intel drops the "80" prefix.) IBM AT's and clones run the coprocessor at ⅔ the speed of the cpu. Thus the original 6 megahertz AT ran the 287 at 4 megahertz (slower than the PC!) and the coprocessor on the 8 megahertz AT runs at 5.33 megahertz. These machines require a 287-6. The newer PS/2 machines run the cpu and coprocessor equally fast. A PS/2 model 50 or 60 requires a 287-10. Computers based on the 386 usually run the 387 at the same speed as the 386. The 387 is available in 16 and 20 megahertz models, with higher speeds planned for the future.

Actually, the situation with 386-class machines is a little more complicated. The 386 was commercially available before the 387. Planning for this event, Intel built the 386 so that it could work with the 287 as well as the 387. A number of the first 386 machines to reach market were built to use the 287. The sockets for the 287 and 387 are different, so you can't simply plug a 387 into an older machine. The 387 is internally faster than the 287 and is built to run at a higher clock speed. As a ball-park figure, the slowest (16 megahertz) 387 is about three times the speed of the fastest (10 megahertz) 287. Frankly, if you are interested in number crunching, don't burden a state-of-the-art 386 with a 287 coprocessor.

- *There is no advantage to buying a coprocessor with a faster rating than you need.*

Table 1-1. Coprocessor speed ratings.

Coprocessor	*Speed (Mhz)*	*Intel Part Number*
8087	5	8087
	8	8087-2
	10	8087-1
287	6	80287-6
	8	80287-8
	10	80287-10
387	16	80387-16
	20	80387-20

In addition to the standard speeds, various vendors "hand-test" coprocessors and pick out ones that can be run safely above their rated speeds. These high-speed chips are often sold in conjunction with "speed-up" boards. Such boards can be a very cost-effective path to faster number crunching—especially on AT-class machines.

Processors and Coprocessors

The "brain" of any computer is its "cpu," or central processing unit. For the IBM PC, and many other "second generation" personal computers, the "brain" is an Intel 8088. A complete, general purpose central processing unit built into a single chip, the 8088 has a complete instruction set for 8- and 16-bit integer arithmetic, programming logic, and input and output. Like most microprocessors, the 8088 lacks the advanced mathematical instructions found in large, mainframe computers.

The Intel 8087 Numeric Data Processor extends the instruction set of the Intel 8088 by adding sophisticated new mathematical instructions. The 8087 high-speed hardware carries out mathematical operations that would require thousands of lines of code if implemented in software. The 8087 hardware can operate 10 to 200 times faster than equivalent software.

From a programmer's viewpoint, the 8087 adds additional instructions to the 8088's repertoire and makes available additional processor registers. Why not include all the capabilities on one chip, rather than create an add-on device? There are several reasons:

- The 8087 is an extraordinarily sophisticated computational device, including 75,000 transistors on a single chip. Even though the 8087 is "limited" to numerical processing, it is much more complex (and more expensive) than the general-purpose 8088. Building two separate chips holds down development costs and allows users and system manufacturers to tailor-fit systems for different uses.

- The 8088 (and its 16-bit bus sibling, the 8086) were available to the general market for several years before the first delivery of the 8087. In designing 16-bit personal computers, several manufacturers left an open socket, labeled the "coprocessor socket" on the IBM PC, so that machines could be upgraded easily when the 8087 became available.

- Because the 8087 and 8088 are two devices, they execute instructions simultaneously. As a practical programming matter, this means that while the 8087 completes one numerical computation, the 8088 prepares the next.

In the remainder of this chapter, we describe the capabilities of the 8087 in a general way. Chapter 3 provides a much more detailed technical discussion.

Overview of the 8087

The 8087 serves as a *coprocessor* with the 8088. The 8087 "watches" instructions as they are received by the 8088. The 8087 processes its own instructions, while allowing 8088 instructions to pass by. The 8088 also watches all instructions, processing its own, while allowing 8087 instructions to pass by. The 8088 does provide one important service for the 8087. On seeing an 8087 instruction, the 8088 calculates any necessary memory address and makes the address available to the 8087. The 8088 then proceeds immediately to the next instruction. In this way, the coprocessor design allows the 8087 and 8088 to execute instructions simultaneously, thus considerably enhancing total system performance.

The central feature of the 8087's architecture is eight 80-bit data registers. These registers are organized as a classic "pushdown stack," an organizational technique that leads both to fast vector operations and to efficient code generation by high-level language compilers. (Chapter 3 includes an extensive discussion on the operation of the pushdown stack.) The 80-bit register width allows the 8087 to perform extremely accurate calculations. While the 8087 instruction set recognizes seven different data types in memory, all data is automatically converted to an 80-bit internal representation when brought into the 8087. This frees the programmer from most worries about converting between data types.

Instruction Classes

Each of the 8087's 68 instructions fall into one of six classes. (The classification scheme is a convenient way of describing the capabilities of the 8087. You needn't remember the classifications in order to use the 8087.) The six classes are:

Data transfer (discussed in Chapter 4). These instructions move data back and forth between the 8087 and memory and shuffle data internally among the 8087 registers.

Arithmetic (discussed in Chapter 4). At the heart of the 8087 instruction set are the operations for addition, subtraction, multiplication, and division—plus some extras such as square root and absolute value.

Transcendental (discussed in Chapter 10). The 8087 hardware has built-in capabilities for computing logarithms and trigonometric functions. (These instructions are rarely found even on large-scale mainframes.)

Constants (discussed in Chapters 4 and 10). Seven of the most frequently used constants, such as 0, 1, and pi, are built into the 8087.

Comparison (discussed in Chapters 6 and 7). These instructions are used for making less than/equal to/greater than, and other similar tests.

Processor control (discussed in Chapter 12). This class of instructions gives the programmer total control over the behavior of the 8087. Some of these instructions are also used in conjunction with the comparison instructions and 8088 branching instructions to control program flow.

Data Types

The seven regular 8087 data types are examined in depth in Chapter 5. However, for most ordinary 8087 programming considerations, only a few facts are really important. The only data types directly available in BASIC are integer, single precision, and double precision. Generally, only the latter two are used to hold numerical data. If your principal use of the 8087 is scientific programming, you need remember only three facts about data types:

1. *Single precision* numbers (called *short real* in 8087 terminology) have six or seven decimal digits of accuracy and occupy four bytes of memory.
2. *Double precision* numbers (called *long real* in 8087 terminology) have 15 or 16 decimal digits of accuracy and occupy eight bytes of memory.
3. *Temporary real* numbers are used internally by the 8087 for all calculations. They retain better than 18 decimal digits of accuracy. When stored in memory, a temporary real occupies 10 bytes.

If you are primarily a number cruncher, these three data types will probably account for 95 percent of your use. However, the 8087 recognizes four additional data types:

1. *Integer* numbers (called *word integer* in 8087 terminology) occupy two bytes of storage and are used principally to index arrays and other data structures. BASIC and the 8087 use the same representation for integer data.
2. A *short integer* occupies four bytes. While the largest (signed) word integer is 32,768, a short integer can be as large as two billion.

3. A *long integer* occupies eight bytes. A long integer has two or three more digits of accuracy than a double precision real number and can hold values as large as 10^{18}.

4. *Packed decimal* representation is used for business and data processing operations. A packed decimal uses 10 bytes of memory and holds 18 decimal digits. Unlike the three preceding data types, the packed decimal form uses decimal rather than binary representation. Each of the digits 0—9 is represented by four binary bits. These decimal digits are then "packed" two to a byte.

By way of contrast, the types of data recognized by the 8088 hardware are limited to one- and two-byte binary integers and short packed decimal values. All the numerical processing in pre-8087 BASIC and other high-level languages is performed by software created from operations on integers. The 8087 eliminates the need for such software. Not only are 8087-based systems faster, but programs use up much less space and numerical results are more reliable.

How Does My Computer Access the Power of the 8087?

In the next chapter we discuss software for the 8087. In order to understand why some software is 8087-compatible—and why some isn't—it helps to review the basics of the 8088/8087 co-operative set-up.

The instruction set for the 8088 was designed to be extended at a later date. One of the 8088's instructions is called the *escape* instruction. The 8088 knows that the escape instruction really calls for an operation on the 8087, so it essentially ignores this instruction and allows the 8087 to process it. The instructions used by the 8087 are different varieties of the 8088 escape.

When both the 8088 and 8087 are installed, we can think of the combination as one large computer with expanded capability. Software that uses the escape instruction internally must have an 8087 present in order to operate correctly. Software built "pre-8087" simply does not use the escape instruction and therefore does not take advantage of the new capacity.

If you are writing your own programs at the machine language level, you'll know whether or not you've used the escape instruction. Most of the time you use a computer, such intimate internal detail isn't under your control. Next, we discuss some of the varieties of 8087-compatible—and incompatible—software.

Buying and Building 8087-Compatible Software

What special considerations apply when buying or building software for use with the 8087? Your first question will always be, "What software works?" Your second question, "How well?"

Compatibility—The Technical Details

Suppose we could look at a program that had been translated into our computer's "machine language." The program uses either the machine language instructions that drive the 8087, the "escape instructions" mentioned above, or it doesn't. If it doesn't use these instructions, then the 8087 is irrelevant. The program will run with or without an 8087 and will run at the same speed either way. If the program does use 8087 instructions, then the 8087 must be present, of course.

As it turns out, there is a second issue, equally important for compatibility, which hinges on a detail of software design. All computers represent numbers internally as particular patterns of 0's and 1's. Different computers use different patterns for the same number. For the most part, we don't care which pattern the computer uses, since we don't see the individual 0's and 1's anyway. The important thing is that the computer's hardware knows how to interpret its own patterns. (As it happens, the representation used on the 8087 is essentially the new IEEE industry standard. For the curious, we show what the 8087's representation looks like in Chapter 3.)

Until the introduction of the 8087, personal computers based on the 8088 family had hardware for integer arithmetic only. Since there was no hardware "with an opinion" on how non-integers should be represented, each software designer was free to choose his or her own patterns. In practice, this meant that whoever built translators for programming languages (compilers, interpreters, and assemblers) made the decision for everyone using a particular language. Since Microsoft has been the principal supplier of programming languages for 16-bit computers, the vast bulk of software uses the patterns chosen by Microsoft.

Unfortunately, *the Microsoft pattern and the Intel 8087 pattern are different.*

The result of this conflict is that pre-8087 software and 8087-compatible software cannot trade data represented in their respective internal formats. With your 8087 in place, you can safely use either pre-8087 or 8087-compatible software. If you try to combine programs produced with pre-8087 and 8087-compatible translators, you will usually get garbage. Further, if you try to exchange data between such programs you will get garbage if the data was stored using the computer's internal format. If the data is not stored in the internal format, then the programs can probably exchange data. There is no general rule as to whether a conflict will occur between two pieces of software; you need to know the particulars of each program.

There exists one prominent example of automatic translation between Intel 8087 and Microsoft Binary Format. If you use the 8087 version of Microsoft QuickBASIC (Version 3.0 or 4.0) and compile using the "/MBF" switch, QuickBASIC will assume that external files are in Microsoft Binary Format while internal computation is done in 8087 format. (See QuickBASIC (Version 4.0) *Learning and Using QuickBASIC,* page 210, and *Basic Reference Guide,* pp 132-133, 275-276.)

There are three possible scenarios for the interaction between hardware and number formats. First, numbers can be stored in 8087 format and the software uses the 8087. Second, numbers can be stored in 8087 format and the software *emulates* the 8087. Third, numbers can be stored in Microsoft Binary Format or some other non-8087 arrangement, in which case an 8087 can't be used. The different arrangements are useful in different situations.

Suppose we are writing a very heavy-duty, number-crunching program. It might make sense to require the 8087 on the grounds that without a coprocessor the program will simply be too slow to be useful. In this case, we compile or assemble our programs using the 8087 number format and using 8087 instructions. This produces the fastest, and most compact, program possible. The tradeoff is that we limit our market to users who own a coprocessor.

Suppose that it just isn't reasonable to limit our market to 8087 owners. Our next option is to store numbers in 8087 format and write software that uses the coprocessor if one is present and emulates the coprocessor in software otherwise. Microsoft has made this option especially easy if you are programming in QuickBASIC, C, or FORTRAN. Each of these compilers will produce executable programs that automatically try to use an 8087 and go for 8087 emulation only if they can't find one.

Finally, we might ignore the 8087 entirely in our program and just let the software use Microsoft Binary or some other format.

It certainly sounds like choice number two ought to win every time. Isn't 8087-or-emulation the best of both worlds? In fact, there are some tradeoffs. When the cpu has to do floating point arithmetic in software, it spends a great deal of time shifting bits around. A carefully designed number format can speed this up *a lot.* So when Microsoft designed Microsoft binary, or Borland designed the six-byte real of Turbo Pascal, they weren't ignoring the 8087 format out of stubborness or ignorance. Software emulation of 8087 format is *really* slow when compared with the other formats. (However, the 8087 software format is usually somewhat more accurate.) Thus, we might opt for a non-8087 format if only a few users will have a coprocessor. It's interesting to note that in the upgrade from QuickBASIC 3.0 to QuickBASIC 4.0, Microsoft abandoned Microsoft binary in favor of 8087 format. (Functions to translate back and forth between Microsoft binary and 8087 format are supplied.)

Why wouldn't we always choose 8087-or-emulation over 8087 only? Usually, we would! However, there are some arguments against it. First, 8087-or-emulation mode runs a tad slower than 8087 only. Although with the latest versions of the Microsoft compilers the difference is really too trivial to be of concern. Second, 8087-or-emulation programs require extra memory to store the emulator code. Third, you can only get 8087-or-emulation if you're using a language translator equipped to produce this option.

Using Packaged Programs

Packaged programs come in four flavors with respect to 8087 use. These flavors reflect the translation possibilities discussed above. First, some programs just don't touch the 8087. (I'd be a little nervous about a word processor advertising 8087 use!) Second, some programs require an 8087. These are usually very heavy-duty number-crunchers. Third, some programs come in both an 8087 and a non-8087 version. Good examples are Microsoft QuickBASIC (Version 3) and Borland's Turbo Pascal (Version 3). Both of these come with two disks, one with an 8087-only version and one with a non-8087 version. This method gives both 8087 owners and non-owners the fastest possible program, at the expense of having to supply an extra disk. It's worth knowing that the two versions will sometimes give slightly different answers, with the 8087 version generally being more accurate.

Finally, a program may be "8087 optional," meaning it uses the 8087-or-emulator mode discussed above. The most prominent example is Lotus 1-2-3 (Version 2 and later). A note of caution in reading magazine software benchmarks is called for here. Frequently, speed comparisons of a non-8087 program versus an 8087-or-emulator program run in emulator mode (without a coprocessor) are presented. Remember that emulator mode is slow. Even if the non-8087 program looks like a speed winner without the 8087, the 8087-or-emulator might well win by a large margin on your 8087-equipped machine.

Choosing a Compiler or Assembler

Typically, the choice of a language translator revolves around three questions. Which language do you want to use? (An argument that is best evaded here.) How fast is the translator and how good are the associated programming and debugging tools? Which translator produces the fastest executable programs?

Assembly Language

The fastest, most compact, programs are written in assembly language. Sometimes such power is the over-riding consideration. However, an assembly language program typically takes 10 times the number of lines of code as the same program written in a high-level language such as BASIC or FORTRAN. As a result, it'll probably be 100 times harder to debug! All of the assembly language programs in this book are in the form of routines that can be called from a high-level language. For most number crunching, a very small part of the program accounts for almost all the computation time. By using assembly language routines for these few critical lines only, we get nearly all the speed advantage of assembly language and most of the ease of use advantage of a high-level language.

The programs in this book were written for Microsoft's MASM Macro Assembler. Originally assembled using Version 4.0, they were re-assembled using Version 5.0. Execution speed and program size should be all but identical no matter what assembler you use. However, Version 5.0 of MASM includes two important upgrades over earlier Microsoft (and IBM) products. MASM 5.0 supports the 386/387 instruction set. Of greater importance, MASM 5.0 supports Microsoft's wonderful debugger, CodeView. Among its many fine features, CodeView allows you to examine the internal contents of the 8087 between steps in your program. (Earlier debuggers, Debug and Symdeb didn't support the 8087.)

Fast Compilers

Fast compilers such as QuickBASIC and Turbo Pascal provide excellent programming environments and fast compilation. The code they produce is reasonably fast, but not completely suped-up. Depending on the program and the machine, an assembly language routine can beat one of these fast compilers by a factor of 4 to 10. So here we have an obvious candidate for rolling in a few critical assembly language routines.

Optimizing Compilers

An optimizing compiler tries to generate the fastest possible code, at the expense of compilation itself being relatively slow. One of the design goals for the 8087 was to make it easy for compilers to make efficient use of the coprocessor and some of the new compilers do produce quite efficient code. Optimizing compilers for personal computers have improved enormously in the past few years (since the last edition of this book). Microsoft's FORTRAN, Version 4.0 and later, and C, Version 5.0 and later, are good examples of powerful optimizing compilers. In the next chapter, you'll see that these compilers can sometimes generate essentially "perfect" code. By "perfect" we mean that the code is as fast as the best assembly language program. Of course the compilers don't usually do that well. Still, I've found that a good assembly language program rarely beats an optimizing compiler by more than a factor of two.

2

Benchmarks

With the advent of the 8087, moderate-to-large scale numerical computing can now be done on a microcomputer. The 8087 increases the computational range of the microcomputer by one to two orders of magnitude.

The 8087 brings the "minimum-efficient-scale" of computing down to the personal level. In the past, a mainframe computer that cost 100 times more than a personal computer would have been thousands or tens of thousands times faster. While the 8087 remains several times slower than powerful mainframes, an 8087-equipped PC also costs tens or hundreds of times less. So today, the 8087 has made the personal computer a cost effective number cruncher.

Historically, large computers have always been more cost efficient, in terms of raw computational power, than smaller computers. Very large mainframes are more cost efficient than minis; minis are more cost efficient than micros. Just as the advent of "super-mini" computers a few years ago closed most of the gap between minicomputers and mainframes, the 8087 closes most of the gap between personal and minicomputers. To help you draw your own conclusions, speed benchmarks for a range of machines appear below.

Benchmarks can help us both in the choice of hardware and in the choice of a language translator. We present two sets ot benchmarks in this chapter. First, we run a standardized program on several different kinds of hardware. Second, we run programs written using several different translators on standardized hardware.

Naturally, you should remember that benchmark programs provide at best a rough guide.

Hardware Benchmarks

For many years, the standard measure of floating point operations has been the *Whetstone*. The Whetstone is a specific mixture of additions, multiplications, trigonometric, and other operations. We used the Whetstone benchmark program supplied by Microsoft as part of its FORTRAN package. Microsoft FORTRAN Version 4.00A was used to produce both an 8087-only executable file and a no-8087 executable file. We then timed both versions on a variety of machines. Figure 2-1 shows speed relative to an IBM-PC without a coprocessor.

The machines used for Figure 2-1 were a 4.77 megahertz IBM PC with a 4.77 megahertz 8087; an 8 megahertz PC Limited 286 with a 5.33 megahertz 287 (marked "AT clone"); a 10 megahertz IBM PS/2 model 30 (a 8086 machine) with a 10 megahertz 8087; a PS/2 model 60 (a 286 machine) with a 10 megahertz 287; and a 16 megahertz PS/2 model 80 (a 386 machine) with a 16 megahertz 387. Since the same executable file was used on all machines, the code is optimized for the 8088/8086 machines. Code generated specifically for the newer machines would show slightly better performance for the 286 machines and notably better performance for the 386 machine.

Based on the Whetstone benchmark, and quite a few other programs, I've developed some rough rules of thumb that you may fine useful (see Table 2-1). Rate a plain IBM PC/XT without coprocessor as a 1.0. Any other 8088/8086 machine is rated approximately at it's clock speed divided by 5, adding maybe 20 percent for the 16-bit bus of the 8086. Thus the PS/2 model 30 rates about a 2.5. I mentally rate an 8 megahertz AT as a 4 on the same scale. A 16 megahertz 386 machine gets a 10, but it would rate more highly if running code written specifically for the 386.

So what does the coprocessor buy us in this scheme? It varies a lot because the fraction of time a program spends on number crunching versus housekeeping varies tremendously. For really heavy-duty number crunching, I rate the 8087 on a PC as a 10. Faster 8087's rate proportionally higher. For a given clock speed, the 287 runs just about as fast as the 8087. In fact, the 287 sometimes seems to be slower, but this is usually more than made up for by the faster cpu. A 387 gets a high rating both because of its higher clock speed and because internally it's about twice as fast as the earlier coprocessors. So I rate a 16 megahertz 387 as being about six times as fast as a 5 megahertz 8087 or 287.

All these ratings are affected somewhat by memory speed (especially on 386 machines) and are affected a lot by the instuction mix. Nonetheless, they ought to get you in the ball park, say within 50 percent.

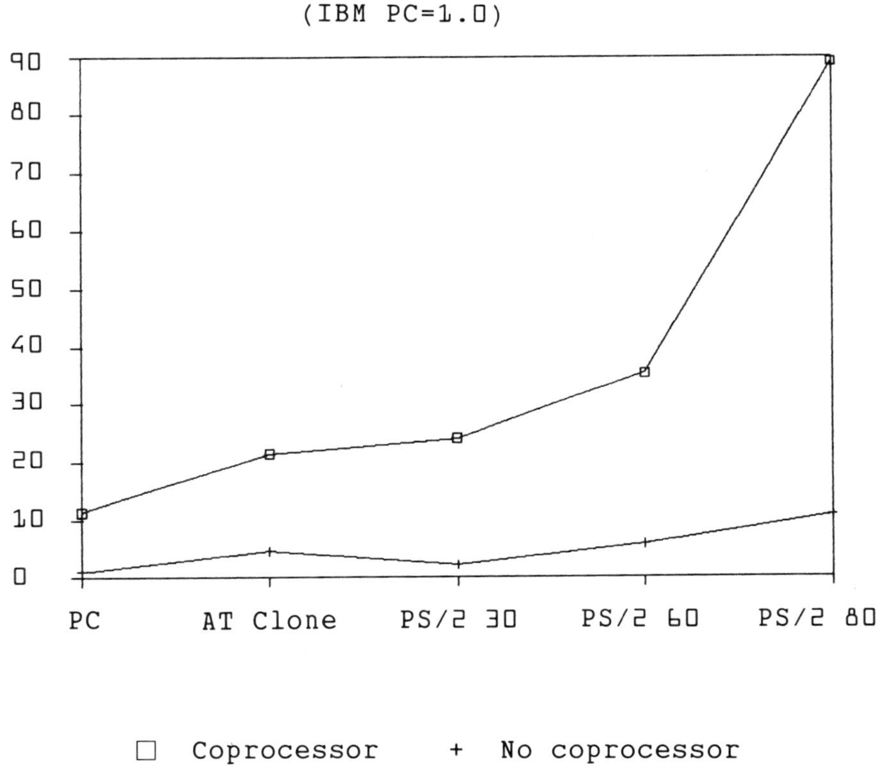

Figure 2.1. Double precision whetstones.

Table 2-1. Author's highly subjective speed Rules of Thumb.

Machine	*CPU rating*	*Coprocessor rating*
PC	1.0	10.0
AT	4.0	10.0
PS/2 30	2.5	20.0
PS/2 60	5.0	20.0
PS/2 80	10.0	60.0

Translator Benchmarks

The choice of compiler or assembler is just as important as the choice of hardware. Benchmarking software is a rather more precarious endeavor than benchmarking hardware. The problems are twofold. First, compilers don't really all do the same thing. Consider the square root. FORTRAN and BASIC take either single or double precision square roots. C will compute only a double precision square root. Turbo Pascal always uses a six byte real without the 8087 and always uses double precision with the 8087. Second, software houses are continually improving their product. Even without an 8087, Microsoft's QuickBASIC beats Microsoft interpreted BASIC by perhaps a factor of 40.

Having set out the appropiate caveats, we'll set out two sets of benchmarks. The first benchmark gives timings for a 50 by 50 matrix multiplication. The second benchmark computes 5,000 square roots. All benchmarks were run on our 8 megahertz AT "clone." Microsoft QuickBASIC and Borland's Turbo Pascal are both Version 3.0. Microsoft FORTRAN is Version 4.00A. Microsoft C was timed on a beta-test copy of Version 5.0. (A "beta-test" copy is a preliminary version of the compiler.)

Table 2-2. Software benchmarks for 50 by 50 matrix multiplication (time in seconds).

	Coprocessor	*No-coprocessor*
Assembly language	7.80	—
C	6.97	30.04
FORTRAN	6.98	30.92
QuickBASIC	18.51	39.49
Turbo Pascal	30.50	56.75

Table 2-3. Software benchmarks for 5,000 square roots (time in seconds).

	Coprocessor	*No-coprocessor*
Assembly language	0.35	—
C	0.99	2.92
FORTRAN	0.64	0.59
QuickBASIC	0.87	1.52
Turbo Pascal	0.64	13.40

As noted in the last chapter, an optimizing compiler can make quite a difference.

Two interesting anomolies appear in Tables 2-2 and 2-3. Note that the C and FORTRAN compilers beat the time given for the assembly language matrix multiplication program. Of course, a compiler can never actually beat the best possible assembly language program. In this case, we're seeing two things. First, the assembly language program isn't the "best possible." (It appears later in the book.) The routine handles a variety of data types and uses some modular subroutines, since it's intended primarily to demonstrate techniques. Second, for this simple program, these optimizing compilers do generate "optimal code." In this particular case the best a "perfect" assembly language routine could do is reach a tie.

The second anomaly is that the no-coprocessor FORTRAN program marginally beats the coprocessor version on the square root problem. I haven't any explanation for this one, but I am hoping for an answer from a wise reader!

More Benchmarks

Sometimes you get to pick your computer. How does an 8087-equipped personal computer compare with "other people's" equipment? The comparisons below repeat our benchmarks on several popular combinations of hardware and software.

Please don't read these comparisons as "better" or "worse." The hardware used runs from an Apple II+ to an IBM 3081. The Apple isn't as fast as the PC, but then it doesn't cost as much. An IBM 3081 is faster than the PC, but it won't fit on your desk.

The comparisons are run on four machines outside the IBM compatible line:

- **Apple II +**—Many people's favorite first-generation personal computer. Both programs used the Apple's built-in Applesoft BASIC interpreter.
- **DEC 2060**—A moderate size mainframe computer used by many universities to provide time-sharing services. (Manufactured by Digital Equipment Corporation.) Both programs were executed using compiled BASIC. DEC-2060 BASIC includes a matrix multiplication function that we used for the first program.
- **VAX 780**—A 32-bit "super-mini" computer, very popular for moderate size number crunching applications. (Manufactured by Digital Equipment Corporation.) These test programs were written in the popular scientific language FORTRAN, and executed using the VAX's optimizing compiler.
- **IBM 3081**—The IBM 3081 is a very large mainframe computer costing millions of dollars. Both programs were written using the "Stanford BASIC" interpreter. We again used a built-in matrix multiplication function for the first program.

The benchmark results appear in Table 2-4.

Table 2-4. Micro, mini, and mainframe speed benchmarks (time in seconds).

Program/Computer	*50 by 50 matrix multiplication*	*5,000 square roots*
IBM PC w/8087	8	0.35
Apple II+ BASIC	1796	130
DEC 2060 BASIC	5.2	0.40
VAX 780 FORTRAN	1.6	0.20
IBM 3081 BASIC	0.11	0.26

As we cautioned above, you need to be careful about benchmarks. The 8087 routines make optimal use of the 8087's potential. (The 8087 routines appear in later chapters, so you can examine their innards if you wish.) The programs on the other machines use standard programming techniques, and so make moderate to excellent use of the hardware's potential.

Caveats notwithstanding, Table 2-4 tells us quite a bit about how to classify an 8087-equipped personal computer. When it comes to number crunching, the 8087 doesn't just make a fast micro—it creates the equivalent of a slow super-mini or a slow mainframe computer!

Let's conclude this chapter with a few more rules of thumb.

- An 8087 speeds up a 8088/8086 or 386 machine by about a factor of 10.
- A 287 speeds up a 286 machine by a factor of 6, but on an "AT" where the coprocessor runs at 2/3 the speed of the cpu, you only get a factor of 4. If you are using a 286-based machine for number crunching, investigate adding a 287 "speed-up" board.
- A 16 megahertz 386 machine without a coprocessor is about as fast as a 5 megahertz IBM PC with a coprocessor.
- A 16 megahertz 386/387 using an optimizing compiler outperforms an IBM PC using interpreted BASIC by about 1,000 to 1.

3

Introduction to 8087/287/387 Architecture

This chapter provides a detailed, technical description of 8087 (and 287 and 387) architecture. The 8087 instruction set is described in Chapters 4 and 10. (For hardware and electronic details about the 8087, see Intel's *iAPX 86,88 User's Manual,* the definitive source on the 8087. For hardware and electronic details about the 287, see Intel's *iAPX 286 Programmer's Reference Manual.* For the 387, see Intel's *80386 Programmer's Reference Manual* and *80387 Programmer's Reference Manual.*)

More detail is given in this chapter than the typical 8087 user need be concerned with. You may want to browse through this chapter and then proceed directly to the description of the simple instruction set in Chapter 4.

Coprocessor Organization

The 8087 is designed as a *coprocessor* for the cpu. Both the 8087 and the cpu "look" at each instruction fetched from memory. The 8087 acts on its own instructions and ignores those belonging to the cpu. When the cpu sees an 8087 instruction, which is a cpu ESCape instruction, it calculates the address of any data referenced by the instruction and reads—but ignores—one byte of data from this address. Otherwise, the cpu treats the 8087 instruction as a null operation. The 8087 copies the address calculated by the cpu and uses it to store or fetch data to and from memory. In this way, the co-processor design allows the 8087 and the cpu to execute simultaneously, considerably enhancing total system performance.

To ensure properly coordinated parallel operation, 8087/8088 programs must follow the following synchronization rules:

- The cpu must not change a memory location referenced by an 8087 instruction until the 8087 is finished. The cpu is free to change its own internal registers and flags.
- A second 8087 instruction must not be fetched until the current operation is complete. (Under special circumstances it is possible to safely violate this rule, but such circumstances do not generally occur in application programs.)

These synchronization rules are implemented slightly differently on the 8087 and the 287/387. We'll cover the 8087 first.

Synchronization, obedience to both rules of the 8087, is achieved through judicious use of the 8088 WAIT instruction. The WAIT instruction tells the 8088 to suspend processing until the TEST line becomes active. (The 8088 checks the TEST line status once every microsecond.) When the 8087 begins an instruction, it sets the TEST line to inactive. It then resets the TEST line to active when the instruction is complete.

The programmer has responsibility for seeing that the first rule is obeyed. To ensure synchronization, code an FWAIT instruction after an 8087 instruction and before an 8088 instruction whenever the two instructions access the same memory location. (Except that the FWAIT may be omitted if neither instruction changes the memory location.) FWAIT generates an 8088 WAIT instruction. (Use of the mnemonic "FWAIT," for "floating wait," is a software convention.) FWAIT holds the 8088 until the 8087 operation is complete, thus preventing violation of the first rule.

Responsibility for implementing the second rule is left to the assembler. The assembler automatically places a WAIT instruction in front of every 8087 instruction. (Except those few instructions mnemonics that explicitly indicate "no-wait." These mnemonics begin with "FN" rather than "F.") Thus the 8088 will suspend processing and not fetch another 8087 instruction so long as a previous 8087 instruction is still being executed.

Programs violating either of the two rules will have unpredictable results. Possible outcomes include the computer coming to a dead halt (if you are lucky), and having random numbers presented as final results (if you are not so lucky).

Synchronizing the 287 and the 387

Synchronization of the 287/387 is more completely automatic than on the 8087. The 286/386 takes responsibility for the second synchronization rule.

The 286/386 checks electronically to see if the 287/387 is busy before sending it an instruction. (Processor control instructions are an exception. See Chapter 10.) Therefore, unlike 8087 systems, the assembler need not code a WAIT instruction before a 287/387 instruction. Omission of the WAIT instruction increases efficiency in two small ways. First, memory is saved because every WAIT omitted saves one byte of code. Second, executing a WAIT takes three "clock cycles" on a 286 and six clock cycles on a 386, so each WAIT omitted saves between a quarter and a half a microsecond. Note that the programmer retains responsibility for implementing the first synchronization rule through judicious application of the FWAIT instruction.

If you want your programs to run on all three coprocessors, you have to follow the 8087 synchronization rules. For this reason, most assemblers always obey the 8087 synchronization rules and produce WAIT instructions for you. Thus half a microsecond or so is wasted in return for remaining compatible with several million 8088/8086 machines. Microsoft's MASM assembler, Version 5.0 and later, will omit the WAIT instructions if you give the .286 directive.

What Happens If the Coprocessor Isn't There?

Suppose you execute an 8087 instruction on a system without a coprocessor? 8088 and 286 systems will just continue blithely along, essentially treating the 8087 instruction as a null operation. Things are a bit better on the 386. The 386 has internal flags that indicate if there is a 387 attached, a 287 attached, or neither. Assuming that the operating system has done its job, if you execute a coprocessor instruction when none is present an exception will be generated and the operating system can take appropriate action. (If the manufacturer has included 387 emulation software, then the appropriate action may be to emulate the 387 in software. To the user, this looks as if a very slow 387 is present.)

If you execute a WAIT instruction when there isn't an 8087 present, the cpu will continue to execute the same WAIT instruction while waiting for you to go out and buy it a coprocessor. (Since 8087 programs almost always include some WAIT instructions, they will usually hang the computer if the 8087 isn't there.)

Internal 8087 Registers

Five internal data areas are accessible by the 8087 programmer. These are the *register stack*, the *status word*, the *control word*, the *tag word*, and the *exception pointers*.

8087 computation is organized around eight 80-bit data registers. These registers form a pushdown stack, called the *register stack*. The register at the top of the stack is referred to as ST or ST(0); the register immediately below the top is ST(1); and so forth through ST(7). Many 8087 instructions implicitly reference ST(0) or both ST(0) and ST(1). Many instructions also push data onto or pop data off of the stack. (The stack is actually organized as a chain, so that ST(0) is "below" ST(7). It is the programmer's responsibility to prevent stack overflow or underflow on the 8087 and 287. The 387 can detect such a stack error automatically. (See below.) Stack operations are described in detail in Chapter 4.

The 16-bit *status word* shows the current state of 8087 operations. We make extensive use of the *condition code* bits in the status word, which indicate the result of 8087 comparison operations. The status word also shows whether any exceptions (computational errors) have occurred, whether the 8087 is busy, whether the 8087 has requested to interrupt the 8088, and which of the eight stack registers is currently the top of the stack. These elements are primarily used for systems programming. Figure 3.1 shows the layout of the status word.

The 387 status word differs slightly from the earlier models. Bit 6 (SF), reserved on the 8087/287, now indicates if a stack fault has occurred. If SF = 1, then C1 = 1 indicates stack overflow and C1 = 0 means stack underflow. In addition, the name of bit 7 has been changed from "Interrupt Request" (IR) to "Error Summary Status" (ES).

The 16-bit *control word* allows a number of 8087 options, described below under "control options," to be set under program control. These include the exception and interrupt-enable masks, which are primarily of interest to systems programmers. Other options, defining rounding, infinity, and precision controls, are occasionally used to control the results of numerical operations. Figure 3.2 shows the layout of the control word.

The *tag word* has two bits for each stack register to indicate whether the contents of the register are valid, zero, special, or empty. The *exception pointers* show the current instruction and operand. Neither the tag word nor exception pointers are normally of any interest to application programmers.

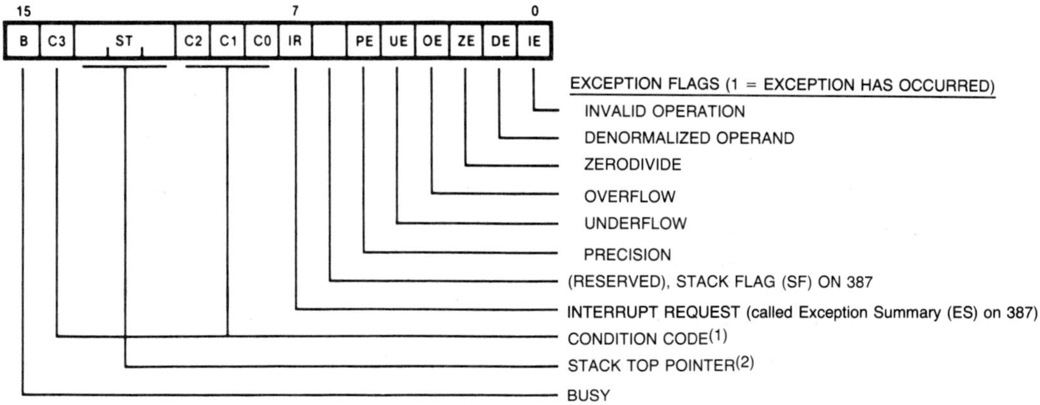

(1) See descriptions of compare, test, examine and remainder instructions for condition code interpretation.

(2) ST values:
000 = register 0 is stack top
001 = register 1 is stack top
•
•
•
111 = register 7 is stack top

Figure 3-1. Status Word. (Used with permission of Intel Corporation.)

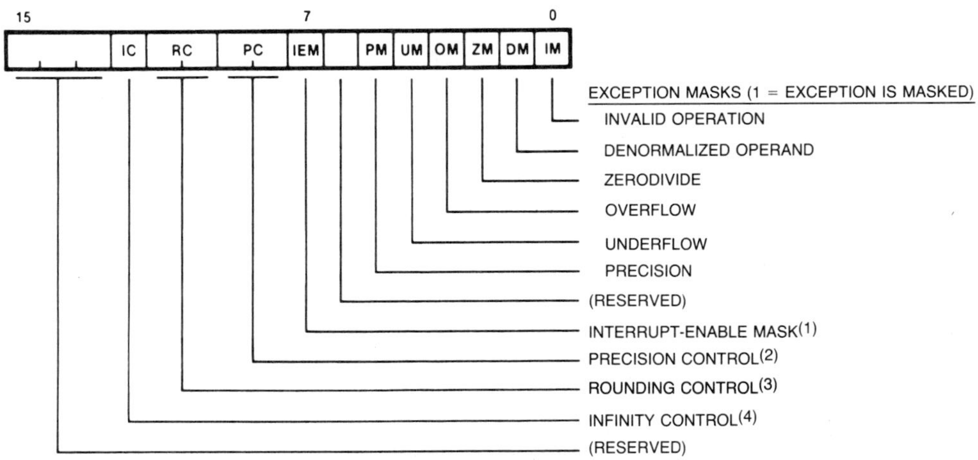

(1) Interrupt-Enable Mask:
0 = Interrupts Enabled
1 = Interrupts Disabled (Masked)

(2) Precision Control:
00 = 24 bits
01 = (reserved)
10 = 53 bits
11 = 64 bits

(3) Rounding Control:
00 = Round to Nearest or Even
01 = Round Down (toward $-\infty$)
10 = Round Up (toward $+\infty$)
11 = Chop (Truncate Toward Zero)

(4) Infinity Control:
0 = Projective
1 = Affine
(ignored on 387)

Figure 3-2. Control Word. (Used with permission of Intel Corporation.)

Control Options

By manipulating the control word, you can change the way the 8087 handles rounding, infinity, and precision.

The 8087 offers four methods of rounding off answers that cannot be represented exactiy in the available number of bits. The options are *round to nearest, round down* (toward minus infinity), *round up* (toward infinity), and *chop* (truncate toward zero). *Round to nearest* is the default.

The 8087, unlike most computers, has a well-defined representation of infinity. The 8087 produces the proper result when calculating mathematical functions with infinite arguments, at least when a mathematically well-defined result exists. For example, 5/infinity yields zero. Both positive and negative infinity may be represented.

Two modes of "infinity control" are offered on the 8087 and 287: *affine closure* and *projective closure.* Under affine closure, positive and negative infinity are regarded as being at opposite "ends" of the number line. Under projective closure, positive and negative infinity are considered equal, as if the two "ends" of the number line bent around and came together. Relative comparisons between finite numbers and infinity are permitted under affine closure, but not under projective closure. Projective closure is the default.

The 387 always uses affine closure and ignores the value of infinity control bit in the control word.

Precision on the 8087 can be set to 64, 53, or 24 bits of accuracy, corresponding to the temporary real, double precision, and single precision data types. This option is offered so that the 8087 may comply with certain industry standards that offer only reduced accuracy, and so that 8087 computation can be made compatible with less accurate computers. Aside from the compatibility issue, the only value in using less than the full 64 bits of accuracy is the educational value of learning that more accuracy is better. Default precision is 64 bits.

Exception Masking

Various important computational errors are trapped by the 8087. When such an error occurs, the 8087 raises an *exception* condition. Exceptions may be *unmasked* ("unmasked" means exposed to the 8088), in which case a program interrupt occurs to permit user supplied exception handling software to take control. Usually, however, exceptions are *masked* (hidden from the 8088). The 8087 holds onto any masked exception and executes an internal error correction procedure. For example, if your program attempts to divide a number by zero, the 8087 will set the answer to infinity under exception masking.

Table 3-1 presents the six exceptions and the most common masked response. Note that execution is never halted by a masked response. As a default, all exceptions are masked.

Table 3-1. Common masked response to 8087 exceptions.

Exception	*Most Common Masked Response*
Zerodivide	Return properly signed infinity
Overflow	Return properly signed infinity
Underflow	Denormalize result
Denormalized	Memory operand—proceed as usual
	Register operand—convert to unnormal (8087/287), proceed (387)
Precision	Round result

Note: The terms "denormal" and "unnormal" are defined under Special Data Types, below.

Number Systems

The 8087 "understands" floating point, integer, and packed decimal numbers. For number crunching, floating point numbers are by far the most important.

Floating Point Numbers

In order to accommodate a wide range of values, computers store numbers in a "floating point" or "real" representation. Essentially, floating point is the computer's version of scientific notation. For example, in standard scientific notation the fraction "negative one-half" can be written out as

$$-5.0 \times 10^{-1}$$

Scientific notation splits the representation of a number into three sections. The "sign field" tells us the sign of the number, in the case above the leading "−" indicates a negative number. Next, the "significand field," 5.0 above, gives the number's significant digits. (The significand field is also called the "mantissa.") The third section is the "exponent" field. The "-1" above tells us to multiply the significand by ten to the minus one power, or, equivalently, to shift the decimal point one place to the left.

The 8087 stores floating point numbers in a form of scientific notation. The exact bit patterns used are laid out for the computer's convenience so they are a little less than obvious to humans. Fortunately, we almost never need concern ourselves with such minute detail. While exact bit patterns are covered below, there are really three facts to know about each data type:

1. How many bytes of memory are used up to store a number?
2. How many digits of accuracy are retained in a number?
3. How wide is the range of numbers which can be represented? That is, how large an exponent can be used?

The answers to 1 through 3 are shown in Table 3-2.

Data Types

The seven regular 8087 data types are shown in Table 3-2. A brief discussion of the use of each type appears below.

Table 3-2. 8087 data types.

Data Type	*Bits*	*Significant Digits*	*Range*
Word Integer (BASIC Integer)	16	4	−32,768 to 32,767
Short Integer	32	9	-2×10^{9} to 2×10^{9}
Long Integer	64	18	-9×10^{18} to 9×10^{18}
Packed Decimal	80	18	18 decimal digits + sign
Short Real (BASIC Single Precision)	32	6 or 7	10^{-37} to 10^{38}
Long Real (BASIC Double Precision)	64	15 or 16	10^{-307} to 10^{308}
Temporary Real	80	19	10^{-4932} to 10^{4932}

Short real. Short real corresponds to BASIC's single precision data type. Micros have less storage than mainframe computers. Since real-world data rarely has more than six or seven digits of accuracy, this data type is commonly used for economical storage of basic input data.

Long real. Long real corresponds to BASIC's double precision data type. As a rule, most calculations should be done in double precision in order to minimize the effect of round-off error in intermediate steps.

Temporary real. Whatever the data type in memory, the 8087 converts all numbers to the temporary real format for internal use. The significand of the temporary real format holds 64 bits, so that every other data type can be loaded into a temporary real without loss of precision.

By designing the 8087 around the temporary real concept, Intel has simplified the application programmer's life in several important ways:

- Since all data types are converted to temporary real by the hardware, the programmer rarely need worry about explicit type conversions. It is just as easy for the programmer to multiply a double precision floating point number by a packed decimal number as it is to multiply two integers. (Of course, when storing a number back in memory, the programmer remains responsible for ensuring that the destination data type is large enough to hold the result being stored.)
- The range for temporary reals is (almost) infinite. The exponent range is 10 to the ± 4932. As a result, overflows and underflows are almost always caused by a bug in either the data or the program, and only rarely indicate a numerical computing error.
- The temporary real has 19 significant digits. Even when a long series of intermediate calculations produces significant cumulative roundoff error, the loss of 3 or 4 digits of accuracy still leaves an accurate double precision answer. With the 8087 onboard, an IBM Personal Computer is more accurate than most IBM mainframes!

Word integer. Word integer corresponds to BASIC's integer data type. A word integer occupies two bytes of storage and is principally used to index arrays and other data structures.

Short integer. A four-byte integer. Not usually used in numerical programming.

Long integer. An eight-byte integer. Not usually used in numerical programming.

Packed decimal. Packed decimal representation is used for business and data processing operations. A packed decimal uses 10 bytes of memory and contains 18 decimal digits. Unlike the three preceding data types, the packed decimal form uses a decimal rather than a binary representation. Each of the decimals 0—9 is represented by four binary bits. These decimal digits are then "packed" two to a byte.

Business and data processing programs generally spend much more time converting data between external (ASCII) and internal (binary) representation than doing arithmetic. Conversion between ASCII and packed decimal representation is quite easy. (Also, some data processing languages, such as COBOL, use packed decimal representation as a standard data type.)

Data Type Hardware Representations

The 8087 knows exactly where each and every little bit goes. This is fortunate, because the physical and logical orders in which numbers are placed in memory differ. It is fairly easy for this difference to confuse us human types. However, the physical layout is easier for the machinery to handle and isn't relevant to programmers, except, on occasion, when trying to debug a machine language program. The description of the exact hardware representations is included here for the sake of completeness.

Logically, all the data types are laid out left to right. The left-most bit is the most significant. Thus, a 16-bit integer is represented by a string of 16 bits running from the high-order bit 15 on the left to the low-order bit 0 on the right. Each of the seven data types is laid out in this way, as illustrated by Figure 3.3.

Physically, the right-most logical byte comes first. For example, suppose a 16-bit integer is stored in memory locations 100 and 101. The low-order bits, 7-0, are in byte 100, and the high-order bits, 15-8, are in byte 101. The same "reversal" holds for all the data types. This format is used throughout the 8088/8086 family and is common to many microprocessors. See Figure 3.4.

Floating Point Representation

8087 floating point representation makes a number of concessions to the computer's convenience.

- Numbers are represented, unsurprisingly, by a string of binary bits rather than decimal numbers.

- The position of the "binary point" is implicit. Since computer memory contains only zeros and ones, there is no convenient way to explicitly write in a decimal point. In ordinary scientific usage we write 153.7 as 1.537E2. (Computers typically use "E" in this context to indicate multiplication by a power of ten.) If our type font had no period, we might agree to write 153.7 as 1537E2 and agree that a decimal point is implicit after the first digit. On the 8087, the binary point is assumed to appear immediately to the right of the most significant bit of the significand.

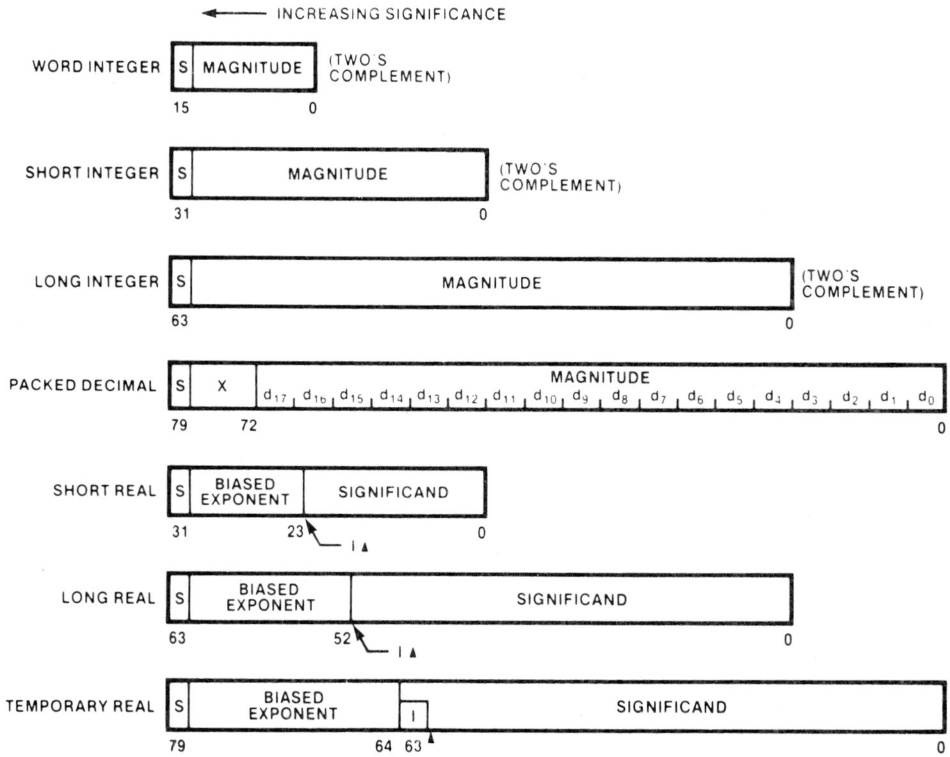

NOTES:
S = Sign bit (0 = positive, 1 = negative)
d_n = Decimal digit (two per byte)
X = Bits have no significance; 8087 ignores when loading, zeros when storing.
▲ = Position of implicit binary point
I = Integer bit of significand; stored in temporary real, implicit in short and long real
Exponent Bias (normalized values):
Short Real: 127 (7FH)
Long Real: 1023 (3FFH)
Temporary Real: 16383 (3FFFH)

Figure 3.3. 8087 data type bit patterns.
(Used with permission of Intel Corporation.)

- Floating point numbers are represented in a "normalized" format. The leading bit of a floating point number is always a one. The computer shifts the significand left or right, while decreasing or increasing the exponent, in order to maintain this format. (However, see *Special Data Types,* below, for some exceptions.)

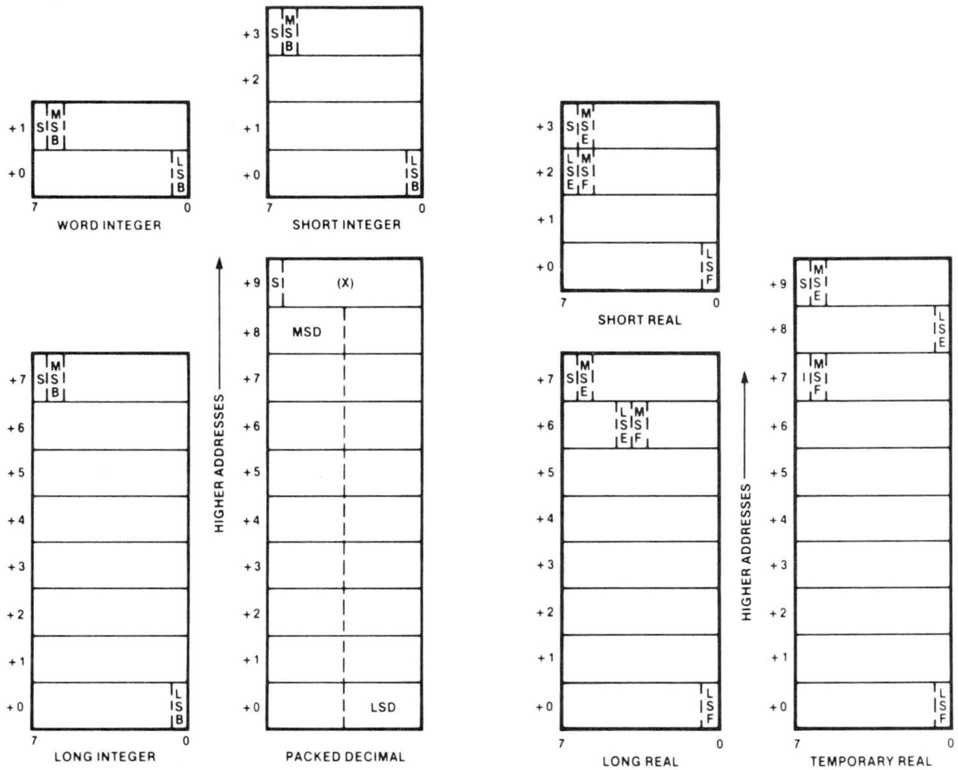

S: Sign bit
MSB/LSB: Most/least significant bit
MSD/LSD: Most/least significant decimal digit
(X): Bits have no significance

S: Sign bit
MSE/LSE: Most/least significant exponent bit
MSF/LSF: Most/least significant fraction bit
I: Integer bit of significand

Figure 3.4. 8087 data type byte patterns.
(Used with permission of Intel Corporation.)

- Since single and double precision numbers are always normalized, the leading bit is always a one and therefore needn't be stored. It isn't. The leading bit *is* stored in the 80-bit temporary real format.
- Exponents in scientific notation can be either positive or negative. Rather than store an explicit sign bit for exponents, the 8087 uses a "biased exponent." The exponent field holds the sum of the true exponent and a positive constant. For example, the exponent stored in a single precision real number is the true exponent plus 127. The exponent bias, chosen to provide the widest possible range given the number of bits assigned to

hold the exponent, is 127 for single precision, 1023 for double precision, and 16383 for temporary real. To illustrate floating point representation, the significand of 2.0 is "[1]00..." (where the "[1]" indicates the leading 1 is assumed but not stored and "00..." indicates enough zeros to fill out the rest of the significand field). The exponent of 2.0, for single precision, is 128. Examples of significand and exponent fields for other numbers are: ½ is "[1]00..." and 126; 3.0 is "[1]10..." and 128; and 4.0 is "[1]00..." and 129.

- Zero is represented by all exponent and significand bits set to zero. (The sign bit may be either positive or negative, without significance for any arithmetic or comparison operation.)

Integer Representation

The three integer types are represented in "two's complement" format. Positive numbers are simply binary integers. Negative numbers are represented in the following way: If X is a positive integer, then −X is written as (NOT X)+1. The left-most bit of an integer is always a one for negative integers and 0 for zero or a positive integer.

Packed Decimal Representation

Packed decimal numbers are integers represented with a sign and exactly 18 decimal digits. Bits 0-3 hold the least significant digit, that is, the "one's place." Bits 4-7 hold the "ten's place," and so forth. Bits 72-78 are unused. (If an additional digit were stored here, it would not always be possible to convert a packed decimal number into an eight-byte integer.) The high-order bit, bit 79, holds the sign. If a decimal digit is not in the required range 0-9, the result of using the packed decimal number is undefined.

As an exercise, try writing out a number in each of the seven formats. Figure 3.5 gives the hexadecimal representation of −127 for each format. (Note that 127 is 01111111 in binary or 7F in hexadecimal.)

Special Data Types

On most computers, every bit pattern represents a valid numerical value. In contrast, the 8087 reserves a large class of bit patterns to represent special non-numerical values. For almost all applications programs, these special data types can be safely ignored. Here is a brief description of these types:

WORD INTEGER

FF	81
1	0 BYTE

SHORT INTEGER

FF	FF	FF	81
3	2	1	0 BYTE

LONG INTEGER

FF	FF	FF	FF	FF	FF	FF	81
7	6	5	4	3	2	1	0 BYTE

PACKED DECIMAL

80	00	00	00	00	00	00	00	01	27
9	8	7	6	5	4	3	2	1	0 BYTE

SHORT REAL

C2	FE	00	00
3	2	1	0 BYTE

LONG REAL

C0	5F	C0	00	00	00	00	00
7	6	5	4	3	2	1	0 BYTE

TEMPORARY REAL

C0	05	FE	00	00	00	00	00	00	00
9	8	7	6	5	4	3	2	1	0 BYTE

Figure 3.5. 8087 hexadecimal representation of -127.

Denormal: Real numbers are usually stored in the normalized format described above. An underflow occurs when the result of an operation would require a negative biased exponent. Rather than merely set the result to zero, the 8087 "stretches" the precision of the result by setting the exponent field equal to zero and shifting the significand right the appropriate number of places. Thus, denormal numbers can be recognized, when stored in memory, by the zero exponent field together with a non-zero significand field. A denormal is converted to an unnormal when loaded into the 8087 from memory or used in an arithmetic operation. Denormals are perfectly acceptable as operands for arithmetic instructions. (With the critical exception of transcendental operations which assume without checking that operands are normals. [The 387 does check for denormals.])

Unnormal: When a denormal is used in an arithmetic operation, the result is an unnormal. Unnormals exist only in temporary real format and can be recognized by a zero in bit 63 (as opposed to one for a normal). Unnormals are also perfectly acceptable in arithmetic operations. (Except that transcendental operations and unnormals don't mix.) The result of an operation on an unnormal is a normal when possible and an unnormal otherwise. The existence of denormals and unnormals provide a major convenience to the applications programmer. Frequently, numerical algorithms create very small intermediate results. Most computers either halt with an underflow signal or set the intermediate result equal to 0.0. In contrast, 8087 routines continue to execute while maintaining maximum possible accuracy.

The 387 does not generate unnormals. It produces normals in situations where earlier coprocessors produced unnormals. In the extraordinarily unlikely event that an unnormal somehow gets read into a 387, an invalid operation exception occurs. (The moral seems to be that the unnormal data type probably wasn't necessary in the first place.)

Zero: Zero hardly seems like a special data type. However, it is very useful to know how the processor treats operations involving zeros. Real zeros may be signed either positive or negative, but the sign is always ignored. The 8087 is extraordinarily well behaved when using zero in arithmetic operations. Where most processors would come to an unpleasant halt, the 8087 produces a sensible answer; for example, the result of 7/0 is infinity and the result of 0/0 is indefinite.

Pseudo-zero: Under certain rare circumstances, temporary reals may end up containing a type known as a pseudo-zero. The pseudo-zero behaves mostly like a zero. For most purposes, this type may be safely ignored. (The 387 does not generate pseudo-zeros.)

Infinity: The real formats include the values plus and minus infinity. These are represented by a biased exponent of all ones and a significand with a leading one and trailing zeros. Infinity can be used as an argument for most 8087 arithmetic operations. Infinity in a register is tagged special (in the tag word).

Real indefinite: The 8087 produces the value indefinite as the masked response to an invalid operation. A real indefinite is indicated by a negative sign bit, all ones in the biased exponent, and a significand with two leading ones followed by trailing zeros. Indefinite in a register is tagged special.

Integer and packed decimal indefinite: For each integer type, the largest negative number (for example, -2^{15}) also represents indefinite. Packed decimal indefinite is represented by 16 leading ones with the trailing bits undefined. Use of integer and packed decimal indefinite should be avoided, as the 8087 treats integer indefinite as the largest negative number and gives undefined results after loading a packed decimal indefinite from memory.

NAN (Not-A-Number): Any value, except infinity, with a string of ones for the biased exponent is a member of the class NAN (Not-A-Number). NANs propagate through arithmetic operations. Thus you can design software that treats members of this class as being "special" in any way you'd like (except for real indefinite which is reserved for the use described above). For example, particular NANs might be used to indicate unassigned memory locations while debugging a program or missing data in a statistical or accounting problem.

On the 387, NANs are further subdivided into *signaling NANs*, and *quiet NANs*. The basic idea is that when the 387 hits a signaling NAN in an arithmetic operation it raises the invalid operation exception; in contrast, operations on quiet NANs continue and the NAN is propagated. The 387's built-in response to using a NAN is to create a quiet NAN. For example, if your program picks a particular quiet NAN to mean "data not available," then all calculations based on a "not available" datum will be executed without interruption and the final result will also be a NAN. Signaling NANs have a zero as the first bit of the significand, where quiet NANs have a one. Real indefinite is one particular quiet NAN.

In the next chapter, we turn away from architectural detail and begin writing our first useful programs.

4

Simple Instruction Set

We write our first program in this chapter: a simple routine to calculate the sum of an array of numbers. Before preparing our program, we discuss the 8087's basic instructions.

The 8087 has six instruction groups: *data transfer, arithmetic, transcendental, constants, comparison,* and *processor control.* We discuss data transfer, a few of the comparison instructions, and the basic arithmetic operations in this chapter. We defer discussion of the less frequently used instructions until Chapter 10. This chapter is divided into five sections. In the first section, we take a close look at the 8087 register stack. The next three sections look at the 8087 data transfer instructions, the 8087 basic arithmetic instructions, and the basic comparison instructions. In the last section we build our first program.

The Stack Mechanism

The 8087 has eight 80-bit registers for holding data internally. On most computers, these registers would be numbered 0, 1, 2, 3, 4, 5, 6, and 7; and a typical instruction would be something like "add register 3 to register 4 and leave the sum in register 3." The 8087 uses a more elegant system for accessing registers—the *stack.*

The stack method is invariably described by analogy to the plate holders found in cafeterias. A stack of plates is loaded on a spring with only the top plate visible. If you put a plate on the stack, all the other plates move down and only the new plate is accessible. Remove the top plate and all the ones below move up one place. On a computer, the action of adding an item to a stack is called a *push* (all the data is pushed down one position), and removing the top item is called a *pop* (all the data pops up one position). For the sake of efficiency, a computer doesn't actually move data up and down.

Instead the computer changes a pointer which indicates which register is at the top of the stack.

The register on top of the 8087 stack is called *ST or ST(0).* The 8087 also allows you to reference registers below the stack top. The piece of data immediately below the stack top is called *ST(1);* one further down is ST(2); and so on through *ST(7).* As we push and pop data from the stack, these names become attached to different registers.

Figure 4.1 illustrates the stack in action. Initially, the stack is empty. Next, we push the number 3.14 onto the stack. Now, ST(0) has the value 3.14 and ST(1) through ST(7) are undefined. Suppose we push 2.18 onto the stack. ST(0) holds 2.18 and ST(1) holds 3.14. If we pop the stack, then ST(0) will again point to the value 3.14.

Notice that the stack mustn't grow to be more than eight deep, since the 8087 has only eight internal registers. The 8087 leaves responsibility for watching the depth of the stack in your hands. If a program does nine pushes in a row, you'll get incorrect answers—but no error messages. (Technically, the 8087 registers are organized as a chain rather than a stack. On the ninth push, ST(7) becomes ST(0) and the previous contents of ST(7) are lost.)

Data Transfer Instructions

Data transfer instructions move data from memory into the 8087 (load), from the 8087 into memory (store), and between 8087 registers (exchange). Inside

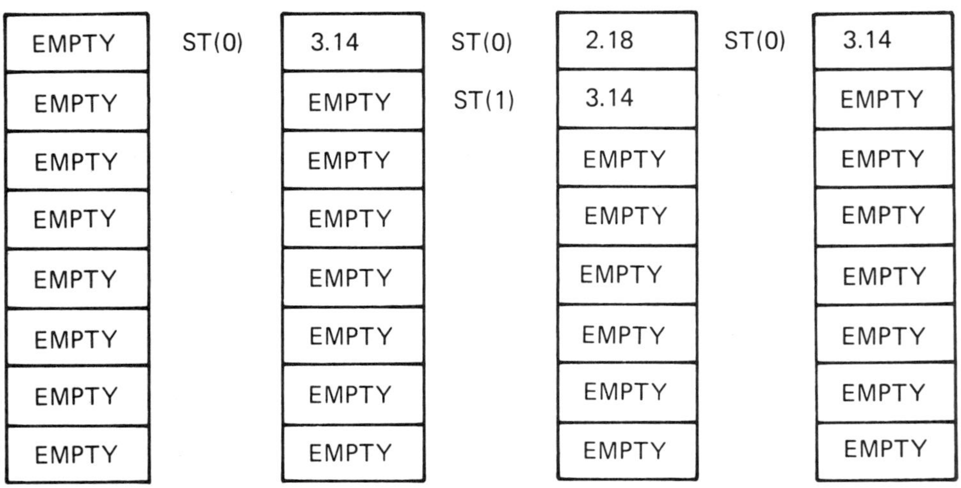

Figure 4.1. 8087 stack mechanism.

the 8087 all data is held in temporary real format. In memory, operands fall into one of the seven data types discussed in Chapters 1 and 3. As data moves into or out of the 8087, it is automatically converted between temporary real and other formats. Three rules summarize the way the 8087 distinguishes among the different types of data.

- Data stored internally in an 8087 register is always temporary real.
- Different instructions reference real, integer, and packed decimal types.
- Within a given type, the 8087 distinguishes between arguments of different precision according to the amount of memory space the argument occupies. For example, an instruction which operates on reals treats an operand referencing a four-byte memory location as a single precision number and an operand referencing an eight-byte memory location as a double precision number.

The data transfer instructions are summarized in Table 4-1.

Table 4-1. 8087 data transfer instructions.

	Real Transfers
FLD	Load real
FST	Store real
FSTP	Store real and Pop
FXCH	Exchange registers
	Integer Transfers
FILD	Integer load
FIST	Integer store
FISTP	Integer store and pop
	Packed Decimal Transfers
FBLD	Packed decimal (BCD) load
FBSTP	Packed decimal (BCD) store and pop

(Used with permission of Intel Corporation.)

The typical execution time, on an IBM PC, XT, or compatible, appears to the right of the instruction name in the discussion below. (Throughout the book, execution times are given for an IBM PC unless specified otherwise.) Execution time for an instruction depends on the clock speed of the computer and on the width of the data bus. The times below are calculated for an 8088 running at approximately 5 megahertz. Faster clock speeds will execute proportionately faster. Thus the FLD instruction takes about 13 microseconds on an IBM PC, but only about six microseconds on a 10 megahertz computer.

Sixteen-bit bus computers (8086, 186, and 286) save roughly two "clock ticks" for each byte transferred to or from memory, when compared to eight-bit bus computers (8088, 188). For example, an instruction which transfers a double precision number between memory and the 8087 will run about 3 microseconds faster on an 8086/8087 than on an 8088/8087. A 386/387 running on a 32-bit bus saves even more time. (The exact difference across the 8088/386 spectrum spent on memory access depends on whether the computer's memory is slowed down by "wait states" as well as the bus width.)

Except for differences in clock speed and bus width, instruction execution uses equal amounts of time on an 8087 and a 287. In contrast, 387 clock counts are typically 1/3 to 1/2 those of the 8087.

Together with the introduction of each instruction, we present "typical" execution times for a 5 megahertz 8088/8087 system and for a 16 megahertz 386/387 system—the latter in curly brackets "{ }". Actual execution time will vary depending on data and the construction of a system's memory. The variation is likely to be considerably greater for a 387 then for an 8087.

Real Transfer Instructions

FLD source — 13 {1} microseconds

FLD (load real) *pushes* the source data onto the stack by changing the top of stack pointer to point to the next available register and then copying the source data into this register. The source may be either a *real-memory* location or an 8087 register. FLD is the basic instruction for moving data into the 8087.

FST destination — 23 {3} microseconds

FST (store real) copies the contents of the top element of the stack into the indicated destination, either an 8087 register or a single or double precision memory location. Data moved into memory is automatically converted to single or double precision format. FST does not affect the depth of the stack or its contents. FST cannot be used to store a temporary real in memory.

FSTP destination — 23 {3} microseconds

FSTP (store real and pop) stores the top element of the stack and then *pops* the top of the stack. Unlike FST, FSTP will move a temporary real into memory.

The "pop" is accomplished in two steps. First, the register currently at the top of the stack is marked "empty" (in the tag word). Second, the top of stack pointer is changed to point to the register logically "below" the current top of stack. Thus the instruction FSTP ST(0) pops the stack with no effective transfer.

FXCH destination 3 {1} microseconds

FXCH (exchange registers) exchanges the stack top with the designated destination register. If the destination is not specified, ST(1) is assumed. Thus, FXCH with no destination swaps the contents of the two registers at the top of the stack.

Integer and Packed Decimal Data Transfer Instructions

FILD source 12 {4} microseconds

FILD (load integer) *pushes* the integer memory operand onto the stack (converting it to a temporary real).

FIST destination 21 {5} microseconds

FIST (store integer) rounds the value held in ST(0) and stores the resulting integer in the destination memory location. (A copy of the value is made before rounding so that the contents of ST(0) remain unchanged.) The destination may be either a word or short integer. You cannot store a long integer with FIST.

FISTP destination 21 {5} microseconds

FISTP (store integer and pop) rounds the top of stack element and stores it in the destination memory location. The top of stack is then *popped.* Unlike FIST, FISTP will store into a long integer memory location.

FBLD source 69 {17} microseconds

FBLD (load packed decimal) *pushes* the memory source location onto the top of the stack, converting the operand from packed decimal to temporary real. No check is made to see that the data is a valid packed decimal number. The result of loading invalid data is undefined and should be carefully avoided. (The "B" in FBLD comes from an alternative name for packed decimal representation, "BCD or Binary Coded Decimal.")

FBSTP destination 117 {33} microseconds

FBSTP (store packed decimal and pop) converts the contents of the top of stack register into packed decimal representation and transfers the converted number to the destination memory location. The top of stack is then *popped.* If the top of stack element is not already an integer, it is converted to one by adding 0.5 and truncating. This rounding operatlon sometimes differs from FIST, which operates under 8087 rounding control. Rounding control can be effectively invoked by preceding FBSTP with FRNDINT, which rounds the stack top to an integer. (FRNDINT is described in Chapter 10.)

Basic Arithmetic Instructions

The 8087 has 21 basic arithmetic instructions, summarized in Table 4-2. Of these, 18 provide varieties of addition, subtraction, multiplication, and division. In addition to the standard use of these four basic operations, the 8087 also allows "reversed" subtraction and "reversed" division.

Table 4-2. 8087 arithmetic instructions.

	Addition
FADD	Add real
FADDP	Add real and pop
FIADD	Integer add
	Subtraction
FSUB	Subtract real
FSUBP	Subtract real and pop
FISUB	Integer subtract
FSUBR	Subtract real reversed
FSUBRP	Subtract real reversed and Pop
FISUBR	Integer subtract reversed
	Multiplication
FMUL	Multiply real
FMULP	Multiply real and pop
FIMUL	Integer multiply
	Division
FDIV	Divide real
FDIVP	Divide real and pop
FIDIV	Integer divide
FDIVR	Divide real reversed
FDIVRR	Divide real reversed and pop
FIDIVR	Integer divide reversed
	Other Operations
FSQRT	Square root
FSCALE	Scale
FPREM	Partial remainder
FRNDINT	Round to integer
FXTRACT	Extract exponent and significand
FABS	Absolute value
FCHS	Change sign

(Used with permission of Intel Corporation.)

In normal subtraction, the destination is replaced by the destination minus the source. In reversed subtraction, the destination is replaced by the source minus the destination. Reversed division operates analogously. (No reversed operations are needed for addition and multiplication, since both operations are commutative.)

Including the reversed operations, there are six basic arithmetic instructions. Each instruction comes in three formats: *real, real-and-pop,* and *integer.* Thus, there are 18 total instructions.

Arguments in the *real* format may take the *stack form,* the *register form,* or the *real-memory* form. In the stack form, the destination is always ST(1) and the source is always ST(0). In the register form, one argument is the stack top, ST(0), and the other is any 8087 register. In real-memory form, the destination is ST(0) and the source is a location in memory. Only *single precision* and *double precision* types may be used in the real-memory form.

The *real-and-pop* format uses the *register form.* After the operation, the stack is popped. For example, FADDP ST(1),ST adds the top two stack elements, stores the sum one element below the top of stack, and pops the stack. After execution, the original contents of the stack top have been discarded, the contents of ST(1) are replaced by the sum, and the register that was formerly ST(1) pops up to the top of the stack.

The *integer* format references a *word integer* or *short integer* location in memory as the source. ST(0) is the destination.

Implicit Operands

Stack operands may be either *implicit* or *explicit.* For example, in the stack form ST is always assumed to be the source and ST(1) is assumed to be the destination. For purposes of illustration, implicit arguments are shown below in curly brackets, as in {ST}, even though these operands are not coded in actual programs.

Use of implicit arguments can lead the unwary programmer into great confusion. Unfortunately, an instruction with two implicit arguments has a different meaning from the same instruction followed by (the implied) explicit arguments. By convention, use of two implicit arguments tells the assembler that you wish to pop the register stack after executing the instruction. For example, the instruction "FADD" implies the source is ST and the destination is ST(1). But the assembler translates the instruction as "FADDP ST(1),ST", which is quite different from "FADD ST(1),ST". You can avoid a lot of trouble by *not* taking "advantage" of this convention. Instead, make both arguments explicit.

The various combinations of instruction formats are summarized in Table 4-3.

Table 4-3. 8087 arithmetic instruction formats.

Instruction Form	*Mnemonic Form*	*Operand Forms destination, source*	*Example*
Classical stack	F*op*	{ST(1),ST}	**FADD**
Register	F*op*	ST(i),ST or ST,ST(i)	**FSUB ST,ST(3)**
Register pop	F*op*P	ST(i),ST	**FMULP ST(2),ST**
Real memory	F*op*	{ST, short-real/long-real}	**FDIV AZIMUTH**
Integer memory	FI*op*	{ST, word-integer/ short-integer}	**FIDIV N_PULSES**

NOTES: Braces { } surround *implicit* operands; these are not coded and are shown here for information only.

op =		
	ADD	destination←destination + source
	SUB	destination←destination − source
	SUBR	destination←source − destination
	MUL	destination←destination * source
	DIV	destination←destination ÷ source
	DIVR	destination←source ÷ destination

(Used with permission of Intel Corporation.)

Addition Instructions

FADD {ST(1),ST} 18 {2} microseconds

FADD {ST,}real-memory 25 {2} microseconds

FADD ST(i),ST or ST,ST(i) 17 {2} microseconds

FADDP ST(i),ST 18 {2} microseconds

FIADD {ST,}integer-memory 27 {4} microseconds

FADD (add real), FADDP (add real and pop), and FIADD (add integer) add the source operand to the destination operand and leave the sum in the destination. In addition, FADDP pops the stack.

Subtraction Instructions

FSUB {ST(1),ST} 18 {2} microseconds

FSUB {ST,}real-memory 25 {2} microseconds

FSUB ST(i),ST or ST,ST(i) 17 {2} microseconds

FSUBP ST(i),ST 18 {2} microseconds

FISUB {ST,}integer-memory 27 {4} microseconds

FSUB (subtract real), FSUBP (subtract real and pop), and FISUB (subtract integer) subtract the source operand from the destination operand and leave the difference in the destination. In addition, FSUBP pops the stack.

FSUBR {ST(1),ST} 18 {2} microseconds

FSUBR {ST,}real-memory 25 {2} microseconds

FSUBR ST(i),ST or ST,ST(i) 17 {2} microseconds

FSUBRP ST(i),ST 18 {2} microseconds

FISUBR {ST,}integer-memory 27 {4} microseconds

FSUBR (reversed subtract real), FSUBRP (reversed subtract real and pop), and FISUBR (reversed subtract integer) subtract the destination operand from the source operand and leave the difference in the destination. In addition, FSUBRP pops the stack.

Multiplication Instructions

FMUL {ST(1),ST} 28 {3} microseconds

FMUL {ST,}real-memory 34 {2} microseconds

FMUL ST(i),ST or ST,ST(i) 28 {3} microseconds

FMULP ST(i),ST 28 {3} microseconds

FIMUL {ST,}integer-memory 28 [5} microseconds

FMUL (multiply real), FMULP (multiply real and pop), and FIMUL (multiply integer) multiply the source and destination operands and leave the product in the destination. In addition, FMULP pops the stack.

Division Instructions

FDIV {ST(1),ST} 4 {6} microseconds

FDIV {ST,}real-memory 48 {6} microseconds

FDIV ST(i),ST or ST,ST(i) 40 {6} microseconds

FDIVP ST(i),ST 41 {6} microseconds

FIDIV {ST,}integer-memory 49 {8} microseconds

FDIV (divide real), FDIVP (divide real and pop), and FIDIV (divide integer) divide the destination operand by the source operand and leave the quotient in the destination. In addition, FDIVP pops the stack. Note that FIDIV yields a temporary-real quotient.

FDIVR {ST(1),ST} 41 {6} microseconds

FDIVR {ST,}real-memory 48 {6} microseconds

FDIVR ST(i),ST or ST,ST(i) 40 {6} microseconds

FDIVRP ST(i),ST 41 {6} microseconds

FIDIVR {ST,}integer-memory 49 {8} microseconds

FDIVR (divide real reversed), FDIVRP (divide real reversed and pop), and FIDIVR (divide reversed integer) divide the source operand by the destination operand and leave the quotient in the destination. In addition, FDIVRP pops the stack. Note that FIDIVR yields a temporary-real quotient.

Miscellaneous Arithmetic Instructions

FSQRT {ST} 37 {8} microseconds

FSQRT (square root) replaces the top of stack with its square root.

FABS {ST} 3 {1} microseconds

FABS (absolute value) sets the sign of the top of stack element to positive.

FCHS {ST} 3 {1} microseconds

FCHS (change sign) changes the sign of the top of stack element.

One more instruction really belongs in this chapter, even though it is a constant instruction and constant instructions are covered in Chapter 10. However, this instruction is simple and extremely useful. It is:

FLDZ {ST} 3 {1} microseconds

FLDZ (load zero) *pushes* a zero onto the top of the stack.

Comparison Instructions

The 8087 includes a number of instructions for making size comparisons between numbers on the register stack. These instructions are used for tasks such as identifying the largest number in an array or for determining whether a number is less than, equal to, or greater than zero. We describe the instructions here. Illustrative programming examples appear in Chapter 5.

The 8087 instruction set includes six comparison and one examine instruction. All the instructions operate on the stack top. Most compare the stack top to a specified source operand. There are four possible outcomes of a comparison operation: ST > source, ST < source, ST = source, or ST and source are non-comparable. The comparisons are reported by setting the condition code bits C3 and C0 in the status word, as indicated in Table 4-4. The condition code can be examined by using the processor control instruction, FSTSW, discussed below. The cpu conditional jump instruction used after FSTSW is also shown in Table 4.4

Table 4-4. Condition code setting following comparison.

C3	*C0*	*Order*	*CPU Conditional Jump*
0	0	ST > source	JA
0	1	ST < source	JB
1	0	ST = source	JE
1	1	non-comparable	JP

(Used with permission of Intel Corporation.)

Note that *non-comparable* results from using NANs or projective infinity. Non-comparable usually indicates a previous overflow or illegal operation.

FCOM {ST,ST(1)} 9 {1} microseconds

FCOM {ST,}ST(i) 9 {1} microseconds

FCOM {ST,}real-memory 17 {2} microseconds

FCOM (compare real) compares the stack top to the source and sets the condition code bits. Temporary real format may not be used in the real-memory form.

FCOMP {ST,ST(1)} 10 {1} microseconds

FCOMP {ST,}ST(i) 10 {1} microseconds

FCOMP {ST,}real-memory 17 {2} microseconds

FCOMP (compare real and pop) executes a FCOM and then pops the stack, discarding the contents of the stack top.

FCOMPP {ST,ST(1)} 10 {2} microseconds

FCOMPP (compare real and pop twice) executes a FCOM and then pops the stack twice. Thus, to compare two numbers in memory, push both onto the stack and then use a FCOMPP.

If the comparison instructions hit a NAN, they raise an invalid operation exception. For consistency with arithmetic operations, quiet NANs should not generate exceptions. Rather than change the operation of existing comparison instructions, as was done with the arithmetic instructions, Intel added three new comparison instructions. These *unordered comparison* instructions work just like the preceding instructions except that, (1) quiet NANs do not cause an exception, and (2) the instructions only work on the stack, not memory.

FUCOM {ST,ST(1)} {2} microseconds

FUCOM {ST,ST(i)} {2} microseconds

FUCOM (unordered compare real) *(387 only)* is equivalent to FCOM except that quiet NANs do not raise the invalid operation exception.

FUCOMP {ST,ST(1)} {2} microseconds

FUCOMP {ST,ST(i)} {2} microseconds

FUCOMP (unordered compare real and pop) *(387 only)* executes a FUCOM and pops the stack, discarding the contents of the stack top.

FUCOMPP {ST,ST(1)} {2} microseconds

FUCOMPP (unordered compare real and pop twice) *(387 only)* executes a FUCOM and pops the stack twice.

FICOM {ST,}integer-memory 19 {4} microseconds

FICOM (compare integer) compares the stack top to a word integer or short integer in memory.

FICOMP {ST,}integer-memory 19 {4} microseconds

FICOMP (compare integer and pop) executes a FICOM and then pops the stack.

FTST {ST} 9 {2} microseconds

FTST (test) compares the stack top to zero.

FXAM {ST} 4 {2} microseconds

FXAM (examine) examines the top of stack and sets the condition code bits C0, C1, C2, and C3 to indicate what sort of value is being held. (The various "sorts" were discussed in Chapter 3.) Table 4-5 shows the possible combinations.

Table 4-5. Condition code settings following FXAM.

Condition Code				*Interpretation*
C3	*C2*	*C1*	*C0*	
0	0	0	0	+ Unnormal
0	0	0	1	+ NAN
0	0	1	0	Unnormal
0	0	1	1	− NAN
0	1	0	0	+ Normal
0	1	0	1	+ ∞
0	1	1	0	− Normal
0	1	1	1	− ∞
1	0	0	0	+ 0
1	0	0	1	Empty
1	0	1	0	− 0
1	0	1	1	Empty
1	1	0	0	+ Denormal
1	1	0	1	Empty
1	1	1	0	− Denormal
1	1	1	1	Empty

(Used with permission of Intel Corporation.)

In order to make use of comparison instructions, we need to retrieve the condition code bits. The condition codes are retrieved with the processor control instruction, FSTSW.

FSTSW word-integer 5 {1} microseconds

FSTSW (store status word) stores the 8087 status word at the two-byte destination location. All the comparison instructlons set bits in the status word; FSTSW is used to move the status word into memory so that the appropriate bits can be examined and appropriate action taken. Generally, FSTSW should be followed by an FWAIT, to ensure that the condition codes are actually stored in memory before the program proceeds.

FSTSW AX 5 {1} microseconds

FSTSW AX (store status word in AX) *(287 and 387 only)* stores the status word in directly in the 286 or 386 AX register rather than in memory. As we will see in the next chapter, this is really where we usually want to put the status word in preparation for a jump instruction. FSTSW is automatically synchronized so that it need not be followed by an FWAIT.

This completes our coverage of the basic 8087 instruction set. For most programs, these instructions are sufficient. More advanced 8087 instructions are discussed in Chapter 10.

Our First Program—Adding Up an Array of Numbers

Our first program is picked to show off the speed and ease in using the 8087.

To write a complete 8087 program, we need a number of details that we haven't covered. For example, we really ought to specify how the routine gets its arguments from BASIC. In the interest of preserving everyone's sanity, we are going to cheat just this once by leaving out some details. Therefore, the program below won't run as it stands. (The program appears in full in Chapter 7.)

We assume that, elsewhere in the program, someone has already defined a single precision array named ARRAY. Our task is to add up the numbers stored in ARRAY and place a single precision result in a variable named DSUM. The integer variable N has the number of elements in ARRAY. (ARRAY goes from ARRAY(0) to ARRAY(N-1)). A fragment of a BASIC program to do the job follows:

```
DEFDBL D
DEFINT I
DSUM=0
  FOR I=0 TO N-1
  DSUM=DSUM+ARRAY(I)
  NEXT I
```

Notice that we collected the sum in a double precision variable to ensure getting at least single precision accuracy for the final answer.

Our 8087 code appears below. The program assumes that ARRAY is an array of single precision memory locations, that N holds a non-negative integer, and that DSUM is a double precision memory location. Everything on a line after a semicolon is a comment. We have used comments to number the lines and mark each instruction as either a cpu or an 8087 instruction.

```
              MOV    CX,N          ;1  {cpu}
              FLDZ                 ;2  {8087}
              JCXZ   DONE_ADDING   ;3  {cpu}
              MOV    BX,0          ;4  {cpu}

LOOP-TOP:     FADD   ARRAY{BX}     ;5  {8087}
              ADD    BX,4          ;6  {cpu}
              LOOP   LOOP_TOP      ;7  {cpu}

DONE-ADDING:  FSTP   DSUM          ;8  {8087}
```

The program uses the following strategy: place the number of array elements in the 8088 register CX. Subtract one from this register each time through the adding-up loop and quit when the register hits zero. Use cpu register BX to keep track of where we are in ARRAY. (Cpu instructions are covered in detail in the next chapter.) A line-by-line explanation of the program follows:

1. `MOV CX,N`. Load N into the CX register. (The cpu instruction "LOOP", in line 7, subtracts 1 from the CX register. When CX hits zero, the program has gone all the way through the array, so we will jump out of the loop.)
2. `FLDZ`. Push a zero onto the 8087 stack. We accumulate the running total in the top of stack element.
3. `JCXZ DONE_ADDING`. If CX (that is, N) is zero, jump to DONE_ADDING before entering the loop.
4. `MOV BX,0`. Set the BX register equal to zero. BX is used as an index for ARRAY. When BX equals zero, we get the first element of array.
5. `LOOP_TOP: FADD ARRAY[BX]`. Add the current element of ARRAY into the running sum we are accumulating in the top of the stack.
6. `ADD BX,4`. Add 4 to the count in BX. Why? Single precision numbers occupy four bytes, so we have to move along ARRAY four bytes at a hop. (Some things are just naturally more clumsy in assembly language than in a higher level programming language.)
7. `LOOP LOOP_TOP`. The LOOP instruction subtracts one from CX. If CX is still positive, the program "loops" to LOOP-TOP, otherwise we proceed to the next instruction, falling out of the bottom of the loop since we must have already added up all N numbers.
8. `DONE_ADDING: FSTP DSUM`. Store the answer in DSUM.

Besides the fact that it was a lot easier to write the BASIC program, what's the difference between BASIC and our 8087 code? One, the 8087 program is a little more accurate, though on most problems we'd probably never notice the difference. Two, the 8087 is quite a bit faster. The assembly language program using the 8087 beats QuickBASIC by about a factor of two. (It beats QuickBASIC without an 8087 by a factor of six to twelve, depending on the version of QuickBASIC.)

5

Introduction to Assembly Language Programming

Before the era of the 8087, all personal computer thinking was done with a general purpose microprocessor such as the Intel 8088. A number crunching personal computer combines the mathematical power of the 8087 with the general programming capabilities of a cpu. The 8087 needs the cpu to talk to the outside world. In this chapter, we discuss 8088 (etc.) programming.

This brings us to a dilemma. The 8087 is a simple, elegant machine. The 8088 is a complex, elegant machine. Chapters 4 and 10 of this book present a complete, detailed description of the 8087 instruction set. A similar description of the 8088 instruction set would require a book, and wouldn't be very interesting to readers who just want to crunch numbers. On the other hand, you can't get to the 8087 except through the 8088.

As a compromise, we discuss just those 8088 features needed to get through to the 8087. We don't attempt to cover all features of the 8088 or to talk about assembly language programming in general. This chapter is oriented toward the BASIC programmer; the experienced assembly language programmer is asked to forgive the occasional simplification. (If you are already comfortable with 8088 assembly language, you can skip this chapter entirely.) For full details on the 8088 (and 8086 family) we recommend:

iAPX 88 Book by Intel;
iAPX 86,88 User's Manual, by Intel;
iAPX 286 Programmer's Reference Manual, by Intel;
The 8086 Primer, by Stephen P. Morse, Hayden Book Company;
IBM PC Assembly Language, by Leo J. Scanlon, Robert J. Brady Co.;
80386 Programmer's Reference Manual, by Intel;

80387 Programmer's Reference Manual, by Intel;
The 80386/387 Architecture, by Stephen P. Morse, Eric J. Isaacson, and Douglas J. Albert, John Wiley.

The last is particularly recommended if you want to learn about the "why" of various design features.

The 8088 and 8086 use the same machine language instructions. A couple of minor new wrinkles were added for the 188 and 186 cpus. The big change arriving with the 286 was the availability of protected mode. And the 386 adds a huge set of powerful new instructions and addressing modes. For most of this chapter, we'll discuss cpu programming in mostly terms of the 8088. This is really all that's necessary because:

- *If it runs on an 8088, it will run on the newer chips as well.*
- *The 8087/287/387 primarily expects the attached cpu to deliver memory addresses; it doesn't really care about addressing modes and how the cpu accomplishes its task.*

Well, these two points aren't entirely true. We'll return to them at the end of the chapter.

Overview of the 8088

Machine language instructions are much less powerful than BASIC commands. (A typical line of BASIC might be equivalent to 10 to 100 lines of machine language instructions.) Consequently, it's easy to understand what a single line of 8088 code does, but it can be very tedious to put together enough lines to do anything useful. For example, suppose we want to copy the data in integer variable A into integer variable B. In BASIC we write:

```
B=A
```

8088 code might be:

```
MOV   AX,A   ;MOVE CONTENTS OF LOCATION A INTO REGISTER AX
MOV   B,AX   ;MOVE CONTENTS OF REGISTER AX INTO LOCATION B
```

A and B are integer variables in both sets of code, but there the similarity ends. We see the following differences:

- BASIC uses mathematical notation. 8088 notation takes the form of a command to the cpu.
- BASIC deals directly with the variables of interest. The 8088 uses internal registers as intermediaries. In this example, the data in A is trans-

ferred into a register named "AX" and then transferred from the AX register into B.

- Anything following a semicolon is a comment in assembly language. BASIC uses the apostrophe and REM statement for this purpose.

Suppose we wanted to deal with single precision numbers instead of integers. In BASIC, we declare the variables A and B to be of the appropriate type. Thereafter, B = A works equally well for any type of variable. 8088 code would have to be modified, leading us to some further differences.

```
MOV   AX,A     ;MOVE THE FIRST HALF OF A INTO AX
MOV   B,AX     ;MOVE AX INTO THE FIRST HALF OF B
MOV   AX,A+2   ;MOVE THE SECOND HALF OF A INTO AX
MOV   B+2,AX   ;MOVE AX INTO THE SECOND HALF OF B
```

- BASIC deals with data a number at a time. The 8088 works either on a word (two bytes) or a byte at a time. Since a single precision number occupies two words, two sets of MOV operations are required to move a single precision number. (The 386 provides instructions to move four bytes at a time.)
- Unlike BASIC, which thinks in terms of variables, *the 8088 fundamentally thinks in terms of memory locations.* In the instruction "MOV AX,A","A" represents a memory location to be assigned by the assembler. "A + 2" means the memory location 2 bytes after "A". "A + 2" does not mean add 2 to the value stored in A.

8088 Program Structure

An 8088 assembly language program is structured into procedures, code segments, and data segments.

Each separate program module is identified to the assembler as a *procedure* by the PROC and ENDP directives (discussed below). The assembler remembers the location of each block of code identified so that the module can be called as a subroutine from another 8088 assembly language program or by use of the BASIC CALL statement. Normally, each procedure is a self-contained unit intended to perform one task in a larger program.

Programs written for the 8088 segregate code and data into different areas of memory called segments. While any number of segments may reside in memory simultaneously, only one *code segment* and one *data segment* (plus a stack and an extra segment described below) may be active at any one time. Segments are identified to the assembler with the SEGMENT and ENDS directives (discussed below). Segments are limited in length to 64K bytes. (In certain programming modes, segments on the 386 can be as large as 4 gigabytes.)

One way to think of an assembly language program is that we write out an exact picture of how memory looks before execution begins. Some areas of memory hold program constants or are set aside to hold results produced by the computer. These areas are placed in data segments. Other areas of memory hold the executable code, as translated from assembly language into machine language, by the assembler. The code is logically organized into procedures. One or more procedures is then placed in each code segment. When we run the program, the computer places each segment, as a block, in memory and then begins execution.

To master the 8088, one must understand:

1. General registers
2. Memory addressing
3. Labels and data definition
4. Some basic 8088 instructions
5. Comparisons
6. Branching
7. Segments
8. Memory stack
9. Subroutine branching and returns
10. Assembler directives

General Registers

The 8088 has eight general registers, each of which holds one 16-bit word. The registers are named AX, BX, CX, DX, SI, DI, BP, and SP. In the MOV examples above, any of these registers could have been used in place of AX. However, each register has various special purposes in addition to its general role. The special uses of interest to us are:

AX and DX—Register AX is sometimes called the accumulator. A few 8088 instructions will only work with AX. Instructions that produce a double length result, such as multiplication, place the result in AX and DX.

BX, SI, and DI—base and index registers (see Memory Addressing below).

CX—count register (see Branching below).

BP and SP—stack pointers (see Memory Stack below).

In addition, registers AX, BX, CX, and DX can each be treated as a pair of 8-bit registers. The high-order bytes are addressed as AH, BH, CH, and DH and the low-order bytes are addressed as AL, BL, CL, and DL. Most 8088 operations can operate on either a word at a time or a byte at a time. Moving a byte into AH, for example, changes the high-order half of AX without affecting the low-order half.

The AH half of AX also has a special use in moving "flags" around (see Branching below).

Memory Addressing

In the "MOV AX,A" instruction above, "A" represents a particular memory location called the *displacement.* The first byte of memory is numbered 0, the second 1, and so forth. The assembler figures out the number of the memory location for A and sticks the number into the instruction. Note that the 8088 addresses bytes, not words, so the first word begins at 0, the second at 2, the third at 4. (It is perfectly acceptable to store a byte at 0, a word at 1 and 2, and so forth. Words don't have to fall on even-numbered locations. However, the 8086 side of the 8088/8086 family will run a tiny bit faster when words do fall on even locations.)

If we want to use the byte after location A we code "A+1". Analogously, the word after location A is "A+2", and the byte before location A is addressed as "A−1".

Just as BASIC allows indexed arrays, the 8088 allows us to index memory. In BASIC the first element of an array A is A(0), the second A(1), and so forth. To pick different elements at different points in the program we code A(I), and set the variable I appropriately. In 8088 code we index memory by indicating that the value held in one of the registers is to be added to the displacement in calculating the address. We tell the 8088 which register to use by placing its name in square brackets, as in A[BX]. Further, we can "double index" memory by placing a second register in square brackets, as in A[BX][SI]. Thus, if A is location 75, the BX register holds 150, and the SI register holds *1000,* A[BX][SI] is location 1225.

Unfortunately, we are somewhat restricted in which registers can be used as indexes. If we use one register, it can be BX, SI, or DI. If we use two registers, one must be BX and the other can be either SI or DI. (Actually, BP can be used rather than BX as an index, but this is generally not done for reasons that become clear when we discuss the memory stack.)

Thus, a memory address consists of a displacement and zero, one, or two index registers. The displacement may be omitted, in which case a displacement of zero is assumed. This usage is quite common, because when we call a subroutine from BASIC, BASIC passes the subroutine the address of each argument. If we call a subroutine with an argument A(0), the subroutine might place the address of A(0) into the BX register, use the SI register to hold an index, and address the array by [BX][SI] with no displacement.

Note some critical differences between indexing in BASIC and indexing in assembly language. In BASIC if the index is 17, we get the 18th (started at zero, remember) element of the array, regardless of whether the array is of type integer, single precision, or double precision. In machine language if the index is 17, we get the 18th byte, not the 18th element of the array. Depending on the type of data being used, consecutive elements have indexes 0, 2, 4..., 0, 4, 8..., or 0, 8, 16....Also, in BASIC we can specify multi-dimensional arrays. 8088 indexing is all one-dimensional.

When the displacement is added to the value of the index registers the result is a 16-bit logical address. Therefore, the address must be between 0 and (2^{16})—1, or 64K. It is no coincidence that programming languages often limit an array to 64K.

Most operations specify a register and a memory location. Instructions can also specify two registers, as in

```
MOV AX,BX   ;MOVE THE CONTENTS OF THE BX REGISTER INTO AX
```

Some instructions allow one argument to be an *immediate operand.* An immediate operand is a constant built right into the instruction—the value is used "immediately," in contrast to being fetched from memory. For example, to set the register AX to zero and the value of memory location A to minus one:

```
MOV    AX,0
MOV    AX,-1
```

8088 instructions such as MOV can operate either a byte at a time or a word at a time. In truth, MOV is really two separate instructions, "move word" and "move byte." The assembler looks at the specified operands to decide which instruction we mean. Most of the time the assembler can figure out whether we want a byte or a word by examining the specifications used to define the memory location (see Labels and Data Definition below). Sometimes there aren't any such specifications, such as when we use an index register without a displacement, and sometimes we want to override the original specifications. To order the assembler to think in terms of a byte or a word, use the "PTR" (pointer) directive. We indicate that location A is a byte or a word by saying "BYTE PTR A" or "WORD PTR A." So to move an integer whose location is held in BX into a location held in SI we might code:

```
MOV    AX,WORD PTR [BX]
MOV    WORD PTR [SI],AX
```

Labels and Data Definition

An assembly language program consists of a series of one-line commands. Commands are actually of two sorts: instructions and assembler directives. A command may be preceded by an optional identifying label. To label an instruction, begin the line with the desired label and a colon. The program can jump to a labeled instruction in much the same way as a program can GOTO a line number in BASIC. To label a line containing a directive, begin the line with the desired label, but omit the colon.

```
THIS_IS_A_LABEL: MOV AX,A
```

Assembler directives do not generate any machine language code. Instead they give the assembler information or ask it to perform a task, such as setting aside a memory location to be used as data storage. For example, the assembler directive "DW" sets aside two bytes of storage. It can be followed by an initial value and the storage area can be labeled.

```
A DW 37
```

Setting aside and labeling memory is somewhat analogous to the BASIC statement DIM. "DW" stands for "define word." To define a word with no initial value, tell the assembler "DW?". We can also define a series of words with a directive like "DW 3,5,?, -2". Or we could set aside 10 uninitialized words with "DW 10 DUP(?)". Since an address is actually represented by a 16-bit integer, we can also initialize a memory location to contain the address of some other instruction, as in

```
POINT_TO_A_LABEL DW THIS_IS_A_LABEL
```

The 8088 deals with bytes and words. To set aside one or more bytes, we use the "define byte" instruction, DB. The 8087 deals with many more data types. Table 5-1 shows all the storage allocation directives.

The assembler knows how much memory is supposed to be associated with a particular storage allocation directive. This knowledge is used in two ways. First, if you set aside storage using Define Byte, as in "A DB 5" and then try to use a word instruction, as in "MOV AX,A", the assembler will warn you of a type mismatch. If you intend to move the two bytes at A and A + 1, you can override this mechanism by using the instruction "MOV AX, WORD PTR A".

Table 5-1. Storage allocation directives.

Directive	*Interpretation*	*Bytes*	*Pointer type*	*Data types*
DB	Define Byte	1	BYTE PTR	byte
DW	Define Word	2	WORD PTR	word integer
DD	Define Doubleword	4	DWORD PTR	short integer, short real
DQ	Define Quadword	8	QWORD PTR	Long integer, long real
DT	Define Tenbyte	10	TBYTE PTR	Packed decimal, temporary real

(Used with permission of Intel Corporation.)

Second, the assembler uses the storage allocation directives to decide whether 8087 instructions should operate on single or double precision data. For example:

```
FLD     DWORD PTR A
```

loads a single precision number located at bytes A, A + 1, A + 2, and A + 3 onto the 8087 stack. The instruction

```
FLD     QWORD PTR A
```

loads a double precision number located at bytes A through A +7.

We can also label a memory location without setting aside storage by using the directives *EQU* and *THIS WORD*. "THIS WORD" takes on the value of the next memory location and "EQU" assigns a value to a name. For example:

```
A       DW       10 DUP (?)
B       EQU      THIS WORD
        DW       30 DUP (?)
```

These instructions set aside 40 words of storage. If A ends up being located at byte 100 of memory, then B will reference location 120.

Some Basic 8088 Instructions

In this section, we cover a few of the most common 8088 instructions, concentrating on those instructions we need later for programs.

ADD destination,source

ADD (Add) adds the destination and the source and places the sum in the destination.

AND destination,source

AND (Logical and) does a bit by bit "and" operation. Bit "i" in the destination is set to one if bit "i" is one in both source and destination, otherwise it is set to zero.

DEC destination

DEC (Decrement) subtracts one from the destination.

INC destination

INC (Increment) adds one to the destination.

LDS destination,source

LDS (Load pointer using DS) loads the word at address source into the destination register and the word at address source+2 into the DS (data segment) register. The primary use is in accessing data given a segment and offset. (See below.) For example, if the offset of X is stored at address A and the segment is stored at A+2, then `LDS BX,A` followed by `MOV AX,[BX],` moves the value of X into the AX register.

LEA destination,source

LEA (Load Effective Address) loads the address specified as the source into the destination register. (As opposed to MOV, which moves the *contents* of the source address.)

LES destination,source

LES (Load pointer using ES) is like LDS, but the segment goes into the ES (extra segment) register.

MOV destination,source

MOV (Move) copies the value of the source into the destination.

MUL source

MUL (Multiply) multiplies the source by AL or AX. If the source is a byte, it is multiplied by AL, and the result is placed in AH and AL (that is, the 16-bit answer that occupies AX). If the source is a word, the 32-bit answer is placed (upper 16 bits) in DX and (lower 16 bits) in AX. Both operands are treated as unsigned binary numbers. The source cannot be an immediate operand.

OR destination,source

OR (Logical inclusive or) does a bit by bit "or" operation. Bit "i" in the destination is set to one if bit "i" is one in either the source or the destination, otherwise it is set to zero.

SHL destination,source

SHL (Shift logical left) shifts the bits in the destination to the left. Bits that move out on the left "fall off the end" and zeros are moved in on the right. The source can either be "1," in which case the destination is shifted left one bit, or it can be CL, the lower half of the CX register, in which case the destination is shifted left the number of places indicated by the value held in CL.

Notice that shifting a number left one place is the same as multiplying the number by two. It turns out that we frequently have need to multiply by two or by a power of two. The SHL instruction takes only six microseconds, while the MUL instruction takes about 30.

SHR destination,source

SHR (Shift logical right) shifts the bits in the destination to the right. Bits that move out on the right "fall off the end" and zeros are moved in on the left. The source can either be "1," in which case the destination is shifted right one bit, or it can be CL, in which case the destination is shifted right the number of places indicated by the value held in CL.

- Don't shift left or right by more than 31 bits. One, the 8088 and the 286 treat shifts of more than 31 bits differently. Two, there are only 16 bits in a word anyhow.

SUB destination,source

SUB (Subtract) subtracts the source from the destination and places the difference in the destination.

XCHG destination,source

XCHG (Exchange) swaps the contents of the source with the destination register.

Comparisons

Controlling the flow of a program is easier in BASIC than in assembly language. In BASIC, we would jump to line 100 when A is greater than B with a statement combining a comparison and a conditional jump, such as

```
IF A>B THEN GOTO 100
```

In assembly language, the comparison and branching are two logically separate steps. First, we use a comparison (or other) operation to set "flags" inside the 8088. Then, we execute a branching instruction which examines the flags and jumps if it sees the right ones "flying." The 8088 has six internal "flags." These flags can be thought of as occupying six out of the 16 bits of a "flag register." The flags, their position, and meaning are:

CF —bit 0—carry flag

PF —bit 2—parity flag

AF —bit 4—auxiliary carry flag

ZF —bit 6—zero flag

SF —bit 7—sign flag

OF—bit 11—overflow flag

The flag names are suggestive of their general use. We care about the flags for two reasons. First, 8088 comparison instructions set some of the flags to zero or one. Second, 8087 comparison instructions indirectly set some of the flags.

The 8088 compares two numbers by using the CMP instruction.

CMP destination,source

CMP (Compare) compares the destination to the source, setting the flags to indicate the result of the comparison. The flags are read by the jump instructions outlined in Table 5-2.

The 8087 does its own comparisons, but relies on the 8088 for program branching. To set up an 8088 branch following an 8087 comparison, we need to set the 8088 flags. SAHF is used for this purpose.

SAHF

SAHF (Store register AH into flags) sets SF, ZF, AF, PF, and CF from bits 7, 6,4, 2, and 0 of AH.

Branching

JMP address

The 8088 jump instruction is analogous to GO TO in BASIC. The program jumps from its current position to the address specified by the jump.

The 8088 also has 18 conditional jump instructions. These instructions cause a jump to the specified address only if the flags have a certain pattern, otherwise execution continues with the next instruction. For example, if we execute a "JG SOME_LABEL" following a CMP, the program goes to SOME_LABEL if the destination was greater than the source, and continues on to the next instruction otherwise. Table 5-2 describes the conditional jump instructions.

One warning: an 8087 comparison sets different bits than an 8088 comparison. See below.

A simple program illustrates 8088 branching technique. Suppose we want to add up an array of 100 integers in memory and put the answer in a location called SUM.

```
            MOV AX,0        ;CLEAR OUT AX TO HOLD THE
                              RUNNING SUM
            MOV CX,100      ;PUT A COUNT INTO CX
            MOV BX,0        ;USE BX AS AN INDEX REGISTER
NEXT_ADD:   ADD AX,ARRAY[BX]
            ADD BX,2        ;POINT BX AT THE NEXT ELEMENT
            DEC CX          ;SUBTRACT ONE FROM THE COUNTER
            CMP CX,0        ;IS THE COUNTER ZERO YET?
            JG  NEXT_ADD    ;IF NOT, ADD ANOTHER ELEMENT
            MOV SUM,AX
ARRAY       DW  100 DUP(?)
SUM         DW  ?
```

Because looping is so important, the 8088 has specialized instructions for this sort of routine.

Table 5-2. 8088 conditional jump instructions.

Mnemonic	*Condition tested*	*"Jump if..."*
JA/JNBE	(CF OR ZF) = 0	above/not below or equal
JAE/JNB	CF = 0	above or equal/not below
JB/JNAE	CF = 1	below/not above nor equal
JBE/JNA	(CF OR ZF) = 1	below or equal/not above
JC	CF = 1	carry
JE/JZ	ZF = 1	equal/zero
JG/JNLE	((SF XOR OF) OR ZF) = 0	greater/not less nor equal
JGE/JNL	(SF XOR OF) = 0	greater or equal/not less
JL/JNGE	(SF XOR OF) = 1	less/not greater nor equal
JLE/JNG	((SF XOR OF) OR ZF) = 1	less or equal/not greater
JNC	CF = 0	not carry
JNE/JNZ	ZF = 0	not equal/not zero
JNO	OF = 0	not overflow
JNP/JPO	PF = 0	not parity/parity odd
JNS	SF = 0	not sign
JO	OF = 1	overflow
JP/JPE	PF = 1	parity/parity equal
JS	SF = 1	sign

NOTE: "above" and "below" refer to the relationship of two unsigned values: "greater" and "less" refer to the relationship of two signed values. (Used with permission of Intel Corporation.)

JCXZ address

JCXZ (Jump if CX equals zero) takes a conditional branch if the CX register equals zero. In the program above, "CMP CX,0" and "JG NEXT_ADD" test the

CX register at the bottom of the loop. We could instead use JCXZ to test the CX register at the top of the loop, as we illustrate below. The choice between testing at the bottom versus the top of a loop is largely a matter of style. We use both styles in this book to provide you with a variety of examples. However, as a matter of good programming practice, you may want to choose one style or the other and stick with it.

```
            MOV   AX,0        ;CLEAR OUT AX TO HOLD THE
                                RUNNING SUM
            MOV   CX,100      ;PUT A COUNT INTO CX
            MOV   BX,0        ;USE BX AS AN INDEX REGISTER
NEXT_ADD:   JCXZ  DONE        ;GO TO DONE IF CX EQUALS 0
            ADD   AX,ARRAY[BX]
            ADD   BX,2        ;POINT BX AT THE NEXT ELEMENT
            DEC   CX          ;SUBTRACT ONE FROM THE COUNTER
            JMP   NEXT_ADD    ;GO TO NEXT_ADD
DONE:       MOV   SUM,AX

ARRAY       DW    100 DUP(?)
SUM         DW    ?
```

LOOP address

LOOP (Loop on CX) subtracts one from CX and then jumps to the address if CX is not equal to zero. Thus LOOP is like a BASIC FOR-NEXT loop with a FOR statement "FOR initial-value TO 1 STEP −1". We could further modify the original program by replacing "DEC CX", "CMP CX,0", and "JG NEXT_ADD" with "LOOP NEXT_ADD".

You should be warned that the conditional jumps in Table 5-2, JCXZ, and LOOP all have one limitation. They only work when the target is within plus or minus 127 bytes. Usually, the target is close enough that the limitation isn't binding. (The assembler will warn you if the target is too far away.) Unconditional jumps (JMP) don't have this limitation, so, if you do get stuck, the solution is to write in an extra, close-by, unconditional JMP as the target of the conditional jump instruction.

8087 Branching

An 8087 comparison sets the internal 8087 condition codes. These condition codes must be transferred into the 8088 flags prior to executing a conditional jump instruction. Because the 8087 condition codes do not exactly parallel the 8088 flags, a little more programming is required following an 8087 comparison than following an 8088 comparison.

Making an 8087-comparison based decision involves three steps.

- Execute an 8087 instruction to set the 8087 condition codes.
- Transfer the 8087 condition codes through memory and into the 8088 flags, using FSTSW and SAHF.
- Execute an 8088 branching instruction.

The 8087 processor control instruction FSTSW, store status word, stores the 8087 condition codes, among other things, into a two-byte area of memory. (FSTSW must be followed in this usage by the processor control instruction FWAIT.) After the FSTSW, the second byte of the memory area holds the condition code bits in just the right position to be loaded into an 8088 register and then dropped into the 8088 flags. The 8088 does not have four separate branching instructions corresponding to the four combinations of C3 and C0, the two condition code bits set by the 8087 comparison instructions. The 8088 instruction JB jumps if C0 is on and JE jumps if C3 is on. Thus a fragment of code to consider all possible outcomes of the condition codes might look like this:

```
;ASSUME STATUS-WORD IS A 2-BYTE AREA OF SCRATCH MEMORY
                        DEFINED ELSEWHERE

; DO A COMPARISON TO SET CONDITION CODES
       FSTSW      STATUS_WORD
       FWAIT
;NOW GET CONDITION CODES INTO FLAGS
       MOV        AH, BYTE PTR STATUS_WORD+1
       SAHF
;NOW BRANCH AND TAKE ANY APPROPRIATE ACTIONS
       JB         LESS_OR_NON_COMP
       JE         EQUAL
;COME HERE FOR GREATER THAN
EQUAL:   ;COME HERE FOR EQUAL
;
LESS_OR_NON_COMP:
             JE   NON_COMP
;COME HERE FOR LESS THAN
NON_COMP:
;COME HERE FOR NON-COMPARABLE
```

Figure 5.1 shows how the bits in the 8087 status word are mapped into the cpu flags by the sequence FSTSW STATUS_WORD, MOV AH, BYTE PTR STATUS_WORD + 1, SAHF. Only five of the eight possible bits are mapped into

8087 Status Word (bit)		CPU Flag
B (7)	→	SF
C3 (6)	→	ZF
-- (4)	→	AF
C2 (2)	→	PF
C0 (0)	→	CF

Figure 5.1. Mapping of 8087 status word bits into cpu flags.

cpu flags. Two of the five aren't of much interest. The busy flag (bit 7) just tells whether the 8087 is busy. Bit 4 is the middle of the three bits which hold the register number of the stack top, which is really of little use!

Once you've transfered the status word bits into the cpu flags, you can use the cpu conditional jump instructions for controlling program flow. Table 5.3 shows the mapping from 8087 comparisons to cpu jump instructions. Jump Above (JA) jumps for greater than. (Be sure to use JA, not JG (Jump Greater than).) If you know in advance that the results will never be "non-comparable," then Jump Below (JB) and Jump Equal (JE) work as expected. However, if non-comparable is a possibility, then you need to go through a sequence of jumps like the one that appears above.

Table 5-3. Mapping of 8087 comparison into cpu flags and jumps.

C3	*C0*	*Order*	*CPU Flags*	*CPU Jcond*
0	0	ST>source	ZF=0 AND CF=0	JA
0	1	ST<source	ZF=0 AND CF=1	JB (non-comparable ruled out)
1	0	ST=source	ZF=1 AND CF=0	JE (non-comparable ruled out)
1	1	non-comparable	ZF=1 AND CF=1	

On a 287 or 387, the three instructions "FSTSW, FWAIT, and MOV" could all be replaced by the new instruction "FSTSW AX".

Segments

8088 registers are 16 bits wide. Since 2^{16} is only 64K, the designers of the 8088 had to find a "trick" to allow more memory to be addressed. The solution is to make up addresses in two parts: a *segment* and an *offset.* The segment part of the address picks a starting location in memory. The offset then specifies a memory position relative to that starting address. The way the segment part of the address is interpreted differs across the 8088 through 386 spectrum. However, it is always the cpu's responsibility to combine the segment and the offset into an *effective address,* which the 8087 can use. If we want our programs to run across all the addressing modes of all the cpus, we have to avoid making any assumptions about what the cpu does with the segment address. All of our subroutines do just that.

The 8088 has four segment registers: *CS,* code segment; *DS,* data segment; *SS,* stack segment; and *ES,* extra segment. (The 386 adds two further "extra segment" registers, FS and GS.) Every memory reference must include not only an offset, but either an implicit or explicit reference to a segment register. All references to code use CS as the segment register. References to data assume the DS register unless overridden. Sometimes we explicitly override with the ES register to reference a second data segment. For example, if A is the offset of a word in the DS segment and B is the offset of a word in the ES segment, we can add the two with the sequence MOV AX,A, ADD AX,ES:B. One segment in memory serves as a stack.

On the 8088, the *stack segment* register, SS, gives the location of the stack segment. The *stack pointer* register, SP, points to the top of the stack. The stack grows (upside) down in memory, progressing toward location zero as it grows. Since the stack is just an area in memory, we can access data on it with any of the usual 8088 instructions. For example, "MOV BX,SP" and "MOV WORD PTR SS:[BX],0" will move the offset of the stack top into register BX and then replace the element on top of the stack with a zero.

Usually, however, we use the stack manipulation instructions PUSH and POP.

PUSH source

PUSH (Push) subtracts two from the stack pointer, SP, and then transfers two bytes from the source into the word at SS:SP.

- In one particular instance, PUSH SP, the 8088 and 286/386 give different results. The 286 and 386 push the value the stack pointer held before the subtraction—the 8088 pushes the value after the subtraction. To preserve compatibility, do not use the instruction PUSH SP!

POP destination

POP (Pop) transfers two bytes from SS:SP to the destination and then adds two to SP. POP effectively undoes the previous PUSH.

- As an aid to manipulating data on the stack, whenever you code BP as a base register, as in "[BP] + 10", the 8088 assumes you want the stack segment rather than the data segment.

Let's put together a useful example. Suppose that a high-level language has pushed the address, segment and offset, of the variable A onto the stack. Suppose that in our subroutine the offset of this address is given by the contents of BP plus the constant A. (Note A is a constant in our program, not the value of the original variable.) We can load the contents of A into AX through the following two instruction sequence.

```
LES BX,[BP].A
    ;put segment and offset into ES:BX


MOV AX,ES:[BX]
    ;move word pointed to by ES:BX
```

Subroutine Branching and Returns

BASIC has the GOSUB and RETURN. The 8088 has CALL and RET. We describe the 8088 calling and returning mechanism here. The next chapter treats the BASIC-to-8088/8087 routine-calling mechanism in depth.

CALL far-procedure-name

CALL near-procedure-name

CALL (Call a subroutine) is actually two instructions: one for calling subroutines in another segment, CALL far; and one for calling subroutines within the current code segment, CALL near. BASIC always uses a far CALL. Near CALLs are used by Turbo Pascal (Version 3.0).

CALL far pushes CS and IP (the *instruction pointer,* which holds the address of the next instruction) onto the stack. The address of the code segment of the subroutine and the location of the subroutine within the segment are taken from the procedure-name argument. (The assembler fills these in automatically.) CS is set to the address of the new code segment and execution begins at the beginning of the new subroutine.

CALL near pushes IP onto the stack and jumps to the location given as the procedure name.

RET immediate-operand

RET (Return) effectively undoes a CALL. The assembler codes a RET to undo either a far CALL or a near CALL, depending on whether the current procedure is marked FAR or NEAR. (See Assembler Directives below.) In a FAR return, the top two words are popped off the stack. The first gives the address of the next instruction and the second a new value for CS. In a NEAR return, one word is popped off the stack and then used as the address of the next instruction. In either case, "immediate-operand" additional bytes are popped off the stack. (The stack operates on words, not bytes. However, addresses are always specified in bytes. So, to pop one extra word, code "RET 2".) The immediate-operand is optional.

Note that PUSH/POP and CALL/RET are matched pairs, much like FOR/NEXT or WHILE/WEND in BASIC or parentheses in mathematics. If the pairing is mismatched, things go very wrong.

Assembler Directives

Assembler directives aren't actually 8088 instructions. Rather, they supply the assembler program with necessary information. We've already met some of the most important assembler instructions above under "Labels and Data Definition." The other important directives follow:

```
label SEGMENT attributes
      .
      .
      .
label ENDS
```

SEGMENT and ENDS (END Segment) define the enclosed series of code or data definitions to be a segment named "label". The segment may optionally be given attributes that provide information to the LINK program. At a minimum, a data segment should have the attribute 'DATA' (including the single quotes) and a code segment should have the attributes PUBLIC 'CODE'. These attributes provide compatibility with Microsoft's high-level languages.

ASSUME CS:segment-label 1,DS:segment-label 2,
SS:segment-label 3,ES:segment-label 4

ASSUME promises the assembler that the segment registers will contain the indicated segment addresses. (It's the programmer's responsibility to see to it that the promise is kept at execution time.) Since a section of code always has a code segment, "CS:..." must always be present, the three remaining ASSUME specifications appear as needed.

```
label   PROC FAR
        .
        .
        .
label   ENDP
```

PROC (PROCedure) and ENDP (END Procedure) mark the boundaries of a procedure just as SEGMENT and ENDS mark the boundaries of a segment. FAR signals the assembler that the procedure will be called with a CALL FAR instruction. When the assembler sees a RETurn instruction, it generates a RET FAR. (For a NEAR procedure, code NEAR in place of FAR).

PUBLIC symbol

EXTRN name:type

PUBLIC and EXTRN (EXTeRNal) are used to supply information necessary for linking together separately assembled or compiled programs. Information about a symbol defined to be PUBLIC is made available to other programs. EXTRN tells the assembler to treat "name," which has been defined in another program, as being of type "type." The following example shows the most common use of PUBLIC and EXTRN.

```
          program1

          PUBLIC LABEL1

LABEL1    PROC     FAR
          .
          .
          .
LABEL1    ENDP

program2

     EXTRN LABEL1:FAR
     CALL LABEL1
```

Any label declared PUBLIC can be accessed by any program declaring the same name to be EXTRN. A label which is to be used by separately assembled programs should be declared PUBLIC. The declaration should be made exactly once, in the program where the label is defined. Any number of other programs may declare the label EXTRN. In particular, the name of an assembly language procedure should be declared PUBLIC if the procedure is to be called as a BASIC subroutine.

SEGMENT/ENDS and PROC/ENDP are also matched pairs. Since these directives carry labels, the assembler will probably catch the error if you omit a half of either pair.

END

END marks the end of the entire assembly language program.

Macro Programming

While programming in assembly language, one frequently sees sequences of code that appear repeatedly with little or no variation. In our case, the declarations and other instructions appearing at the beginning and end of subroutines are pretty much the same whether the subroutine adds an array or computes a square root. Programs are easier to read, and more likely to work, if we can define the necessary instructions once and then call up the definition as needed. In this section we present a (very) brief introduction to macro programming.

INCLUDE filename

INCLUDE tells the assembler to start reading from file filename and then return to the current file. Typically, filename might contain a series of macro definitions.

label MACRO arg1,arg2

any statements

ENDM

This defines a *macro* named "label" with arguments arg1 and arg2. After the definition, whenever "label foo1,foo2" appears, the sequence of instructions appearing between MACRO and ENDM will be repeated, substituting "foo1" for "arg1" and "foo2" for "arg2."

LOCAL name1, name2

Defines "name1" and "name2" to be local variables within the body of a macro.

IF arg

any statements

ELSE

any statements

ENDIF

If arg is non-zero (at assembly time), then the code between IF and ELSE is assembled; otherwise the code between ELSE and ENDIF is assembled. Variants that we also use are **IFDEF,** which causes assembly if arg is defined and **IFNDEF,** which causes assembly if arg is not defined.

IRP dummyname,<parameter1,parameter2,...>

any statements

ENDM

IRP causes the statements between IRP and ENDM to be repeated once for each parameter, substituting the parameter for dummyname. (Note that, unfortunately for clarity, both macros and IRPs end with ENDM.)

.ERR

.ERR generates a fatal assembly error.

.OUT message

.OUT prints message on the screen.

.286

.286 tells the assembler to recognize non-privileged 286 and 287 instructions, as well as 8088 and 8087 instructions. ("Privileged" instructions are reserved for the use of the operating system.)

.386

.386 tells the assembler to recognize non-privileged 386 and 387 instructions, as well as 8088/286 and 8087/287 instructions.

286 Instruction Extensions

While the 286 has extraordinarily more power than the 8088 family, there are very few differences relevant to 8087 or 287 programming. Essentially, any program written for the 8088/8087 will run unchanged on the 286/287, but not vice versa. Several of the noteworthy features of the 286 are:

1. There are quite a few new instructions on the 286. See the *iAPX 286 Programmer's Reference Manual.*
2. The 286 runs much faster than the 8088. For example, use of the MOV instruction to transfer a word from memory to a register requires 3 clock ticks on the 286 versus 17 to 25 clock ticks on the 8088. The speed advantage of the 286 is somewhat less on other instructions, so the actual advantage of a 286 over an 8088 will vary from program to

program. As a ballpark estimate, figure that a 286 running at 8 megahertz is four times as fast as a 5 megahertz 8088.

3. The 286 is really two computers on one chip. When running in *Real Address Mode,* the 286 differs little from the 8088 family, except for its greater speed. When running in *Protected Virtual Address Mode,* the 286 is more like a minicomputer than a micro. The 286 can run several simultaneous tasks for several users. It can address 16 megabytes of real memory and over a gigabyte of virtual memory.

Use of Protected Mode involves a fundamental change in the way memory is addressed. However, so long as your programs don't make any assumptions about the interpretation of segment registers, your programs should work equally well in either Real or Protected Mode. Obviously, some program must set up the segments initially and that program must distinguish between Real and Protected Mode. In this book, we leave this problem to BASIC or some other high-level language. So while you'll need separate versions of BASIC for Real and for Protected Mode, the routines here should work equally well with either.

In the interests of full disclosure, three caveats should be noted. First, a Protected-Mode operating system may require some new assembler directives to provide information to the LINK program. Second, one minor program in the next chapter, STACKERR, makes a call to DOS. This will probably need to be changed under a new operating system. Third, at the time of writing the new Microsoft Protected-Mode operating system (OS/2) hadn't been released, so we haven't actually been able to test our routines in Protected Mode.

386 Instruction Extensions

If the 286 is like a small minicomputer, the 386 is like a small mainframe. The 386 can address up to four gigabytes (4,000 megabytes) of real memory and 64 terabytes (64 million megabytes!) of virtual memory. The 386 can imitate both the 8088 and the 286 and adds quite a few new instructions. From the application programmer's viewpoint, the biggest change is that a single segment can be four gigabytes long. As a practical matter, this means that programs can assume all their data lies in one segment. However, all the programs in this book assume that addresses are 16 bits long, not the 32 the 386 permits. So the programs will run just fine on a 386, but will require a bit of fiddling if you want to take advantage of the enormous new segment size.

6

Using the Assembler and High-Level Languages

We cover four topics in this chapter. First, we discuss the use of the macro assembler and the CodeView debugger. Second, we explain the conventions for linking up an assembly language routine with high-level language programs. The third section of the chapter reviews the use of Microsoft QuickBASIC, FORTRAN, and C, and Borland's Turbo Pascal. In the fourth part of the chapter we present several assembly language macros that are used throughout the book. Each of the topics in the chapter could be the subject of its own book, so we are going to limit coverage to only those elements either directly germane to 8087 use or necessary for understanding the programs later in the book.

If you're an experienced assembly language programmer, you can pretty much skip this chapter. You might want to skim the fourth section. At a minimum, read the next short subsection.

A Quick Summary for the Experienced Programmer

All the assembly language programs in this book are written as subroutines that can be called from a high-level language or another assembly language program. Variables are passed by reference using long addresses. The calling program must push onto the memory stack the segment and the offset of each variable, in order from left to right. The calling program then makes a FAR Call to the subroutine (except Turbo Pascal, which makes a NEAR Call).

The file SUBROUT.MAC contains several macros and is INCLUDEd at the front of each routine. The macro "SUBROUTINE foo, <arg1,arg2,...>" defines a subroutine named "foo" with arguments "arg1," "arg2," etc. The address of "arg1" can be found on the stack at location [BP].arg1. The offset is stored at [BP].arg1 and the segment at [BP].arg1 + 2. The macro "RETURN foo" returns to the calling program. The macro "CHKSTCK *some_number*" checks to see that at least *some_number* bytes remain on the memory stack and executes a jump to the routine STACKERR if the stack is too small. Macro "PUSHTEMP register,name" pushes the contents of "register" onto the stack at a location that PUSHTEMP defines as [BP].name. "POPTEMP *some_number*" pops *some_number* previous PUSHTEMPs off the stack.

Using the Macro Assembler

Programming for the 8087 affects use of the macro assembler only tangentially. While very early versions of the assembler released by Microsoft (and IBM) did not support the 8087 instruction set, all recent versions do. Versions 4.0 and earlier of the macro assembler require the switch "/R" on the command line, or the ".8087" directive in the source code, in order to recognize 8087 instructions. "/R" or ".8087" also set the assembler to using 8087-format for real numbers rather than Microsoft Binary Format. Version 4.0 does not recognize 386/387 instructions. Except for this last point, Version 4.0 is perfectly adequate for assembly language programming. (Note, however, that there is a bug in assembly of the JMP instruction in Version 4.0. Some of our programs use a short macro named "NEARJMP" to program around the bug. Microsoft knows about the bug and has corrected it in Version 5.0, but not Version 4.5.) To assemble a program "foo.asm" using Version 4.0, give the comand "MASM /R foo;". The equivalent command for Version 5.0 is MASM foo;".

While Version 4.0 is perfectly adequate, Version 5.0 is just incredible. If you do any serious assembly language programming, get Version 5.0 The new version is faster, but of far greater importance, it supports Microsoft's CodeView debugger. CodeView allows you to step through your assembly memory locations, and to examine the contents of the 8087. To assemble program "foo.asm" with Version 5.0, give the command "MASM /Zi foo;" to include information for CodeView or "MASM foo;" when debugging information is no longer needed.

- *The initial release of MASM 5.0 assembles the 387 instructions FSIN, FCOS, FSINCOS, and FPREM1 incorrectly! See chapter 10 for a workaround.*

CodeView and the 8087

CodeView is a powerful and complex program. While it is enormously useful to all programmers, its special appeal to 8087 programmers is that it allows you to examine the inside of the 8087. We'll limit our discussion to this feature.

```
                  1    4
                  |   /
>7                v  /
 Control  1370   / (Affine closure, Round nearest, 64-bit precision)<-2
                /             iem=0 pm=1 um=1 om=0 zm=0 dm=0 im=0<----3
 Status   3820    cond=0000 top=7 pe=1 ue=0 oe=0 ze=0 de=0 ie=0<----5
 Tag      3FFF    instruction=51861  operand=65680  opcode=D807<----7
Stack       ^     Exp   Mantissa              Value
 ST(0)  valid\    BFF6  DD7236000000000 = -0.3378999885171652E-2
>  ^      ^   \     ^    ^                                 ^
   |      |    \     \  /                                  |
   8      9     6     10                                   11
```

Figure 6.1. Examining Contents of the 8087 Using CodeView. (1.) Control word in hexadecimal. (2.) Infinity control, rounding control, and precision control. (3.) Interrupt enable, precision, underflow, overflow, zero divide, denormalized operand, and invalid operation masks. (4.) Status word in hexadecimal. (5.) Condition codes, stack top, precision, underflow, overflow, zero divide, denormalized operand, and invalid operation exception masks. (6.) Tag register. (7.) Address of last 8087 instruction and operand and 8087 opcode (all hexadecimal). (8.) Register name. (9.) Tag value (valid, zero, etc. (10.) Contents in hexadecimal. (11.) Contents as floating point number.

To examine the contents of the 8087, enter "7" at the command line in the dialog window. Since "7" produces several lines of output, you'll probably want to expand the size of the dialog window in order to see everything.

Figure 6-1 shows an annotated example of output from the 7 command. The first and second lines show and interpret the control word. Line three does the same for the status word. The fourth line shows the tag registers and the current instructions. The remaining lines show the contents of the 8087 stack registers, both in hexadecimal and as a floating point number.

Calling a Subroutine

There are many different conventions for passing information to a subroutine. In the interest of simplicity, we have coded all of our routines the same way. Variables are passed by *reference* (This is sometimes also called "call by address.") using long (both segment and offset) addresses. The subroutines are coded for FAR, rather than NEAR, calls (except for Turbo Pascal).

Calling a subroutine requires three tasks. First, we have to set up a list of arguments that can be retrieved by the subroutine. Second, we have to store away a return address in a place the subroutine can find. Third, we jump to the subroutine. The CALL instruction takes care of the latter two tasks. The first is accomplished by pushing the addresses of the arguments onto the 8088 stack.

Calling a subroutine is most easily explained with an illustration. Suppose we wanted to imitate the BASIC instruction:

```
CALL SUB87(A(0),SUM,N)
```

We could use the following assembly language program:

```
          EXTRN     SUB87:FAR                               ;1
          ASSUME    CS:CSEG,DS:DATA_SEG,SS:STACK_SEG        ;2
CSEG      SEGMENT   PUBLIC 'CODE'                           ;3
          MOV       AX,SEG STACK_SEG    ;LOAD ADDRESS OF    ;4
          MOV       SS,AX               ;STACK SEGMENT IN SS;5
          MOV       SP,OFFSET STACK_TOP ;SET SP TO STACK_TOP;6
          MOV       AX,SEG DATA_SEG     ;LOAD ADDRESS OF    ;7
          MOV       DS,AX               ;DATA SEGMENT IN DS ;8
                                        ;KEEP DS IN AX
          PUSH      AX                  ;SEGMENT OF A       ;9
          MOV       BX,OFFSET A         ;PUSH OFFSET        ;10
          PUSH      BX                  ;A                  ;11
          PUSH      AX                  ;SEGMENT OF SUM     ;12
          MOV       BX,OFFSET SUM       ;PUSH OFFSET        ;13
```

```
          PUSH      BX                 ;SUM              ;14
          PUSH      AX                 ;SEGMENT N        ;15
          MOV       BX,OFFSET N        ;PUSH OFFSET      ;16
          PUSH      BX                 ;N                ;17
          CALL      SUB87                                ;18
NEXT_LOCATION:                                           ;19
CSEG      ENDS                                           ;20

DATA_SEG  SEGMENT   'DATA'                               ;21
A         DD        1000 DUP (?)                         ;22
SUM       DQ        ?                                    ;23
N         DW        1000                                 ;24
DATA_SEG  ENDS                                           ;25

STACK_SEG SEGMENT   'STACK'                              ;26
STACK_AREA DW       100 DUP (?)                          ;27
STACK_TOP  EQU      THIS WORD                            ;28
STACK_SEG ENDS                                           ;29

          END                                            ;30
```

1. `EXTRN.` EXTRN tells the assembler that SUB87 is an address defined in another file.
2. `ASSUME CS....` ASSUME promises the assembler we will set up the segment registers appropriately.
3. `CSEG SEGMENT PUBLIC 'CODE'.` Tell the assembler we are beginning the code segment.

4-8. Load the data and stack segment registers. Set the stack pointer, SP. to point to the top of the memory stack.

9-17. Push the segment and then the offset of each argument onto the memory stack. Addresses are pushed in order from left to right.

18. CALL a FAR procedure. The current contents of the CS register and the Instruction Pointer (the address NEXT_LOCATION) are pushed onto the stack. The program then jumps to the location SUB87.
19. When SUB87 returns, execution will resume here.
20. Tell the assembler we are ending the code segment.
21. `DATA_SEGMENT SEGMENT 'DATA'.` Tell the assembler we are beginning the data segment. The compiler is smart enough to know that "OFFSET A" is an address in the data segment and that OFFSET STACK_TOP is an address in the stack segment.
22. `A DD 1000 DUP (?).` Set aside 1000 uninitialized single precision locations for A.

23. `SUM DQ ?`. Set aside one double precision location for SUM.
24. `N DW 1000`. Set aside one word for N, initialized to 1000.
25. `DATA_SEGMENT ENDS`. End the data segment.
26. `STACK_SEGMENT SEGMENT 'STACK'`. Begin the stack segment.
27. `STACK_AREA DW 100 DUP (?)`. Set aside 100 words for the stack.
28. `STACK_TOP EQU THIS WORD`. STACK_TOP is equivalent to the address appearing after the 100 words allocated for the STACK_AREA.
29. `STACK_SEGMENT ENDS`. End the stack segment.
30. `END`. End the program.

The receiving subroutine finds its important information on the memory stack, which is shown in Figure 6.2. Remember that the 8088 stack actually grows upside down in memory, so that as we push addresses onto the stack, SP moves toward zero.

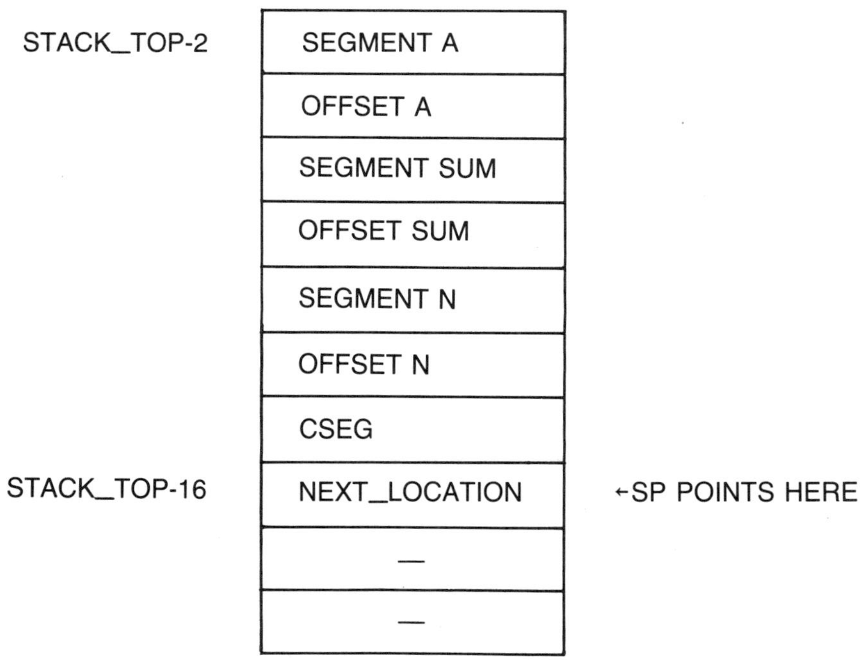

Figure 6.2. Memory stack after subroutine call.

Acting Like a Called Subroutine

Suppose the purpose of SUB87 is to add up N single precision values found in the array A and to return their double precision sum in variable SUM. We could use the following assembly language program.

```
          PUBLIC    SUB87                                ;1
          ASSUME    CS:CSEG                              ;2
CSEG      SEGMENT   PUBLIC 'CODE'                        ;3
SUB87     PROC      FAR                                  ;4
          PUSH      BP                ;SAVE BP           ;5
          MOV       BP,SP                                ;6
          N = 6                       ;DEFINE ADDRESS    ;7
          SUM = 10                    ;OFFSETS           ;8
          A = 14                                         ;9
          LDS       BX,[BP].N         ;DS:BX=ADDR(N)     ;10

          MOV       CX,[BX]           ;CX=N              ;11
          FLDZ                        ;CLEAR ST          ;12
          JCXZ      ALL_DONE          ;CHECK N=0         ;13
          LDS       BX,[BP].A         ;DS:BX=ADDR(A)     ;14
ADD_LOOP:                                                ;15
          FADD      DWORD PTR [BX]                       ;16
          ADD       BX,4              ;NEXT ELEMENT      ;17
          LOOP      ADD_LOOP          ;DO IT AGAIN       ;18
ALL_DONE:                                                ;19
          LDS       BX,[BP].SUM       ;DS:BX=ADDR(SUM)   ;20
          FSTP      QWORD PTR [BX]    ;STORE SUM         ;21
          POP       BP                ;RESTORE BP        ;22
          RET       4*3               ;RETURN            ;23
SUB87     ENDP                                           ;24
CSEG      ENDS                                           ;25
          END                                            ;26
```

1-3. The `PUBLIC`, `ASSUME`, and `SEGMENT` statements supply the usual information to the assembler.

4. `PROC FAR` tells the assembler that this routine will be called with a FAR CALL; information needed to generate the proper type of return instruction in line 18.

5. `PUSH BP`. Save the value of the BP register by pushing it onto the stack for later retrieval. Note this instruction subtracts two from SP, so SP now equals STACK_TOP−18.

6. `MOV BP,SP`. Copy the stack pointer, SP, into BP. The instructions that follow retrieve information from the stack. BP can serve as a base register, as in [BP], while SP cannot.

7-9. Define the symbol `N`, `SUM` and `A` so the `[BP].N` (etc.) is the offset of the address of N on the memory stack.

10-11. Load the address `N` into `DS:BX`, then load the value of `N` into `CX`.

12. Set the running sum, in the 8087 stack-top, equal to zero.

13. Bail out if the array is of length zero.

14. Set `DS:BX` to point to the first element of A.

15-18. Add up the array, elements of which are four bytes apart.

19. Label for `N=0` case.

20. Set `DS:BX` to point to location of `SUM`.

21. Store the running total of `SUM`.

22-26. Restore `BP`, pop the arguments off the stack, return, and close the procedure.

In coding the subroutine, a pattern appears.

- If the subroutine is called with "n" arguments, then the address of argument "i" is stored in [BP]+6+4*(n−i). In other words, the right-most argument has its address stored at [BP]+6; the right-most-but-one is at [BP]+10; one further to the left is at [BP]+14; and so forth. (These addresses are valid *after* we set BP, as in lines 5 and 6, with a PUSH and a MOV.)
- It takes one instruction to retrieve the address of the argument; two to retrieve the argument's value.
- The last instruction should be RET 4*n, where n is the number of arguments.

You can see that a great deal of the code in the subroutine is housekeeping that would be pretty much the same regardless of the contents of the subroutine. The routines in this book use several macros defined later in the chapter. Using these, lines 1-9 would be replaced with "SUBROUTINE SUB87,<A,SUM,N>" and lines 22-25 would be replaced with "RETURN SUB87." A version of this routine using the book's macros appears in the next chapter.

Using High-Level Languages

The assembly language routines in this book are designed to be used with any high-level language that can work with the subroutine calling conventions discussed in the preceding section. Specifically, the routines can be used with Microsoft's QuickBASIC, FORTRAN, and C with the Borland's Turbo Pascal. There is very little about using these languages that is specific to the 8087. In this section of the chapter, we discuss those points that are relevant. We also touch on the general topic of linking assembly language routines, although just enough so that you can easily use the routines in this book.

Using QuickBASIC

To use QuickBASIC with the 8087, you will need Version 3.0 or later. However, Version 4.0 greatly simplifies the process of linking up to assembly language routines and supports the CodeView debugger supplied with the assembler 5.0 package. Version 4.0 can use the standard conventions for passing addresses (particularly of arrays), where Version 3.0 cannot. While it is possible to call an assembly language routine from Version 3.0 through clever use of the VARPTR and PTR86 routines, it is extremely inconvenient. The following description assumes you are using Version 4.0 or later.

QuickBASIC Version 4.0 uses the 8087 automatically whenever one is present. If you are running an old QuickBASIC program that used data binary files, you can start up QuickBASIC with the "/MBF" switch to tell the compiler to use Microsoft Binary Format on files and 8087 format for internal calculations. You can also use the CVSMBF, CVDMBF, MKSMBF$, and MKDMBF$ functions to read and write single and double precision numbers in the old binary format while the remainder of the program uses 8087 format. Programs compiled by QuickBASIC will automatically choose between an 8087, if present, or the 8087-emulator routines.

All of our routines include a reference to a stack checking routine named STACKERR, defined later in this chapter. Whether you build a "Quick Library" for assembly language routines or you use LINK, you should include STACKERR.OBJ on the list of routines to be included.

When using the matrix routines in Chapter 8, QuickBASIC should store matrices in row-order. If you are compiling in memory, turn on the "Arrays In Row Order" button in the "Compile. . ." menu. When using the command line to compile, include the "/R" switch. (For an exception, see "A little more on programing strategy in Chapter 12.)

The DECLARE statement is used to inform QuickBASIC about subroutine calling conventions. For the routines in this book, we want QuickBASIC to think it is calling a Fortran routine and to pass the segment as well as the offset of each variable. Suppose SUM(X,N,DSUM) is a routine in which X is a single precision array, N is an integer, and DSUM is double precision. The proper declaration would be:

```
DECLARE SUB SUM(SEG X AS SINGLE,SEG N AS INTEGER,SEG
   DSUM AS DOUBLE)
```

Some of our routines accept either single or double precision arguments and pass the argument type in a separate variable. Suppose in FOO(X,ITYPE) that X can be either single or double precision and that ITYPE is an integer. In place of "SINGLE" or "DOUBLE", we can use "ANY," which turns off QuickBASIC's type checking. For example,

```
DECLARE SUB FOO(SEG X AS ANY,SEG ITYPE AS INTEGER)
```

If you wish to use CodeView, you must compile using the command line and include the "/Zi" switch. Include the switch "/CO" when invoking the linker.

As an example, suppose we want to compile a QuickBASIC program named CALLSUM.BAS, which calls the assembly language program SUM that appears in the next chapter. CALLSUM.BAS looks like this:

```
DECLARE SUB SUM (SEG A AS SINGLE, SEG N AS INTEGER, SEG DSUM AS DOUBLE)
N% = 1000
REDIM A(N% - 1)
  FOR I = 0 TO N% - 1
  A(I) = I
  NEXT I
CALL SUM(SEG A(0), N%, DSUM#)
PRINT "ANSWER= ", DSUM#
END
```

Assuming we don't plan on using CodeView, we could assemble, compile, link, and run CALLSUM.BAS and SUM.ASM with the following sequence of commands.

```
masm sum;
bc callsum
link callsum+sum+stackerr;
callsum
```

Using FORTRAN

Use of the 8087 with Microsoft FORTRAN, Version 4.0 and later, is pretty much automatic. In fact, by default the compiler assumes you have an 8087. The "/FPi" switch can be used to product 8087-or-emulator code. Our routines assume the large memory model, which is also the default. Our routines expect any integers to be 2 bytes long. (For example, use the $STORAGE:2 metacommand.) Since routine names may be longer than six characters, you should use the $NOTRUNCATE metacommand. Many of the routines can be called with either single or double precision arguments. If both are used in a single program, the FORTRAN compiler produces a warning message, F3607. As long as you are certain that the use of different argument types was intentional, you can ignore the warning.

All of our routines include a reference to a stack checking routine named STACKERR, defined later in this chapter. Thus STACKERR should be included as an object module when using FL or LINK.

While it has nothing specifically to do with the 8087, allocation of large arrays sometimes causes a run-time error due to insufficient stack space. This can often be alleviated by including the "/Gt" switch on the command line.

To use CodeView, compile with the "/Zi" switch.

Our routine SUM could be called by the following FORTRAN program:

```
$NOTRUNCATE
$STORAGE:2
      DIMENSION A(1000)
      REAL*8 DSUM
      N=1000
        DO 1 I=1,N
 1      A(I)=I
      CALL SUM(A,N,DSUM)
      WRITE(6,101)DSUM
 101  FORMAT(' ANSWER= ',D12.6)
      STOP
      END
```

We could assemble, compile, link and run the program with the commands:

```
masm sum;
fl /Gt callsum.for stackerr sum
callsum
```

Using C

The routines in this book were tested using Version 4.0 of Microsoft's C compiler. (However, the benchmarks were done using a beta test copy of Version 5.0, which produces noticeably faster code.) To produce 8087 code with C, use the "/FPi87" switch, or use "/FPi" for 8087-or-emulator code. Use the "/Zi" switch for CodeView.

All of our routines include a reference to a stack checking routine named STACKERR, defined later in this chapter. Thus STACKERR should be included as an object module when using cl or LINK.

Our routines do not use the standard C calling sequence. Rather, you must convince C to use the FORTRAN sequence. Subroutines are reached with FAR calls, arguments are pushed left-to-right and are passed by reference using long addresses. There are quite a few ways to do this in C. (A C theorem states that if there are n ways to do something, there are also n+ + ways.) One method that works is given in the following example.

Suppose SUM(X,N,DSUM) is a routine in which X is a single precision array, N is an integer, and DSUM is double precision. You could declare this function with

```
typedef int far * intfarp;
typedef float far * floatfarp;
typedef double far * doublefarp;
extern void fortran far
  SUM(floatfarp,intfarp,doublefarp);
```

and call it with

```
SUM((floatfarp) X,&N,&DSUM);
```

Our routine SUM could be called by the following C program:

```
#include <stdio.h>

typedef int far * intfarp;
typedef float far * floatfarp;
typedef double far * doublefarp;

extern void fortran far
SUM(floatfarp,intfarp,doublefarp);

#define n 1000
main() {
 static float a[n];
 double dsum;
 int i,num=n;

 for (i=0;i<n;i++) a[i]=i;

 SUM((floatfarp) a,&num, &dsum);

 printf("Answer = %12lf\n",dsum);

return(0);
};
```

We could assemble, compile, link and run the program with the commands:

```
masm sum;
cl /FPi87 callsum.c stackerr sum
callsum
```

Using Turbo Pascal Version 3.0

We used Version 3.0 of Borland's Turbo Pascal in preparing the routines in this book. To use the 8087, you simply use the 8087 version of the program. Linking up the Turbo Pascal is a little more complicated than using the Microsoft languages.

First, Turbo Pascal uses NEAR rather than FAR calls. Second, floating point numbers are all double precision. When assembling any of our routines for use with Turbo Pascal, use the /DTPASCAL switch. This tells the macros appearing later in the chapter to use NEAR calls and to change single precision arguments to double precision. When using our routines that permit either single or double precision arguments, you must specify double precision to avoid errors.)

Linking assembly language routines into Turbo Pascal requires several steps. (For an excellent article, see "Elegant Linkage," by Richard Halpern, in the May 1987 *PC Tech Journal.*) Arguments of routines should be defined with the "var" parameter and should be declared external. We present one example below.

Suppose SUM(X,DSUM,N) is a routine in which X is a single precision array, DSUM is double precision, and N is an integer. You could declare this fuction with

```
const  n=1000;
type vector = array[1..n] of real;
procedure sum(var x:vector; var n:integer;
          var dsum:real); external 'sum.bin';
```

and call it with

```
sum(x,n,dsum);
```

All that is required is to prepare the file SUM.BIN. First, assemble the routine SUM (and STACKERR) using the /DTPASCAL switch. (Remember that object modules prepared this way are incompatible with Microsoft languages. So keep assembler output prepared with and without the /DTPASCAL switch separated.)

Then LINK SUM+STACKERR. (Ignore the "no stack segment" warning message.) Finally, use the utility EXE2BIN SUM to produce SUM.BIN.

Our routine SUM could be called by the following Turbo Pascal program:

```
const  n=1000;
type vector = array[1..n] of real;
procedure sum(var x:vector; var n:integer; var
dsum:real);
          external 'sum.bin';

var
 i,num :integer;
 a :vector;
 dsum :real;

begin;
  num:=n;
  for i:=1 to n do a[i]:=i;
  sum(a,num,dsum);
  writeln('Answer = ',dsum);
end.
```

We could assemble and link the program with the commands:

```
masm /DTPASCAL sum,sump;
masm /DTPASCAL stackerr,stackerp;
link sump+stackerp,sum;
exe2bin sum
```

Then use the 8087 version of Turbo Pascal to compile and run the Pascal program appearing above.

Using Turbo Pascal Version 4.0

Borland's new Version 4.0 of Turbo Pascal considerably simplifies the life of the 8087 programmer. The first improvement over Version 3.0 is that a single copy of the program generates both 8087 and non-8087 code. In order to generate 8087 code, give the {N+} compiler directive. Version 4.0 also adds four new data types. Types "single," "double," and "extended" provide four, eight, and ten byte 8087 reals. Type "comp" is the 8087's eight byte integer.

Version 4.0 still offers the type "real," but its use with the 8087 has undergone a critical change. In Version 3.0, a "real" was stored in a special six byte format in the non-8087 version and as a double precision number in the 8087 version. In Version 4.0 "real" always specifies the six byte format, so it's incompatible with the 8087. Use single or double instead.

Suppose SUM(X,DSUM,N) is a routine in which X is a single precision array, DSUM is double precision, and N is an integer. You could declare this function with

```
const  n=5000;
type vector = array[1..n] of single;
procedure sum(var x:vector; var n:integer; var
dsum:double);
          external;
```

and call it with

```
sum(x,n,dsum);
```

Version 4.0's big improvement for 8087 users in the great stride in ease of linking. Turbo Pascal now accepts object files in the same format as do Microsoft products. (So if you assemble our routines for use with Version 4.0 *do not* use the /TPASCAL switch.) In order for Turbo Pascal to use our object files you need to take three steps. First, give the compiler directives {F+}, to instruct the compiler to use far calls, and {N+}, to generate 8087 code. (Alternately, go to the Options-Compiler menu inside Turbo Pascal and set "Force far calls" to "On" and "Numeric processing" to "Hardware.") Second, give the compiler directive {$L SUM} to instruct the compiler to link in the object file found in SUM.OBJ (or wherever). You need to give one {$L} directive for each assembly language routine you call plus one for any routines referenced by your assembly language routines. For example, because all our routines refer to routine STACKERR, you should always include the directive {$L stackerr}. Third, all assembly language routines must be declared external, including those referenced by one of your assembly language routines—even if the routines are never called directly from Turbo Pascal. Thus if your program uses our routines it should include the statement "procedure stackerr;external".

Our routine SUM could be called by the following Turbo Pascal Version 4.0 routine.

```
const  n=1000;
type vector = array[1..n] of single;
{$L sum}
{$L stackerr}
procedure stackerr;external;
procedure sum(var x:vector; var n:integer; var dsum:double);
          external;
```

```
var
 i,num :integer;
 a :vector;
 dsum :double;

begin;
  num:=n;
  for i:=1 to n do a[i]:=i;
  sum(a,num,dsum);
  writeln('Answer = ',dsum);
end.
```

While our routines have been tested with these four specific compilers, there is no reason you can't use them with any other language translator which follows the appropriate conventions.

The SUBROUT.MAC Include File

All of our assemble language routines begin with INCLUDE SUBROUT.MAC. This includes a file, which appears below, whose main purpose is to define a number of housekeeping macros. The important services are:

- SUBROUTINE FOO,<arg1,arg2,...> defines a routine named FOO whose arguments can be addressed as [BP].arg1, etc.
- RETURN FOO returns from FOO.
- The SUBROUTINE and RETURN macros save and restore several registers, as required by high level language calls.
- CHKSTCK,some_number jumps to routine STACKERR if there are fewer than some_number bytes left on the stack.
- PUSHTEMP arg1,name pushes arg1 into the stack and allows the location to be preferenced by [BP].name.
- POPTEMP,some_number undoes the past some_number of PUSHTEMPs.
- The macro NEARJMP assembles a NEAR JMP instruction to work around a bug in Version 4.0 of Microsoft's Marco Assembler.
- The macro EXTERNAL replaces the assembler directive EXTRN. External routines are automatically defined to be FAR, unless Turbo Pascal is being used.

Several flags can be set by using the "/D" define symbol flag.

- /DTPASCAL tells the macro to use NEAR rather than FAR calls. Since Turbo Pascal uses double precision, the symbol RealLength and RealPtr are set to 8 and "QWORD PRT", in place of their usual values 4 and

"DWORD PTR." Only use /DTPASCAL when assembling for Version 3.0 of Turbo Pascal, never for Version 4.0.

- /DDODEBUG inserts a breakpoint at the beginning of the routine which will be recognized by the utility DEBUG. This allows you to compile a program named foo, give the command DEBUG FOO, start the program, and then have it stop at the beginning of the routine. This is particularly valuable if CodeView isn't available. (And should only be used with DEBUG, not with CodeView!)
- /DNOFWAIT eliminates the FWAIT instruction in the RETURN macro. Ordinarily, the RETURN macro executes an FWAIT to be sure the 8087 is done before the routine relinquishes control. When the FWAIT is unnecessary, either because the program doesn't require it or because a 287 or 387 is handling synchronizatin electronically, execution is slowed down (or if no coprocessor is present, the machine will hang).

The file SUBROUT.MAC appears below. The coding is straightforward, though not always neat. Note that some symbols, such as TEMP_COUNT, are carried across macro definitions and are therefore not defined to be LOCAL. Also, note that we JMP, rather than CALL to STACKERR. This is necessary because we can't make a call without using the stack!

```
CHKSTCK   MACRO     SPACE
          LOCAL     STACKOK
          CMP       SP,SPACE            ;if not enough stackspace
          JAE       STACKOK             ;jump around error call
          JMP       STACKERR            ;inter segment jump
STACKOK:
          ENDM

          TEMP_COUNT=0                  ;initialize TEMP_COUNT

PUSHTEMP  MACRO     TO_BE_PUSHED,NAME_TO_USE
;;TO_BE_PUSHED IS PUSHED ONTO THE STACK AND THE LOCATION
;;RELATIVE TO BP IS PUT IN NAME_TO_USE (IF PRESENT)
          TEMP_COUNT=TEMP_COUNT+1
          PUSH      TO_BE_PUSHED
IFNB      <NAME_TO_USE>
          NAME_TO_USE=-2*TEMP_COUNT
ENDIF
          ENDM

POPTEMP   MACRO     TO_BE_POPPED
IF        TO_BE_POPPED                  ;;assemble if anything to be popped
          ADD       SP,2*(TO_BE_POPPED)
          TEMP_COUNT=TEMP_COUNT-(TO_BE_POPPED)
ENDIF
```

```
          ENDM
external  MACRO     routinelist
LOCAL     arg
          IRP       arg,<routinelist>
IFDEF     TPASCAL
          EXTRN     arg:NEAR
ELSE
          EXTRN     arg:FAR
ENDIF
          ENDM
          ENDM

subroutine MACRO    subname,argumentlist
LOCAL argloc,arg,arglength,retlength,STACKSPACE
                                  ;;establish local macro variables
;;-------------------------------------------------------
;;The subroutine macro handles the bookkeeping involved
;;in being called as a subroutine.
;;Relevant flags are:
;; /DTPASCAL  for Turbo Pascal
;;  (if absent Fortran conventions apply
;; /DFNOWAIT  eliminate final FWAIT from RETURN macro
;; /DDODEBUG  for use with DEBUG (not Codeview)
;;---------------------------------------------------------
          argcount = 0                 ;;count number
          IRP         arg,<argumentlist>;;of arguments
          argcount = argcount + 1      ;;on stack
          ENDM
          arglength = 4                ;;segment & offset
          retlength = 4                ;;far call
          STACKSPACE = 8               ;;BP,DS,SI,DI
IFDEF     TPASCAL
          arglength = 4                ;;segment & offset
          retlength = 2                ;;near call
          STACKSPACE = 4               ;;BP,DS
ENDIF
          argloc = 2 + retlength + arglength*(argcount-1)
          IRP       arg,<argumentlist>  ;;define addresses on stack
          arg = argloc
          argloc = argloc - arglength
          ENDM

          PUBLIC    subname
          EXTERNAL  STACKERR
          ASSUME    CS:CSEG
CSEG      SEGMENT   PUBLIC 'CODE'
IFNDEF    TPASCAL
```

```
subname   PROC      FAR
ELSE
subname   PROC
ENDIF

IFDEF     DODEBUG
          INT       1
ENDIF
          CHKSTCK   STACKSPACE
          PUSH      BP                  ;save BP
          MOV       BP,SP               ;find argument list
IFNDEF    TPASCAL
          PUSHTEMP  SI                  ;SAVE SI
          PUSHTEMP  DI                  ;SAVE DI
ENDIF
          PUSHTEMP  DS                  ;SAVE DS
          ENDM

RETURN    MACRO     subname
IFNDEF    TPASCAL
          TEMP_COUNT = TEMP_COUNT-3
          POP       DS
          POP       DI
          POP       SI
ELSE                                    ;;TurboPASCAL
          TEMP_COUNT = TEMP_COUNT-1
          POP       DS
ENDIF
          POP       BP
IFNDEF    NOFWAIT
          FWAIT                         ;;BE SURE 8087 IS DONE
ENDIF
          RET       4*argcount
subname   endp
cseg      ends
.ERRNZ    TEMP_COUNT                    ;;TEMP_COUNT BETTER BE BACK TO 0
          ENDM

IFNDEF    TPASCAL
          RealPtr EQU DWORD PTR
          RealLength = 4                ;;assume single precision
ELSE
          RealLength = 8                ;;assume double precision
          RealPtr EQU QWORD PTR
ENDIF

NEARJMP   MACRO     TARGET
          DB        0E9H
```

```
        DW          TARGET-$-2
        ENDM
```

The routine STACKERR prints an error message to the screen, sets an error code (depending on the version of DOS), and returns to the operating system.

```
;This subroutine prints an error message and then
;terminates the program
;See the Microsoft Macro Assembler Reference Manual sec 3.2
          PUBLIC    STACKERR
          ASSUME    CS:CSEG
CSEG      SEGMENT   PUBLIC 'CODE'
IFNDEF    TPASCAL
STACKERR  PROC      FAR
          ASSUME    DS:DSEG
          MOV       AX,SEG DSEG
          MOV       DS,AX
          MOV       DX,OFFSET MESSAGE
          MOV       AH,09H                  ;CALL STRING DISPLAY
          INT       21H
ELSE
STACKERR  PROC
ENDIF
          MOV       AH,30H                  ;Check for DOS version
          INT       21H                     ;major version number in AL
          CMP       AL,2                    ;if 2 or higher we can
          JGE       SHORT REPORT            ;use extended terminate
          MOV       AH,0                    ;CALL TERMINATE
REPORT:   MOV       AH,4CH                  ;extended
          MOV       AL,255                  ;error code 255
          INT       21H
STACKERR  ENDP
CSEG      ENDS

IFNDEF    TPASCAL
DSEG      SEGMENT   'DATA'
MESSAGE   DB        "80x87 assembler routine stack too small",13,10,"$"
DSEG      ENDS
ENDIF
          END
```

In the next chapter, we get down to the business of preparing some useful 8087 routines.

7

Simple 8087 Routines

Several fairly simple 8087 routines are presented in this chapter. The purpose of the presentation is twofold. First, the routines themselves are quite useful. For example, our first program can be called from BASIC to add up a series of numbers. Second, we illustrate a number of principles of 8087 subroutine programming including:

- Indexing through a single array.
- Using single precision and double precision arithmetic.
- Indexing through multiple arrays.

The Cookbook—Chapter 7

Program:	**SUM**
Purpose:	Sums up a single precision array.
Call:	CALL SUM(ARRAY,N,DSUM).
Input:	ARRAY—single precision array. N—integer number of elements of ARRAY.
Output:	DSUM—double precision sum of ARRAY.
Language:	8087/8088 assembly language.
Program:	**PRODUCT**
Purpose:	Product of elements of a single precision array.

Call: CALL PRODUCT(ARRAY,N,DPRODUCT).

Input: ARRAY—single precision array.
N—integer number of elements of ARRAY.

Output: DPRODUCT—double precision product of ARRAY.

Language: 8087/8088 assembly language.

Program: GSUM

Purpose: Sums up an integer, single, or double precision array.

Call: CALL GSUM(ARRAY,TYPE,N,SUM).

Input: ARRAY—array to be summed.
TYPE—integer variable giving the length of one element of ARRAY
N—integer number of elements of ARRAY.

Output: SUM—double precision sum of ARRAY.

Language: 8087/8088 assembly language.

Program: VADD

Purpose: Adds two single precision vectors.

Call: CALL VADD(A,B,C,N).

Input: A—input array.
B—input array.
N—integer number of elements of A,B,C.

Output: C—output array, C = A + B.

Language: 8087/8088 assembly language.

Program: VSET

Purpose: Sets array to a constant.

Call: CALL VSET(A,SCALAR,N).

Input: SCALAR—single precision constant.
N—integer number of elements of A.

Output: A—output array, A = SCALAR.

Language: 8087/8088 assembly language.

Program: **ADDSC**

Purpose: Adds scalar to single precision array.

Call: CALL ADDSC(A,SCALAR,B,N).

Input: A—input array.
SCALAR—single precision constant.
N—integer number of elements of A.

Output: B—output array, B = A + SCALAR.

Language: 8087/8088 assembly language.

Program: **SQROOT**

Purpose: Takes square root of vector.

Call: CALL SQROOT(A,B,N).

Input: A—input array.
N—integer number of elements of A,B.

Output: B—output array, B = SQR(A).

Language: 8087/8088 assembly language.

Program: **GCOPY**

Purpose: Copies integer, single, or double precision array.

Call: CALL GCOPY(A,B,TYPE,N).

Input: A—input array.
TYPE—integer giving length of element of A.
N—integer number of elements of A,B.

Output: B—output array, B = A.

Language: 8087/8088 assembly language.

Program: GBCOPY

Purpose: Copies integer, single, or double precision array, backwards.

Call: CALL GBCOPY(A,B,TYPE,N).

Input: A—input array.
TYPE—integer giving length of element of A.
N—integer number of elements of A,B.

Output: B—output array, B = A.

Language: 8088 assembly language.

Program: GADDSAFR

Purpose: Adds two vectors, with error checking.

Call: CALL GADD-SAFR(A,B,C,TYPEA,TYPEB,TYPEC,N,IER).

Input: A—input array.
B—input array.
TYPEA—integer giving length of element of A.
TYPEB—integer giving length of element of B.
TYPEC—integer giving length of element of C.
N—integer number of elements of A,B,C.

Output: C—output array, C = A + B.
IER—integer error indicator.

Language: 8087/8088 assembly language.

Program: REALERR

Purpose: Check array for invalid data.

Call:	CALL REALERR(ARRAY,TYPE,N,IFDEN,IFINF, IFNAN,ELEMENT).
Input:	ARRAY—input array (single or double precision). TYPE—integer giving length of element of ARRAY. N—integer number of elements of ARRAY.
Output:	IFDEN—integer (− 1 if denormal found). IFINF—integer (− 1 if infinity found). IFNAN—integer (− 1 if Not-A-Normal found). ELEMENT—integer, index of last invalid data.
Language:	8087/8088 assembly language.
Program:	**DENTO0**
Purpose:	Replace denormal values with zero.
Call:	CALL DENTO0(ARRAY,TYPE,N).
Input:	ARRAY—input array (single or double precision). TYPE—integer giving length of element of ARRAY. N—integer number of elements of ARRAY.
Output:	ARRAY—denormals replaced with 0.
Language:	8087/8088 assembly language.

Array Indexing

Our first 8087 subroutine sums a series of numbers and returns their total. Assuming that a single precision array named ARRAY, dimensioned ARRAY(N−1), has been defined elsewhere, that N has been set equal to the number of elements of ARRAY, and that DSUM is a double precision variable, a BASIC instruction sequence might look like this:

```
DSUM=0
  FOR I=0 TO N-1
  DSUM=DSUM+ARRAY(I)
  NEXT I
```

An equivalent 8087 routine appears below. We could call it from BASIC with the instruction

```
CALL SUM(ARRAY,N,DSUM)
```

The 8087 routine has three logical sections. First, it must accept the information passed to it from BASIC. Secondly, the routine calculates the sum of the array elements. Third, the answer is passed back into the BASIC variable DSUM.

```
INCLUDE    SUBROUT.MAC
           SUBROUTINE SUM,<ARRAY,N,DSUM>
;  ASSUMPTIONS:   ARRAY IS A REAL ARRAY OF LENGTH N
;                 N IS AN INTEGER
;                 DSUM IS DOUBLE PRECISION
;
           LDS        SI,[BP].N            ;DS:SI=ADDR(N)
           MOV        CX,[SI]              ;CX=N
           LDS        BX,[BP].ARRAY        ;DS:BX=ADDR(ARRAY)
;
;NOW ALL SET UP TO GO
           FLDZ                            ;INITIALIZE ST=0
           CMP        CX,0                 ;HOPE N > 0
           JLE        DONE

;THE NEXT 3 INSTRUCTIONS DO ALL THE HARD WORK

ADD_LOOP:  FADD       RealPtr [BX]         ;DWORD=> SINGLE PRECISION
           ADD        BX,RealLength        ;READY FOR NEXT ELEMENT
           LOOP       ADD_LOOP

DONE:
;
;NOW FILE ANSWER BACK IN DSUM
           LDS        DI,[BP].DSUM         ;DS:DI=ADDR(DSUM)
           FSTP       QWORD PTR [DI]       ;QWORD=> DOUBLE PRECISION
                                           ;DSUM IS NOW PUT AWAY
           RETURN     SUM
           END
```

How long does the addition routine take? Essentially, all the execution time is in the three-instruction "ADD_LOOP." (Calling the subroutine from BASIC, and the beginning and end of the routine obviously takes a little time. But this overhead time is inconsequential for large N.)

The FADD instruction takes approximately 21 microseconds. The ADD instruction uses approximately 1 microsecond. The LOOP instruction requires about 1 microsecond. Thus the routine should take about 23 microseconds per array element. Right?

Wrong, actually. The 8087 and the cpu run in parallel. So, while the 8087 is adding one number, the 8088 is adding to the BX register, decrementing the count in register CX, testing CX, and looping back up. Hence, the routine takes about 21 microseconds per element. Adding 10,000 single precision numbers takes just under one-fourth of a second. How long would a comparable QuickBASIC routine take? Without the 8087, about a second and a half. With the 8087, just under a second.

In addition to the speed advantage, the 8087 produces a more accurate answer because it accumulates in 80-bit temporary real format rather than 64-bit double precision.

SUM is quite a useful subroutine. Of more general importance, SUM illustrates how to write a routine that indexes through a single array. We use a three-part trick. First we load the address of the array into a convenient base or index register (we could have used SI or DI instead of BX) and the count into the CX register. Second, we add RealLength (4) to BX at each step. Third, we use the LOOP instruction to count off the steps.

Operations other than addition are easily written using the same procedure. For example, to take the product of an array of numbers we could do:

```
INCLUDE    SUBROUT.MAC
           SUBROUTINE PRODUCT,<ARRAY,N,DPRODUCT>
;  ASSUMPTIONS:   ARRAY IS A SINGLE PRECISION ARRAY OF LENGTH N
;                 N IS AN INTEGER
;                 DPRODUCT IS DOUBLE PRECISION
;
           LDS       SI,[BP].N            ;DS:SI=ADDR(N)
           MOV       CX,[SI]              ;CX=N
           LDS       BX,[BP].ARRAY        ;DS:BX=ADDR(ARRAY)
;
;NOW ALL SET UP TO GO
           FLD1                           ;INITIALIZE ST=1
           CMP       CX,0                 ;HOPE N > 0
           JLE       DONE


;THE NEXT 3 INSTRUCTIONS DO ALL THE HARD WORK


MULT_LOOP:FMUL       Realptr [BX]         ;DWORD=> SINGLE PRECISION
           ADD       BX,RealLength        ;READY FOR NEXT ELEMENT
           LOOP      MULT_LOOP
```

```
DONE:
;
;NOW FILE ANSWER BACK IN DPRODUCT
         LDS       DI,[BP].DPRODUCT    ;DS:DI=ADDR(DPRODUCT)
         FSTP      QWORD PTR [DI]      ;QWORD=> DOUBLE PRECISION
                                       ;DPRODUCT IS NOW PUT AWAY
         RETURN    PRODUCT
         END
```

The FMUL instruction takes approximately 23 microseconds. Multiplying 10,000 single precision numbers takes about one-fourth of a second. A comparable routine takes QuickBASIC about a second and a half without an 8087 and a second with an 8087. Accuracy of the 8087 PRODUCT subroutine will, under some circumstances, considerably exceed the accuracy of the equivalent BASIC code. The 8087 temporary real exponent allows a much greater range than the double precision exponent, so intermediate overflows or underflows are much less likely to occur with the 8087 routine.

Double Precision Arguments

The choice between single precision and double precision arithmetic requires a tradeoff between accuracy and memory space. Double precision numbers take up twice as much space as single precision numbers, but are somewhat more than twice as accurate. Good numerical programming practice dictates using double precision throughout. Unfortunately, because of storage limitations this is rarely practical. In fact, there is a "folk theorem" to the effect that problem size expands to use up all available space. The following stages of compromise are recommended:

1. If the problem can be done entirely in double precision, do it that way.
2. Hold raw input and final results in single precision—everything else in double precision. There is little loss to storing original input in single precision—real data can rarely be measured with the seven significant digits provided for by single precision storage. The problem with single precision is the loss of accuracy from cumulative errors. Doing all the calculations in double precision is almost as good as holding everything in double precision.
3. Retain critical intermediate steps in double precision. Delay conversion into single precision as long as possible.

Of course, the 8087's 80-bit temporary real format is even more accurate than double precision. The most accurate answers are found by doing as many intermediate calculations as possible within the 8087, storing only final results in memory.

In practice, programs use both single and double precision. (Although Turbo Pascal stores all real variables as double precision.) One advantage of a high-level language is that programs "know" whether variables are single or double precision. Our 8087 routines need to be told. There are two ways, both valuable, to "tell" our routines what precision to use. First, we can write separate routines, one for single and one for double precision. Second, we can write routines which handle both cases and include an extra argument to tell the routine which type of data is being used. The first is easier to write, but the flexibility of the second is sometimes worth the extra effort.

Changing a single precision routine to double precision requires only two simple steps: change the 8087 instructions to reference double precision memory, and change the step size to eight rather than four bytes. Thus, we can change subroutine SUM into a double precision subroutine DSUM by setting RealLength = 8. This is equivalent to substituting:

`FADD QWORD PTR [BX]` instead of `FADD DWORD PTR [BX]`
and
`ADD BX,8` instead of `ADD BX,4`

The second approach to the problem of variable precision is to pass the needed information on to the subroutine. As long as we're solving this problem, we may as well make things a bit more general. Subroutine GSUM accepts a single precision, double precision, or integer vector.

```
INCLUDE   SUBROUT.MAC
          SUBROUTINE GSUM,<ARRAY,ARRAY_TYPE,N,SUM>
;  ASSUMPTIONS:    ARRAY IS AN ARRAY OF LENGTH N
;                  ARRAY_TYPE IS AN INTEGER: 2-INTEGER 4-SINGLE 8-DOUBLE
;                  N IS AN INTEGER
;                  SUM IS DOUBLE PRECISION
;
          LDS       SI,[BP].ARRAY_TYPE   ;DS:SI=ADDR(ARRAY_TYPE)
          MOV       AX,[SI]              ;AX=ARRAY_TYPE
          LDS       SI,[BP].N            ;DS:SI=ADDR(N)
          MOV       CX,[SI]              ;CX=N
          LDS       BX,[BP].ARRAY        ;DS:BX=ADDR(ARRAY)
;
;NOW ALL SET UP TO GO
          FLDZ                           ;INITIALIZE ST=0
          CMP       CX,0                 ;HOPE N > 0
          JLE       DONE
;
ADD_LOOP:
          CMP       AX,2                 ;IS IT INTEGER?
```

```
          JNE       NOT_INTEGER
          FIADD     WORD PTR [BX]
          JMP       NEXT_ELEMENT
NOT_INTEGER:
          CMP       AX,4                ;IS IT SINGLE?
          JNE       NOT_SINGLE
          FADD      DWORD PTR [BX]
          JMP       NEXT_ELEMENT
NOT_SINGLE:                             ;BETTER BE DOUBLE
          FADD      QWORD PTR [BX]
;
NEXT_ELEMENT:
          ADD       BX,AX               ;READY FOR NEXT ELEMENT
          LOOP      ADD_LOOP
DONE:
;NOW FILE ANSWER BACK IN SUM
          LDS       DI,[BP].SUM         ;DS:DI=ADDR(SUM)
          FSTP      QWORD PTR [DI]      ;SUM IS NOW PUT AWAY
          RETURN    GSUM
          END
```

Subroutine GSUM will accept any of the three BASIC numeric variable types. GSUM is slightly more complex than SUM and we have to pass it one extra argument. It may look like GSUM will also be slower, since it has to check ARRAY_TYPE each time through and also jump around extra instructions. However, the comparison and jump only take about five microseconds, so the cpu executes these instructions while the 8087 is working on the addition.

Indexing Through Multiple Arrays

In the routines above, we used the BX register to index ARRAY. This procedure works with a single array, but more complicated problems may require us to keep track of several indexes. Up to three indexes may be kept in the registers BX, SI, and DI. In addition, registers AX, DX, and CX are convenient for holding temporary values. (On a 386, an index may be held in any register—simplifying programming enormously.)

Our next subroutine adds two single precision vectors, returning a single precision vector result.

```
INCLUDE   SUBROUT.MAC
          SUBROUTINE VADD,<A,B,C,N>
;  ASSUMPTIONS:   A,B,C ARE SINGLE PRECISION ARRAYS OF LENGTH N
;                 N IS AN INTEGER
```

```
;
          LDS       SI,[BP].N             ;DS:SI=ADDR(N)
          MOV       CX,[SI]               ;CX=N
          MOV       BX,0                  ;BX=0, USE TO TRACK INDEX
;
;NOW ALL SET UP TO GO
          CMP       CX,0                  ;HOPE N > 0
          JLE       DONE
ADD_LOOP:
          LDS       SI,[BP].A             ;DS:SI=ADDR(A(0))
          FLD       RealPtr [SI][BX]      ;LOAD A(I)
          LDS       SI,[BP].B             ;DS:SI=ADDR(B(0))
          FADD      RealPtr [SI][BX]      ;ADD B(I)
          LDS       SI,[BP].C             ;DS:SI=ADDR(C(0))
          FSTP      RealPtr [SI][BX]      ;C(I)=A(I)+B(I)
          ADD       BX,RealLength         ;READY FOR NEXT ELEMENT
          LOOP      ADD_LOOP
DONE:
;
          RETURN    VADD
          END
```

Subroutine VADD requires just under half a second to add two 10,000 long vectors. Note that while we have specified three vectors, nothing prevents A and B or A and C, or even all three from being the same vector. Thus the command CALL VADD(A,A,A,N) doubles each element of A.

Creating routines to perform subtraction, multiplication, and division requires us only to change the 8087 addition instruction to an 8087 subtraction, or other type of instruction. Thus we can change one line in VADD:

```
C=A+B    :    "FADD RealPtr [SI]"
```

to make VSUB:

```
C=A-B    :    "FSUB RealPtr [SI]"
```

or to make VMULT:

```
C=A*B    :    "FMUL RealPtr [SI]"
```

or to make VDIV:

```
C=A/B    :    "FDIV RealPtr [SI]"
```

(Note VMULT and VDIV perform element-by-element operations, not "matrix operations.")

The same technique we used for changing SUM into GSUM can be used to change VADD into a routine for single precision or double precision or integer vector addition.

Scalar Routines

Mathematical operations frequently involve a scalar and a vector. ("Scalar" is the word mathematicians use for a single number, as opposed to an entire vector of numbers.) The simplest example would be setting an entire vector to a constant, as in A=5. Subroutine VSET performs this service. VSET first loads the value SCALAR onto the 8087 stack and then copies the 8087 register ST into each element of A.

```
INCLUDE    SUBROUT.MAC
           SUBROUTINE VSET,<A,SCALAR,N>
;  ASSUMPTIONS:    A IS A SINGLE PRECISION ARRAY OF LENGTH N
;                  SCALAR IS SINGLE PRECISION
;                  N IS AN INTEGER
;
           LDS       SI,[BP].N           ;DS:SI=ADDR(N)
           MOV       CX,[SI]             ;CX=N
           MOV       BX,[BP]+10          ;BX=ADDR(A)
           LDS       SI,[BP].SCALAR      ;DS:SI=ADDR(SCALAR)
           FLD       RealPtr [SI]        ;PUSH SCALAR ONTO STACK
           LDS       BX,[BP].A           ;DS:BX=ADDR(A)
;NOW ALL SET UP TO GO
           CMP       CX,0                ;HOPE N > 0
           JLE       DONE
VSET_LOOP:
           FST       RealPtr [BX]        ;STORE A(I)
           ADD       BX,8                ;READY FOR NEXT A
           LOOP      VSET_LOOP
DONE:
;
           FSTP      ST(0)               ;GET RID OF SCALAR
           RETURN    VSET
           END
```

A typical mathematical operation is to add a scalar to every element of a vector. Routine ADDSC performs this function.

```
INCLUDE    SUBROUT.MAC
           SUBROUTINE ADDSC,<A,SCALAR,B,N>
;  ASSUMPTIONS:    A,B ARE SINGLE PRECISION ARRAYS OF LENGTH N
;                  SCALAR IS SINGLE PRECISION
;                  N IS AN INTEGER
;
           LDS       SI,[BP].N              ;DS:SI=ADDR(N)
           MOV       CX,[SI]                ;CX=N
           LDS       SI,[BP].SCALAR         ;DS:SI=ADDR(SCALAR)
           FLD       RealPtr [SI]           ;PUSH SCALAR ONTO STACK
           MOV       BX,0                   ;BX=0, INDEXES ELEMENT
;NOW ALL SET UP TO GO
           CMP       CX,0                   ;HOPE N > 0
           JLE       DONE
ADD_LOOP:
           LDS       SI,[BP].A              ;DS:SI=ADDR(A)
           FLD       DWORD PTR [SI][BX]     ;LOAD A(I)
           FADD      ST,ST(1)               ;ADD SCALAR
           LDS       SI,[BP].B              ;DS:SI=ADDR(B)
           FSTP      DWORD PTR [SI][BX]     ;B(I)=A(I)+SCALAR
           ADD       BX,RealLength          ;READY FOR NEXT ELEMENT
           LOOP      ADD_LOOP
DONE:
           FSTP      ST(0)                  ;GET RID OF SCALAR
           RETURN    ADDSC
           END
```

Adapting ADDSC for subtraction, multiplication, and division is straightforward. (Remember, of course, that "A−SCALAR" is quite different from "SCALAR−A!")

Unary Operations

Operations requiring only one argument are said to be "unary" (as opposed to two-argument "binary" operations such as "A + B"). For example we might want to find the square root, absolute value, or negative of the elements of an array. Routine SQROOT, which we used for timing examples in Part I, computes B = SQR(A).

```
INCLUDE    SUBROUT.MAC
           SUBROUTINE SQROOT,<A,B,N>
;  ASSUMPTIONS:    A,B ARE SINGLE PRECISION ARRAYS OF LENGTH N
;                  N IS AN INTEGER
;
```

```
          LDS       SI,[BP].N            ;DS:SI=ADDR(N)
          MOV       CX,[SI]              ;CX=N
          MOV       BX,0                 ;BX INDEXES ELEMENTS
;NOW ALL SET UP TO GO
          CMP       CX,0                 ;HOPE N > 0
          JLE       DONE
SQROOT_LOOP:
          LDS       SI,[BP].A            ;DS:BX=ADDR(A)
          FLD       RealPtr [SI][BX]     ;LOAD A(I)
          FSQRT                          ;FIND SQRT(A(I))
          LDS       SI,[BP].B            ;DS:SI=ADDR(B)
          FSTP      RealPtr [SI][BX]     ;B(I)=SQRT(A(I))
          ADD       BX,RealLength        ;READY FOR NEXT ELEMENT
          LOOP      SQROOT_LOOP
DONE:
          RETURN    SQROOT
          END
```

Routine SQRT is easily changed to compute absolute value or to yield the negative of the input vector by changing FSQRT to FABS or FCHS.

Utility Routines

The speed of the routines above reflects both the 8087's prodigious mathematical ability and the vast speed advantage of 8088 assembly language code over BASIC. It can be very useful to use assembly language routines even for such "non-computational" tasks as copying one array of numbers into another. We can use the 8087's automatic precision conversion to allow the transfer between single precision, double precision, and integer arrays as a bonus.

```
INCLUDE   SUBROUT.MAC
          SUBROUTINE GCOPY,<A,B,TYPEA,TYPEB,N>
;  ASSUMPTIONS:  A,B ARE ARRAYS OF LENGTH N
;                TYPEA IS AN INTEGER: 2-INTEGER 4-SINGLE 8-DOUBLE
;                TYPEB   "
;                N IS AN INTEGER
;
          LDS       SI,[BP].TYPEA        ;DS:SI=ADDR(TYPEA)
          MOV       AX,[SI]              ;AX=TYPEA
          LDS       SI,[BP].TYPEB        ;DS:SI=ADDR(TYPEB)
          MOV       DX,[SI]              ;DX=TYPEB
          MOV       SI,[BP].N            ;DS:SI=ADDR(N)
          MOV       CX,[SI]              ;CX=N
          MOV       SI,0                 ;SI=ELEMENT OF A
```

```
          MOV       DI,0                ;DI=ELEMENT OF B
;
;NOW ALL SET UP TO GO
          CMP       CX,0                ;HOPE N > 0
          JLE       DONE
;
COPY_LOOP:
          LDS       BX,[BP].A           ;DS:BX=ADDR(A)
          CMP       AX,2                ;IS A INTEGER?
          JNE       A_NOT_INTEGER
          FILD      WORD PTR [SI][BX]
          JMP       STORE_IT
A_NOT_INTEGER:
          CMP       AX,4                ;IS A SINGLE?
          JNE       A_NOT_SINGLE
          FLD       DWORD PTR [SI][BX]
          JMP       STORE_IT
A_NOT_SINGLE:                           ;BETTER BE DOUBLE
          FLD       QWORD PTR [SI][BX]
;
STORE_IT:
          LDS       BX,[BP].B           ;DS:BX=ADDR(B)
          CMP       DX,2                ;IS B INTEGER?
          JNE       B_NOT_INTEGER
          FISTP     WORD PTR [DI][BX]
          JMP       LOOP_END
B_NOT_INTEGER:
          CMP       DX,4                ;IS B SINGLE?
          JNE       B_NOT_SINGLE
          FSTP      DWORD PTR [DI][BX]
          JMP       LOOP_END
B_NOT_SINGLE:                           ;BETTER BE DOUBLE
          FSTP      QWORD PTR [DI][BX]
;
LOOP_END:
          ADD       SI,AX               ;READY FOR NEXT A ELEMENT
          ADD       DI,DX               ;READY FOR NEXT B ELEMENT
          LOOP      COPY_LOOP
DONE:
          RETURN    GCOPY
          END
```

GCOPY loads each array element into the 8087 and then dumps it back out again. In this way, type conversion is handled pretty much automatically. On the other hand, if all we really wanted to do was make an identical copy of an array the horsepower of the 8087 isn't really necessary. In fact, for a pure copy without type conversions, GCOPY isn't appreciably faster than QuickBASIC. Our next routine can't do type conversions, but it's a *lot* faster.

Our second utility routine is GBCOPY. GBCOPY is like GCOPY, except that it begins copying an A(N−1) and works down to A(0), rather than vice versa, and that GBCOPY does not perform type conversions.

```
INCLUDE    SUBROUT.MAC
           SUBROUTINE GBCOPY,<A,B,ARRAY_TYPE,N>
;  ASSUMPTIONS:  A,B ARE ARRAYS OF LENGTH N
;                ARRAY_TYPE IS AN INTEGER: 2-INTEGER 4-SINGLE 8-DOUBLE
;                N IS AN INTEGER
;
           LDS       BX,[BP].N            ;DS:BX=ADDR(N)
           MOV       CX,[BX]              ;CX=N
           LDS       BX,[BP].ARRAY_TYPE   ;DS:BX=ADDR(ARRAY_TYPE)
           MOV       AX,[BX]              ;AX=ARRAY_TYPE
           MUL       CX                   ;AX=N*TYPE
           MOV       CX,AX                ;CX=BYTES TO BE MOVED
           LDS       SI,[BP].A            ;DS:SI=ADDR(A)
           LES       DI,[BP].B            ;ES:DI=ADDR(B)
           ADD       SI,CX                ;POINT SI TO LAST WORD
           DEC       SI                   ;BY ADDING N*TYPE-2
           DEC       SI
           ADD       DI,CX                ;POINT DI TO LAST WORD
           DEC       DI
           DEC       DI
           SHR       CX,1                 ;CX=WORDS TO BE MOVED
           STD                            ;SET DIRECTION FLAG TO
                                          ;MOVE TOWARD LOWER ADDRESSES
           REP MOVSW                      ;THIS DOES ALL THE WORK

           CLD                            ;CLEAR DIRECTION FLAG
           RETURN    GBCOPY
           END
```

GBCOPY illustrates two points. First, it demonstrates use of the cpu instruction MOVSW (move string). Second GBCOPY copies backwards, for reasons to be discussed shortly.

To use MOVSW, we need to set up the source address in DS:Si and the destination in ES:SI. We set the direction flag, to indicate the direction of the move — STD for begin at end of the array. (We could use CLD to begin at the beginning.) Finally, we load the number of words to be copied into CX and put the REP (repeat) prefix in front of MOVSW.

Since copying an array is so common, most computers include an instruction like MOVSW. However, it takes a very smart compiler to realize it can use MOVSW. Our routine GBCOPY beats QuickBASIC by a factor of 25! It is also interesting to note that MOVSW is one of the instrctions that Intel has done the most to speed up over the years. On the 8088, the basic execution takes 25 clocks per word. On a 286, this time has been chopped to 5 clocks. The time rose to 7 clocks with the 386, but a new instruction that moves four bytes rather than two in those 7 clocks, MOVSD, was introduced.

Now to the second point. Why move an array backwards anyhow? Consider the following two problems. First, copy A(I+1) into A(I) for an entire array. This can be done either in BASIC:

```
FOR I=0 TO N-2
A(I)=A(I+1)
NEXT I
```

or with GCOPY:

```
N1%=N-1:TYPEA%=4
CALL GCOPY(A(1),A(0),TYPEA%,TYPEA%,N1%)
```

Second, copy A(I) into A(I + 1) for an entire array. One might be tempted do this in BASIC with

```
FOR I=0 TO N-2
A(I+1)=A(I)
NEXT I
```

but this won't work. On the first step, this puts A(0) into A(1). On the next step, when BASIC tries to move A(1), it picks up the value originally in A(0). The original value of A(1) has been wiped out. Correct BASIC code would be

```
FOR I=N-2 TO 0 STEP -1
A(I+1)=A(I)
NEXT I
```

GCOPY(A(0), A(1),TYPEA%,TYPEA%, N1%) would generate the same incorrect results as the first BASIC program. GBCOPY(A(0), A(1), TYPEA%, N1%) works correctly. Since GBCOPY's primary use is copying data from one part of an array to another part of the same array, nothing was lost by omitting the type conversion.

On Errors

Errors that might result from using number crunching subroutines can be loosely grouped into four classes:

- Programming errors in the subroutines.
- Errors in using the subroutines.
- Recoverable precision errors.
- Non-recoverable precision errors.

Programming Errors

Computer hardware does not make mistakes. (Not often, anyway.) People who program computers *do* make mistakes. As you develop your own number crunching routines for the 8087, you'll naturally hit an occasional bug. Be warned that a personal computer is not quite so forgiving when programmed at the machine language level as it is when programmed in BASIC.

About the worst that can happen in a BASIC program, aside from getting the wrong answer, is that BASIC halts the program and prints a somewhat cryptic error message. Usually, BASIC at least tells you what line caused the error.

What's the worst that can happen with an undebugged machine language program? Frequently, you CALL a machine language program and nothing happens . . . nothing *at all* happens. The only thing to do is to hit the reset key (Ctrl-Alt-Del on an IBM PC) and restart the system from scratch.

Unfortunately, things can be even a bit worse. Sometimes the reset key doesn't do anything either. A machine language program can, after all, write into any location in memory—including writing garbage into areas that only DOS is supposed to use. When this happens, the only solution is to power down, leave the machine off for a few seconds, and then turn the power back on. *It pays to be careful in debugging 8087/8088 programs.*

Errors in Using the Subroutines

Even bug-free routines can go wrong if fed invalid input. As a simple example, suppose we feed the wrong value for N to one of the vector routines prepared above. It would be nice if the routines would check for valid input and return an error indication when given garbage.

Consider what our routines do instead. If N gives the correct length of the data arrays, the routines return the correct answer. Notice that special consideration is given to the case of zero length arrays and these are handled properly. Suppose we set N to a negative value. The routines act as if N were zero, but do not report the error. Suppose instead that the arrays are really 100 long, but we mistakenly set N to 50. The routines give the wrong answer, but return to BASIC without other errors. Suppose we commit the reverse error, setting N to 100 when the arrays are only of length 50. The routines will merrily write into an area of memory assigned to something other than the arrays we are supposed to be using. If we are lucky, the routine will overwrite something vital and the machine will stop cold. In this way we will come to suspect there is an error. If we are unlucky, the routine will change totally unrelated variables, causing our final answers to be wrong without giving any indication of a possible problem.

It is an unfortunate fact of life that there is no sure-fire way to catch these kinds of errors in a machine language program, or, for that matter, in many other computer languages. For the routines in this book, we have decided to place all error checking responsibility on the BASIC programmer. However, it is certainly possible to rewrite the routines to catch a few errors. Routine GADDSAFR (General precision ADDition, but SAFeR) illustrates one such approach.

```
INCLUDE   SUBROUT.MAC
          SUBROUTINE GADDSAFR,<A,B,C,TYPEA,TYPEB,TYPEC,N,IER>
;  ASSUMPTIONS: A,B,C ARE ARRAYS OF LENGTH N
;                TYPEA IS AN INTEGER: 2-INTEGER 4-SINGLE 8-DOUBLE
;                TYPEB "       "
;                TYPEC "       "
;                N IS AN INTEGER
;                IER IS AN INTEGER RETURNING 0 IF NO ERROR
;                    1 IF N IS NEGATIVE
;                    2 IF TYPEA,TYPEB,OR TYPEC IS ILLEGAL
;
;CHECK TYPES
          LDS       SI,[BP].TYPEA       ;DS:SI=ADDR(TYPEA)
          MOV       AX,[SI]             ;AX=TYPEA
          CMP       AX,2
          JE        TYPEA_OK
          CMP       AX,4
          JE        TYPEA_OK
          CMP       AX,8
          JE        TYPEA_OK
          JMP       TYPE_ERROR
TYPEA_OK:
```

```
          LDS       SI,[BP].TYPEB        ;DS:SI=ADDR(TYPEB)
          MOV       AX,[SI]              ;AX=TYPEB
          CMP       AX,2
          JE        TYPEB_OK
          CMP       AX,4
          JE        TYPEB_OK
          CMP       AX,8
          JE        TYPEB_OK
          JMP       TYPE_ERROR
TYPEB_OK:
          LDS       SI,[BP].TYPEC        ;DS:SI=ADDR(TYPEC)
          MOV       AX,[SI]              ;AX=TYPEC
          CMP       AX,2
          JE        TYPEC_OK
          CMP       AX,4
          JE        TYPEC_OK
          CMP       AX,8
          JE        TYPEC_OK
          JMP       TYPE_ERROR
TYPEC_OK: JMP       CHECK_N
TYPE_ERROR:
          MOV       AX,2
          NEARJMP   DONE
;
CHECK_N:
          LDS       SI,[BP].N            ;DS:SI=ADDR(N)
          MOV       CX,[SI]              ;CX=N
          CMP       CX,0
          JNE       L                    ;LABEL "DONE" TOO FAR FOR
          NEARJMP   DONE                 ;DIRECT JE
L:        JG        START_ADD
;                                        OOPS, N<0
          MOV       AX,1
          NEARJMP   DONE
;
START_ADD:
;USE AX FOR ELEMENT COUNT FOR A
;    DX FOR ELEMENT COUNT FOR B
;    DI FOR ELEMENT COUNT FOR C
          MOV       AX,0
          MOV       DX,0
          MOV       DI,0


ADD_LOOP:
          LDS       SI,[BP].TYPEA        ;DS:SI=ADDR(TYPEA)
          MOV       SI,[SI]              ;SI=TYPEA
```

```
        LDS     BX,[BP].A           ;DS:BX=ADDR(A)
        ADD     BX,AX               ;DS:BX=ADDR(A(I))
        CMP     SI,2                ;IS IT INTEGER?
        JNE     A_NOT_INTEGER
        FILD    WORD PTR [BX]
        JMP     ADD_B
A_NOT_INTEGER:
        CMP     SI,4                ;IS IT SINGLE?
        JNE     A_NOT_SINGLE
        FLD     DWORD PTR [BX]
        JMP     ADD_B
A_NOT_SINGLE:
        FLD     QWORD PTR [BX]
;
ADD_B:  ADD     AX,SI              ;READY FOR A NEXT TIME

        LDS     SI,[BP].TYPEB       ;DS:SI=ADDR(TYPEB)
        MOV     SI,[SI]             ;SI=TYPEB
        LDS     BX,[BP].B           ;DS:BX=ADDR(B)
        ADD     BX,DX               ;DS:BX=ADDR(B(I))
        CMP     SI,2                ;IS IT INTEGER?
        JNE     B_NOT_INTEGER
        FIADD   WORD PTR [BX]
        JMP     NEXT_C
B_NOT_INTEGER:
        CMP     SI,4                ;IS IT SINGLE?
        JNE     B_NOT_SINGLE
        FADD    DWORD PTR [BX]
        JMP     NEXT_C
B_NOT_SINGLE:
        FADD    QWORD PTR [BX]
;
NEXT_C: ADD     DX,SI               ;READY FOR NEXT B

        LDS     SI,[BP].TYPEC       ;DS:SI=ADDR(TYPEC)
        MOV     SI,[SI]             ;SI=TYPEC
        LDS     BX,[BP].C           ;DS:BX=ADDR(C)
        ADD     BX,DI               ;DS:BX=ADDR(C(I))
        CMP     SI,2                ;IS IT INTEGER?
        JNE     C_NOT_INTEGER
        FISTP   WORD PTR [BX]
        JMP     NEXT_ELEMENT
C_NOT_INTEGER:
        CMP     SI,4                ;IS IT SINGLE?
        JNE     C_NOT_SINGLE
        FSTP    DWORD PTR [BX]
```

```
          JMP       NEXT_ELEMENT
C_NOT_SINGLE:
          FSTP      QWORD PTR [BX]
;
NEXT_ELEMENT:
          ADD       DI,SI               ;READY FOR NEXT C
          LOOP      ADD_LOOPER          ;LOOP ONLY JUMPS 127...
          MOV       AX,0                ;   -NO ERROR-
          JMP       SHORT DONE
ADD_LOOPER:JMP      ADD_LOOP            ;...BYTES
DONE:
          LDS       SI,[BP].IER         ;DS:SI=ADDR(IER)
          MOV       [SI],AX             ;IER=ERROR CODE
          RETURN    GADDSAFR
          END
```

Error checking adds only about 20 lines of code and a negligible increase in execution time. Unfortunately, many illegal input errors still won't be caught. Besides N simply having the incorrect value, any of the arrays might actually be of a different type than that stated; the type, N, or IER arguments might not be integers; or we might call GADDSAFR with the wrong number or order of arguments.

Precision Errors

A fact of life that programmers find most difficult to accept is that *perfectly "correct" programs sometimes give the wrong answer.* Computer arithmetic has only limited accuracy. The 8087 is more accurate than most mainframes. Nonetheless, for any finite degree of precision, there exists some problem for which the degree of precision is insufficient. The problem is somewhat aggravated by the fact that a program will work perfectly with one set of data and not at all with another. With some work, one can even construct a series of numbers which add correctly when added from first to last but give a nonsensical result when added backwards. There are several programming approaches to handling precision errors:

- Ignore the problem and hope no errors ever occur.
- Handle each error as soon as it occurs.
- Set up a general scheme to allow computation to proceed as far as possible.

Ignoring the problem is not quite as silly as it sounds. The 8087 is extremely accurate. Furthermore, the 8087 designers have built in automatic error handling capabilities which operate very sensibly. For most problems, precision errors will not occur. For most precision errors that do occur, the 8087 error handling will apply the correct solution.

As an extreme alternative, the 8087 can be set to stop every time an error occurs. *Exception handling* software can be written to take care of every error on a problem-specific basis. This approach requires you to hand-tailor every subroutine, so it isn't practical for this book. Exception handling routines are discussed in the *Intel iAPX 86,88 User's Manual.*

If you are using an 8087 routine in combination with a high-level language, the exception handler provided with the language will maintain control even while your routine is running. In almost all cases this is perfectly satisfactory. Microsoft's C and FORTRAN provide you a fair amount of control over how exceptions are handled through functions _control87 (C) and SSWRQQ, SCWRQQ, and LCWRQQ (FORTRAN).

If we're not using a commercial exception handler and don't wish to start a major systems programming effort, we can still do quite well by letting the 8087 take the reins and then checking over the resulting output data. The error handling routines in the 8087 hardware always allow execution to continue, while generally indicating errors by producing an answer that is not a "normal" number. All our routines allow the 8087 automatic error handling procedures to maintain control. As a result, the final answers may include an error indication. We need a routine to check whether data is valid or invalid. We would also like to fix those errors for which some obvious fix-up exists. Single and double precision output of the 8087 take one of the following forms, which were discussed at length in Chapter 3:

- Normal—a valid number.
- Denormal—indicates a previous underflow.
- Infinity—may indicate a previous overflow.
- Not-A-Number (NAN)—invalid datum.

Routine REALERR accepts an input array of single or double precision numbers. It returns three integer variables, each of which is set to −1 (true) if any denormal, infinity, or NAN, respectively, is stored in the array, or to 0 (false) otherwise. ELEMENT is an integer variable giving the element number of the last other than normal number found.

Routines REALERR and DENTO0 use some processor control instructions defined in Chapter 10. We include these routines here because of their usefulness for even simple numerical programs.

```
INCLUDE   SUBROUT.MAC
          SUBROUTINE REALERR,
          <ARRAY,ARRAY_TYPE,N,IFDEN,IFINF,IFNAN,ELEMENT>
;  ASSUMPTIONS:  ARRAY IS OF LENGTH N
```

```
;               ARRAY_TYPE IS AN INTEGER: 4-SINGLE, 8-DOUBLE
;               N IS AN INTEGER
;               IFDEN,IFINF,IFNAN ARE INTEGER
;                  RETURNING 0 (FALSE) OR -1 (TRUE)
;               ELEMENT IS AN INTEGER
;
;SET TENTATIVE RETURN VALUES TO ZERO
          LDS       SI,[BP].IFDEN       ;CLEAR IFDEN
          MOV       WORD PTR [SI],0
          LDS       SI,[BP].IFINF       ;CLEAR IFINF
          MOV       WORD PTR [SI],0
          LDS       SI,[BP].IFNAN       ;CLEAR IFNAN
          MOV       WORD PTR [SI],0
          LDS       SI,[BP].ELEMENT     ;CLEAR ELEMENT
          MOV       WORD PTR [SI],0
          LDS       SI,[BP].N
          MOV       CX,[SI]             ;CX=N
          MOV       SI,[BP].ARRAY_TYPE  ;DS:SI=ADDR(ARRAY_TYPE)
          MOV       AX,[SI]             ;AX=ARRAY_TYPE
          LDS       BX,[BP].ARRAY       ;DS:BX=ADDR(ARRAY)
          PUSHTEMP  AX,STATUS_WORD      ;SET ASIDE LOCATION FOR
                                        ;8087 STATUS WORD
;
;NOW ALL SET UP TO GO
          CMP       CX,0                ;HOPE N > 0
          JLE       DONE
;
CHECK_LOOP:
          CMP       AX,4                ;IS A SINGLE?
          JNE       NOT_SINGLE
          FLD       DWORD PTR [BX]
          JMP       CHECK_IT
NOT_SINGLE:                             ;BETTER BE DOUBLE
          FLD       QWORD PTR [BX]
;
CHECK_IT:
          ADD       BX,AX               ;READY FOR NEXT ELEMENT
          FXAM                          ;WHAT DID WE LOAD?
          FSTSW     [BP].STATUS_WORD
          FSTP      ST(0)
          FWAIT
          MOV       DH,BYTE PTR [BP].STATUS_WORD+1
          AND       DH,01000101B        ;BLANK OTHER BITS
          CMP       DH,00000100B        ;NORMAL?
          JE        OK
          CMP       DH,01000000B        ;ZERO?
```

```
          JE        OK
          CMP       DH,00000101B        ;INFINITY?
          JE        INF
          CMP       DH,0                ;UNNORMAL?
          JE        DEN
          CMP       DH,01000100B        ;DENORMAL?
          JE        DEN
;MUST BE NAN
          LDS       SI,[BP].IFNAN       ;DS:SI=ADDR(IFNAN)
          JMP       SET_ERROR
DEN:      LDS       SI,[BP].IFDEN       ;DS:SI=ADDR(IFDEN)
          JMP       SET_ERROR
INF:      LDS       SI,[BP].IFINF       ;DS:SI=ADDR(IFINF)
SET_ERROR:
          MOV       WORD PTR [SI],-1    ;ERROR IS TRUE
          LDS       SI,[BP].N           ;GET N BACK
          MOV       SI,[SI]
          SUB       SI,CX               ;SI= CURRENT INDEX
          LDS       DI,[BP].ELEMENT
          MOV       [DI],SI             ;SET ELEMENT
OK:       LOOP      LOOPER
          JMP       DONE
LOOPER:   JMP       CHECK_LOOP


DONE:
          POPTEMP   1
          RETURN    REALERR
          END
```

REALERR is a little complicated, but is nonetheless quite fast, checking an array of 10,000 numbers in about a quarter of a second.

After execution of REALERR, IFDEN, IFINF, and IFNAN are easily tested with BASIC IF statements. The question remains as to what action should follow as a result of the test. The following general rules can serve as a guide:

- NAN—halt execution with an error message.
- Infinity—Halting execution or allowing it to continue depends somewhat on circumstances. Infinity usually indicates a meaningless value, resulting from either an overflow or from some sort of invalid operation. However, there are occasionally functions for which infinity is a sensible number. Consider evaluating the following function:

  $$1/(1 + 1/x)$$

  As x goes to zero, the function goes to zero. Since the 8087 is designed to report 1 divided by zero as infinity, 1 plus infinity as infinity, and 1 divided by infinity as zero, this function will be correctly evaluated, if we ignore intermediate infinite results. If X equals −1, then the final result will be infinity, as it should be.

- Denormals are a somewhat different case. A denormal indicates that an underflow has occurred. The datum therefore represents a number very close to zero. We can either leave the number as a denormal, in which case the 8087 will continue to treat it as a number very close to zero, or we can set the number to true zero.

Routine DENTO0 replaces all denormals in an array with true zeros.

```
INCLUDE    SUBROUT.MAC
           SUBROUTINE DENTO0,<ARRAY,ARRAY_TYPE,N>
;  ASSUMPTIONS:  ARRAY IS OF LENGTH N
;                ARRAY_TYPE IS AN INTEGER: 4-SINGLE, 8-DOUBLE
;                N IS AN INTEGER
;
           PUSHTEMP  AX,STATUS_WORD        ;SET ASIDE LOCATION FOR
                                           ;8087 STATUS WORD
           LDS       SI,[BP].N
           MOV       CX,[SI]               ;CX=N
           MOV       SI,[BP].ARRAY_TYPE    ;DS:SI=ADDR(ARRAY_TYPE)
           MOV       AX,[SI]               ;AX=ARRAY_TYPE
           MOV       BX,[BP].ARRAY         ;DS:BX=ADDR(ARRAY)
;
;NOW ALL SET UP TO GO
           CMP       CX,0                  ;HOPE N > 0
           JL        DONE
;
CHECK_LOOP:
           CMP       AX,4                  ;IS A SINGLE?
           JNE       NOT_SINGLE
           FLD       DWORD PTR [BX]
           JMP       CHECK_IT
NOT_SINGLE:                                ;BETTER BE DOUBLE
           FLD       QWORD PTR [BX]
;
CHECK_IT:
           FXAM                            ;WHAT DID WE LOAD?
           FSTSW     [BP].STATUS_WORD
           FSTP      ST(0)
           FWAIT
           MOV       DH,BYTE PTR [BP].STATUS_WORD+1
           AND       DH,01000101B          ;BLANK OTHER BITS
           CMP       DH,0                  ;UNNORMAL?
           JE        DEN
           CMP       DH,01000100B          ;DENORMAL?
```

```
          JE        DEN
          JMP       LOOP_BOTTOM
DEN:
          FLDZ                          ;MAKE A ZERO
          CMP       AX,4                ;IS A SINGLE?
          JNE       STILL_NOT_SINGLE
          FSTP      DWORD PTR [BX]
          JMP       LOOP_BOTTOM
STILL_NOT_SINGLE:                       ;BETTER BE DOUBLE
          FSTP      QWORD PTR [BX]
LOOP_BOTTOM:
          ADD       BX,AX
          LOOP      LOOPER
          JMP       DONE
LOOPER:   JMP       CHECK_LOOP

DONE:
          POPTEMP   1
          RETURN    DENTO0
          END
```

One last warning about ignoring the presence of denormals, infinities, and NANs. A few 8087 instructions insist on valid data as input. In particular, *the transcendental instructions discussed in Chapter 10 will produce an undefined result if fed invalid data and will do so without signaling any error condition!*

Our error handling has been limited to single and double precision reals to the exclusion of integers. There are two reasons for this exclusion.

First, if you use 16-bit integers, the only kind available in BASIC, for holding numerical results, you are asking for trouble. Merely multiplying two random integers may result in integer overflow! Floating point arithmetic is every bit as fast as integer arithmetic on the 8087. Use integer variables for subscripts, flags, and subroutine addresses. Otherwise stay away.

Second, the integer data type cannot be set to indicate invalid data in the way real variables can be set. If a number cannot be converted to a valid integer, the 8087 reports the most negative value, −32,768. Both BASIC and the 8087 treat −32,768 as they do any other integer, so invalid data will not be flagged. If integer variables must be used, all results should be checked and execution should be stopped if −32,768 appears.

8

Basic Matrix Operations

Matrix operations occupy the center of the number crunching world. Large scale supercomputers, costing tens of millions of dollars, have special built-in hardware devoted entirely to fast matrix operations. There are even computer languages, such as APL, where the matrix replaces the scalar as the fundamental variable type. Matrices are so important that some versions of BASIC (mostly on large computers) have a special set of "MAT" functions devoted to efficient matrix computation. While the 8087 does not have matrix hardware, its stack design allows for easily written, efficient, matrix subroutines.

We cover matrix operations in two chapters. In this chapter, we prepare routines for the most common matrix operations. Chapter 9 concentrates on advanced methods for solving systems of linear equations and on the related problem of matrix inversion.

The Cookbook—Chapter 8

Program: **COLCOPY**

Purpose: Copy one column of a matrix into a vector.

Call: CALL COLCOPY(A,B,COL,N,M).

Input: A—N by M single precision matrix.
COL—integer column number to be copied.

	N—integer number of rows of A. M—integer number of columns of A.
Output:	B—array N long; B(I) = A(I,COL).
Language:	8088 assembly language.
Program:	**ROWCOPY**
Purpose:	Copy one row of a matrix into a vector.
Call:	CALL ROWCOPY(A,B,ROW,N,M).
Input:	A—N by M single precision matrix. ROW—integer row number to be copied. N—integer number of rows of A. M—integer number of columns of A.
Output:	B—array M long; B(I) = A(ROW,I).
Language:	8088 assembly language.
Program:	**DIAGCOPY**
Purpose:	Copy the diagonal of a square matrix into a vector.
Call:	CALL DIAGCOPY(A,B,N).
Input:	A—N by N single precision matrix. N—integer number of rows of A.
Output:	B—array N long; B(I) = A(I,I).
Language:	8088 assembly language.
Program:	**TRANS**
Purpose:	Transpose a matrix.
Call:	CALL TRANS(A, B,N,M).
Input:	A—N by M single precision matrix. N—integer number of rows of A.

	M—integer number of columns of A.
Output:	B—M by N matrix; B(I,J) = AJ,I).
Language:	8088 assembly language.
Program:	**SQTRANS**
Purpose:	Transpose a square matrix in place.
Call:	CALL SQTRANS(A,N).
Input:	A—N by N single precision matrix. N—integer number of rows of A.
Output:	A—new A(I,J) = old A(J,I).
Language:	8088 assembly language.
Program:	**INPROD**
Purpose:	Inner product of two single precision vectors.
Call:	CALL (A,B,C,N).
Input:	A—N long single precision vector. B—N long single precision vector. N—integer number of rows of A.
Output:	C—double precision scalar; C = inner product of A,B.
Language:	8087/8088 assembly language.
Program:	**GINPROD**
Purpose:	Inner product of two generalized vectors.
Call:	CALL GINPROD(A,B,C,TYPEA,TYPEB, SKIPA,SKIPB,N).
Input:	A—N element vector. B—N element vector. TYPEA—integer giving length of element of A.

	TYPEB—integer giving length of element of B. SKIPA—integer "skip factor" (see text) for A. SKIPB—integer "skip factor" (see text) for B. N—integer number of rows of A.
Output:	C—double precision scalar; C = inner product of A,B.
Language:	8087/8088 assembly language.
Program:	**MATMULT**
Purpose:	Matrix multiplicafion.
Call:	CALL MATMULT(A,B,C,L,M,N).
Input:	A—L by M single precision matrix. B—M by N single precision matrix. L—integer number of rows of A. M—integer number of columns of A, rows of B. N—integer number of columns of B.
Output:	C—L by N single precision matrix; C = AB.
Language:	8087/8088 assembly language.
Note:	Requires procedure GINPROD.
Program:	**GAUSS**
Purpose:	Solve linear equations by Gaussian elimination.
Input:	A—N by N coefficient matrix. Y—N vector. N—number of rows and columns of A.
Output:	X—N vector; X solves equations Y = AX.
Language:	BASIC.
Program:	**GAUSS-SE**
Purpose:	Solve linear equations by Gaussian elimination, using space efficient method.

Input:	A—N by N coefficient matrix. Y—N vector. YSTAR—N vector, scratch space. N—number of rows and columns of A.
Output:	X—N vector; X solves equations Y = AX. A—A replaced with Gaussian reducfion.
Language:	BASIC.

What Is a Matrix?

In computer terms, a matrix is a two-dimensional array. The values in the array can be thought of as being laid out in a rectangular grid, where the first array index is the row number and the second array index is the column number. An example of a "2 by 3" matrix is

5	−7	11
0	2	18

Such a matrix might be stored in BASIC by DIMensioning an array with two rows and three columns. The BASIC statement "DIM A(1,2)" produces a matrix laid out like

A(0,0)	A(0,1)	A(0,2)
A(1,0)	A(1,1)	A(2,1)

Since BASIC arrays are numbered starting at zero, an N row by M column matrix is dimensioned A(N−1, M−1).

Why Are Matrices Interesting?

Invariably, matrix algebra is motivated as notation for solving systems of simultaneous linear equations. This may seem a bit strange, as most of us don't have any great need for solving such systems. The truth is that most interesting numerical computation problems have the same mathematical structure as a system of linear equations. Computational aspects of statistics, differential equations, and constrained optimization all center around linear equations and matrix operations. We briefly lay out the linear equation interpretation of matrices here.

As a sample, consider the following system of two linear equations in two unknowns.

$$18 = 4x_1 + 2x_2$$
$$9 = 2x_1 - 2x_2$$

There is exactly one pair of values for x_1 and x_2 that will make both equations true. To find these values, we draw the two equations on a piece of graph paper. Label the horizontal axis x_1 and the vertical axis x_2. Pick any two values for x_1. Plug each into the top equation and solve for the corresponding value of x_2. Connect the two (x_1, x_2) points to get a straight line. Do the same for the bottom equation. The top equation is true for any (x_1,x_2) point on the first line and the bottom equation is true for any point on the second line. Where the two lines intersect, both equations are true. The point (4.5,0) is the solution to this system of equations.

Matrices provide a compact notation for discussing such systems. In matrix notation, the two equations appear as:

$$y = Ax$$

where y is a 2 by 1 matrix.

$$y = \begin{bmatrix} 18 \\ 9 \end{bmatrix}$$

A is a 2 by 2 matrix

$$A = \begin{bmatrix} 4 & 2 \\ 2 & -2 \end{bmatrix}$$

and x is a 2 by 1 matrix.

$$x = \begin{bmatrix} x_1 \\ x_2 \end{bmatrix}$$

If we are given values for x, we can solve for y by *matrix multiplication.* If we are given values for y, we can solve for x by *solving a system of linear equations.*

Storage Allocation and Memory Access

In order to manipulate matrices, we need to know how the matrix is stored in memory. If A is a 2 x 3 matrix, we can think of it as being logically laid out as in Figure 8.1. Since computer memory is one-dimensional, the six elements are actually arranged consecutively in memory. There are two logical ways to do this: lay things out by row or by column. In *row-order,* the six elements are stored in consecutive order with the second dimension varying most rapidly as we move up in memory. The two-dimensional matrix is place in memory in this order: A(0,0), A(0,1), A(0,2), A(1,0), A(1,1), A(1,2). Each element occupies four bytes for a single precision matrix and eight bytes for double precision.

Another way to say the same thing is that each row is stored in order, placing one row after the next in memory. Suppose the (single precision) matrix A is stored in memory with A(0,0) located at memory address 100. The first row of A will be at locations 100, 104, and 108. The second row will be stored at locations 112, 116, and 120. Figure 8.1 illustrates the two-dimensional matrix to one-dimensional memory mapping for row order.

A(0,0)-100	A(0,1)-104	A(0,2)-108
A(1,0)-112	A(1,1)-116	A(2,1)-120

Figure 8.1 Two-dimensional array.

In general, for an n by m matrix, element (i,j) is stored in position $(i*n+j)*k$, where k equals four for single and eight for double precision.

Notice that a 1 by n matrix, called a *row vector,* and an n by 1 matrix, called a *column vector,* will both be stored in the same locations as an n element one-dimensional array.

The alternative to storage in row order is *column-order,* in which one column is stored after another and the first index varies most rapidly as we move through memory. It doesn't matter terribly much whether we use row or column order, so long as we pick one convention and stick to it. Naturally, designers of computer languages have not so stuck. FORTRAN uses the column convention; C and Turbo Pascal use the row convention; and QuickBASIC gives you a choice (although it defaults to column order). We've let majority rule and written all the routines below under the assumption that matrices are stored in row order. (This means that the routines that explicitly reference a matrix will need a bit of re-writing to be called from FORTRAN.) The routines ROWCOPY and COLCOPY illustrate row and column access. ROWCOPY(A,B,ROW,M,N) copies row ROW of m × n matrix A into an N-long array B. The BASIC code below illustrates ROWCOPY.

```
DEFINT I-N
REM DEFINE M,N,ROW HERE
REDIM A(M-1,N-1), B(N-1)
REM FILL IN VALUES OF A
     FOR I=0 TO N-1
     B(I) = A(ROW,I)
     NEXT I
```

```
INCLUDE    SUBROUT.MAC
           SUBROUTINE ROWCOPY,<A,B,ROW,M,N>
;  ASSUMPTIONS: A IS A SINGLE PRECISION M BY N MATRIX
;               B IS A SINGLE PRECISION ARRAY N LONG
;               ROW,N,M ARE INTEGERS
           LDS       BX,[BP].N              ;DS:BX=ADDR(N)
           MOV       CX,[BX]                ;CX=N
           LDS       BX,[BP].ROW            ;DS:BX=ADDR(ROW)
           MOV       AX,[BX]                ;AX=ROW
           MUL       CX                     ;AX=ROW*N
           SHL       AX,1
           SHL       AX,1                   ;AX=4*ROW*N
           LDS       SI,[BP].A              ;DS:SI=ADDR(A(0,0))
           ADD       SI,AX                  ;SI=ADDR(A(ROW,0))
           LES       DI,[BP].B              ;ES:DI=ADDR(B)
           JCXZ      DONE
ROW_LOOP:
           MOV       AX,[SI]                ;MOVE ELEMENT OF ROW
           MOV       ES:[DI],AX
           MOV       AX,[SI]+2
           MOV       ES:[DI]+2,AX
           ADD       SI,4                   ;NEXT COL
           ADD       DI,4                   ;NEXT B
           LOOP      ROW_LOOP

DONE:
           RETURN    ROWCOPY
           END
```

```
INCLUDE    SUBROUT.MAC
           SUBROUTINE COLCOPY,<A,B,COL,M,N>
;  ASSUMPTIONS: A IS A SINGLE PRECISION M BY N MATRIX
;               B IS A SINGLE PRECISION ARRAY M LONG
;               COL,M,N ARE INTEGERS
           LDS       BX,[BP].M              ;DS:BX=ADDR(M)
           MOV       CX,[BX]                ;CX=M
           LDS       BX,[BP].COL            ;DS:BX=ADDR(COL)
           MOV       AX,[BX]                ;AX=COL
           SHL       AX,1                   ;AX=4*COL
           SHL       AX,1
           LDS       SI,[BP].A              ;DS:SI=ADDR(A(0,0))
           ADD       SI,AX                  ;DS:SI=ADDR(A(0,COL))
           LES       BX,[BP].N              ;ES:BX=ADDR(N)
           MOV       BX,ES:[BX]             ;BX=N
           SHL       BX,1                   ;
           SHL       BX,1                   ;ELEMENT DISTANCE IS 4*N
IFDEF      TPASCAL
           SHL       BX,1                   ;DOUBLE PRECISION
```

```
ENDIF
          LES       DI,[BP].B           ;ES:DI=ADDR(B)
          JCXZ      DONE
COL_LOOP:
          MOV       AX,[SI]             ;MOVE ONE ELEMENT
          MOV       ES:[DI],AX
          MOV       AX,[SI]+2
          MOV       ES:[DI]+2,AX
IFDEF     TPASCAL
          MOV       AX,[SI]+4
          MOV       ES:[DI]+4,AX
          MOV       AX,[SI]+6
          MOV       ES:[DI]+6,AX
          ADD       DI,8
ELSE
          ADD       DI,4
ENDIF
          ADD       SI,BX               ;NEXT COLUMN
          LOOP      COL_LOOP

DONE:
          RETURN    COLCOPY
          END
```

COLCOPY and ROWCOPY illustrate four useful points about moving through a matrix:

- *Column* COL *begins at location 4*COL.*
- Sequential elements in a column are located 4 bytes apart.
- Row ROW begins at location 4*N*ROW.
- Sequential elements in a column are located 4*N bytes apart.

Of course, "8" would replace "4" for a double precision matrix.

A matrix with an equal number of rows and columns is called, for obvious reasons, a square matrix. The elements A(0,0), A(I,1),. . ., A(N−1,N−1) form the *principal diagonal* of the matrix. To illustrate accessing the principal diagonal, we present DIAGCOPY:

```
INCLUDE     SUBROUT.MAC
SUBROUTINE  DIAGCOPY,<A,B,N>
;  ASSUMPTIONS: A IS A SINGLE PRECISION N BY N MATRIX
;               B IS A SINGLE PRECISION ARRAY N LONG
;               N IS AN INTEGER
       LDS       BX,[BP].N      ;DS:BX=ADDR(N)
       MOV       CX,[BX]        ;CX=N
       MOV       BX,CX          ;BX=N
       INC       BX             ;BX=N+1
       SHL       BX,1           ;BX=4*(N+1)
       SHL       BX,1           ;NOTE BX HAS DISTANCE
```

```
                                    ;BETWEEN DIAGONAL ELEMENTS
IFDEF   TPASCAL
        SHL         BX,1
ENDIF
        LDS         SI,[BP].A       ;DS:SI=ADDR(A)
        LES         DI,[BP].B       ;ES:DI=ADDR(B)
        JCXZ        DONE
DIAG_LOOP:
        MOV         AX,[SI]         ;MOVE ONE ELEMENT
        MOV         ES:[DI],AX
        MOV         AX,[SI]+2
        MOV         ES:[DI]+2,AX
IFDEF   TPASCAL
        MOV         AX,[SI]+4
        MOV         ES:[DI]+4,AX
        MOV         AX,[SI]+6
        MOV         ES:[DI]+6,AX
        ADD         DI,8
ELSE
        ADD         DI,4
ENDIF
        ADD         SI,BX           ;NEXT ELEMENT
        LOOP        DIAG_LOOP

DONE:
        RETURN      DIAGCOPY
        END
```

Moving along a diagonal is equivalent to moving over one column and down one row. Note the following two facts about accessing elements of the diagonal of a square matrix:

- Diagonal element i is at location i*4*(N + 1).
- Sequential diagonal elements are 4*(N + 1) bytes apart.

Basic Matrix Operations

Matrix operations fall into six categories:

1. Scalar operations.
2. Element-by-element operations.
3. Matrix transposition.
4. Inner products and matrix multiplication.
5. Solving systems of linear equations.
6. Matrix inversion.

Scalar and Element-by-Element Operations

Operations between scalars and matrices operate by applying the scalar operation to every element of the matrix. For example, if A is an m by n matrix, the mathematical operation B = A + 5 could be done with the BASIC program:

```
DEFINT I-N
REM DEFINE M,N,ROW HERE
REDIM A(M-1,N-1), B(M-1,N-1)
     FOR I=0 TO M-1
          FOR J=0 TO N-1
          B(I,J) = A(I,J) + 5
          NEXT J
     NEXT I
```

It would be straightforward to write routines for scalar operations as well as for element-by-element matrix addition, subtraction, and so forth. However, a slight "trick" of observation suggests an even easier solution. Computer memory doesn't "know" that the m by n storage locations represent a matrix. The locations could equally well represent an n by m element one-dimensional array. *All element-by-element and scalar matrix operations can be done by using vector routines,* as developed in Chapter 7.

For example, consider the following BASIC code, using ADDSC from Chapter 9.

```
DEFINT I-N
REM DEFINE M,N,ROW HERE
REDIM A(M-1,N-1), B(M-1,N-1)
SCALAR=5.0: ISIZE=M*N
CALL ADDSC(A,SCALAR,B,ISIZE)
```

Matrix Transposition

The matrix operation *transpose* exchanges the rows and columns of a matrix. If A is an n by m matrix, then "A transpose" is an m by n matrix such that (A transpose)(i,j) = A(j,i). A transpose is often written A^T or A' (pronounced "A transpose" or "A prime"). A BASIC program to transpose a matrix is straightforward. For example:

```
DEFINT I-N
REDIM  A(M-1,N-1), AT(N-1,M-1)
  FOR I=0 TO M-1
    FOR J-0 TO N-1
    AT(J,I)=A(I,J)
    NEXT J
  NEXT I
```

The subroutine TRANS accomplishes the same task as the BASIC code above. Notice that TRANS requires A and B to be different matrices. If A and B were to occupy the same memory locations, the copying operations would write over some A locations before we were able to read them into B. Subroutine TRANS uses about 6 microseconds per element.

```
INCLUDE    SUBROUT.MAC
           SUBROUTINE TRANS,<A,B,M,N>
;  ASSUMPTIONS:  A IS A SINGLE PRECISION M BY MATRIX
;                B IS A SINGLE PRECISION N BY MATRIX
;                M,N ARE INTEGERS
        LDS     BX,[BP].N     ;DS:BX=ADDR(N)
        MOV     CX,[BX]       ;CX=N
        JCXZ    DONE
        LDS     BX,[BP].M     ;DS:BX=ADDR(M)
        MOV     DX,[BX]       ;DX=M
        CMP     DX,0
        JLE     DONE
        MOV     SI,[BP].A     ;SI=OFFSET(A)
        LES     DI,[BP].B     ;ES:DI=ADDR(B)
ROW_LOOP:
        LDS     BX,[BP].M     ;DS:BX=ADDR(M)
        MOV     CX,[BX]       ;CX=M (COL LENGTH)
        MOV     BX,0          ;BX=0,USE BX FOR A INDEX

COL_LOOP:
        MOV     DS,.A+2       ;DS:SI=ADDR(A)
        MOV     AX,[SI][BX]   ;MOVE 4 BYTES
        MOV     ES:[DI],AX
        MOV     AX,[SI][BX]+2
        MOV     ES:[DI]+2,AX
IFDEF     TPASCAL
        MOV     AX,[SI]+4
        MOV     ES:[DI]+4,AX
        MOV     AX,[SI]+6
        MOV     ES:[DI]+6,AX
        ADD     DI,8
ELSE
```

```
        ADD     DI,4            ;NEXT B ELEMENT
ENDIF
        MOV     AX,BX           ;SAVE A ROW POSITION
        LDS     BX,[BP].N       ;DS:BX=ADDR(N)
        MOV     BX,[BX]         ;BX=N
        SHL     BX,1            ;BX=4*N
        SHL     BX,1
IFDEF   TPASCAL
        SHL     BX,1            ;DOUBLE PRECISION
ENDIF
        ADD     BX,AX           ;NEXT A ELEMENT
        LOOP    COL_LOOP        ;IF NOT DONE

IFDEF   TPASCAL
        ADD     SI,8
ELSE
        ADD     SI,4            ;NEXT COL OF A
ENDIF
        DEC     DX              ;ONE COL DONE
        JG      ROW_LOOP

DONE:   RETURN  TRANS
        END
```

Transposition of a square matrix leads to an important special case. To conserve space, we frequently transpose a square matrix "in place," as in the following BASIC code. Notice that the second FOR loop only runs from the diagonal element to the end of the row. The "lower triangle" of the square gets swapped with the upper triangle.

```
DEFINT   I-N
REDIM A(N-1,N-1)
  FOR I=0 TO N-1
    FOR J=I TO N-1
    SWAP A(I,J) , A(J,I)
    NEXT J
  NEXT I
```

We can think of this code as moving along the diagonal of a matrix and swapping the row from the diagonal point to the right with the column from the diagonal down. Subroutine SQTRANS performs this task. The QuickBASIC code above takes about $35n^2$ microseconds to transpose A in place. SQTRANS requires only $5n^2$ microseconds.

```
INCLUDE   SUBROUT.MAC
          SUBROUTINE SQTRANS,<A,N>
;  ASSUMPTIONS: A IS A SINGLE PRECISION N BY N MATRIX
;               N IS AN INTEGER
          LDS       BX,[BP].N            ;DS:BX=ADDR(N)
          MOV       DX,[BX]              ;DX=N
          MOV       BX,DX                ;BX=N
          SHL       BX,1                 ;BX=4*N
          SHL       BX,1
IFDEF     TPASCAL
          SHL       BX,1                 ;DOUBLE PRECISION
ENDIF
          LDS       BP,[BP].A            ;DS:BP=ADDR(A)
                                         ;WE'RE SHORT OF REGISTERS
                                         ;SO WE'LL USE BP TO POINT
                                         ;TO DIAGONAL ELEMENT
                                         ;BP=ADDR(A)
          CMP       DX,0
          JLE       DONE
DIAG_LOOP:
          MOV       CX,DX                ;DX # OF ELEMENTS LEFT
          MOV       SI,BP                ;SI POINTS TO ROW
          MOV       DI,BP                ;DI POINTS TO COLUMN
ROW_LOOP:                                ;SWAP ROW AND COLUMN
          MOV       AX,[SI]              ;MOVE 4 BYTES
          XCHG      [DI],AX
          MOV       [SI],AX
          MOV       AX,[SI]+2
          XCHG      [DI]+2,AX
          MOV       [SI]+2,AX
IFDEF     TPASCAL
          MOV       AX,[SI]+4            ;MOVE 4 MORE BYTES
          XCHG      [DI]+4,AX
          MOV       [SI]+4,AX
          MOV       AX,[SI]+6
          XCHG      [DI]+6,AX
          MOV       [SI]+6,AX
          ADD       SI,8
ELSE
          ADD       SI,4                 ;NEXT ROW ELEMENT
ENDIF
          ADD       DI,BX                ;NEXT COLUMN ELEMENT
          LOOP      ROW_LOOP             ;IF NOT DONE
          ADD       BP,BX                ;NEXT DIAGONAL ELEMENT
IFDEF     TPASCAL
          ADD       BP,8
```

```
ELSE
            ADD      BP,4
ENDIF
            DEC      DX                  ;NEXT COLUMN IS SHORTER
            CMP      DX,0
            JG       DIAG_LOOP

DONE:       RETURN   SQTRANS
            END
```

Inner Products and Matrix Multiplication

More scientific computation time is spent computing *inner products* than on any other single problem. Inner products are at the heart of both matrix multiplication and matrix inversion. If x and y are vectors, then to find the inner product of x and y one multiplies the two vectors element by element and sums the products, as in the following BASIC program.

```
DEFINT I-N
DEFDBL S
REDIM X(N-1),Y(N-1)
SUM=0
   FOR I=0  TO  N-1
   SUM=SUM+X(I)*Y(I)
   NEXT  I
```

At first glance, the inner product doesn't appear to be a particularly interesting operation. However, consider the specification of our system of linear equations earlier in the chapter. The first equation was

$$y_1 = A_{0,0}x_1 + A_{0,1}x_2$$

Thus y_1 equals the inner product of the first row of A with the vector x. Similarly, the second equation specifies that y_2 equals the inner product of the second row of A with x. In this manner, an entire system of equations can be specified in terms of inner products. This leads to a natural definition of matrix multiplication in terms of inner products.

If C = AB, then Cij equals the inner product of row i of A with column j of B.

Note that this definition implicitly assumes that A and B are *conformable* for multiplication, that is, the number of columns of A equal the number of rows of B. A further natural result of the definition is that if A is a l by m matrix and B is an m by n matrix, then C will be l by m.

BASIC code to multiply two matrices is:

```
DEFINT I-N
DEFDBL S
REM REMEMBER TO DEFINE L,M,N
REDIM A(L-1,M-1),B(M-1,N-1),C(L-1,N-1)
  REM DEFINE MATRICES A AND B HERE
    FOR IROW=0 TO L-1
      FOR JCOL=0 TO N-1
      SUM=0
         FOR K=0 TO M-1
         SUM=SUM+A(IROW,K)*B(K,JCOL)
         NEXT K
      C(IROW,JCOL)=SUM
      NEXT JCOL
   NEXT IROW
```

The innermost lines are executed l*m*n times. For matrices of order 50, that's 125,000 additions and multiplications. You can see why we want these lines to be as efficient as possible!

Notice that we collected the inner product in a temporary variable "SUM," rather than directly in "C(IROW,JCOL)." We did this for two reasons. First, it is somewhat more efficient, since BASIC need calculate the location of C(IROW,JCOL) only l*n times, rather than l*m*n times. Second, and far more important, accuracy is improved greatly by accumulating the sum in double precision even if it is to be stored later as a single precision variable.

Because of the central role of inner products and matrix multiplications in numerical computation, accuracy and speed are vital. We present several 8087 routines written with these objectives in mind. Our first routine forms the inner product of two one-dimensional arrays.

```
INCLUDE    SUBROUT.MAC
           SUBROUTINE INPROD,<A,B,C,N>
;  ASSUMPTIONS: A,B ARE SINGLE PRECISION N ARRAYS
;               C IS A DOUBLE PRECISION SCALAR
;               N IS AN INTEGER
           LDS       BX,[BP].N           ;DS:BX=ADDR(N)
           MOV       CX,[BX]             ;CX=N
           LDS       SI,[BP].A           ;DS:SI=ADDR(A)
           LES       DI,[BP].B           ;ES:DI=ADDR(B)
           MOV       BX,0
           FLDZ                          ;SET RUNNING SUM =0
           JCXZ      DONE
ADD_LOOP:
           FLD       RealPtr [BX][SI]    ;LOAD A(I)
```

```
          FMUL       RealPtr ES:[BX][DI] ;MULTIPLY BY B(I)
          FADDP      ST(1),ST            ;SUM=SUM+A(I)*B(I)
          ADD        BX,RealLength       ;READY FOR NEXT ELEMENT
          LOOP       ADD_LOOP
DONE:
          LDS        BX,[BP].C           ;DS:BX=ADDR(C)
          FSTP       QWORD PTR [BX]      ;C=INNER PRODUCT
          RETURN     INPROD
          END
```

Routine INPROD takes about 57 microseconds per array element.

You might expect our next step would be an 8087 routine to multiply two matrices. Instead of proceeding directly to a matrix multiplication program, we are going to take a short strategic detour. A matrix multiplication subroutine presents two difficulties. First, writing such a routine is complicated by the need to keep track of too many indices. As you can see from the BASIC program above, the program needs to remember IROW, JCOL, K, L, M, N and the locatlons of A, B, and C. Using a direct approach, we would run out of registers rather quickly. Second, a straightforward matrix multiplication routine could be used only on one specific argument type; for example, multiplying two single precision matrices and returning a single precision result.

Our strategic approach is to write a very general inner product routine upon which we can build more complicated programs. Subroutine GINPROD, below, calculates the inner product of two n-element arrays. In addition to specification of the input vectors, GINPROD accepts two kinds of options. The first option allows us to specify either single or double precision input arrays. The second option allows us to tell GINPROD how far apart in memory the elements of each array are spaced. Thus if array A has a "skip" parameter of one, the elements are stored sequentially. If the skip parameter is two, then elements are stored in every other location—with four bytes between elements for a single precision array and eight bytes between elements for a double precision array.

Of what use is the "skip" parameter? Think about accessing a column of a matrix. The elements of an m by n matrix are located 4*m bytes apart. Thus we can move down a column of an m by n matrix by specifying m as the skip parameter.

```
INCLUDE SUBROUT.MAC
          SUBROUTINE GINPROD,<A,B,C,TYPEA,TYPEB,SKIPA,SKIPB,N>
;  ASSUMPTIONS: A,B ARE ARRAYS
;               C IS A DOUBLE PRECISION SCALAR
;               TYPEA,TYPEB,SKIPA,SKIPB,N ARE INTEGERS
;
;               GINPROD TAKES THE INNER PRODUCT OF N ELEMENTS USING
```

```
;               EVERY SKIPA ELEMENT OF A AND
;               EVERY SKIPB ELEMENT OF B

;          Save 6 registers since this routine is called from others
;          Also leave room for one word of temporary storage
           CHKSTCK    12+2
           PUSHTEMP   AX
           PUSHTEMP   BX
           PUSHTEMP   CX
           PUSHTEMP   DX
           PUSHTEMP   SI
           PUSHTEMP   DI
           FLDZ                          ;SET RUNNING SUM=0
           LDS        BX,[BP].N          ;DS:BX=ADDR(N)
           MOV        CX,[BX]            ;CX=N
           MOV        SI,[BP].A          ;SI=OFFSET(A)
           MOV        DI,[BP].B          ;DI=OFFSET(B)
           LDS        BX,[BP].TYPEB      ;DS:AX=ADDR(TYPEB)
           MOV        AX,[BX]            ;AX=TYPEB
           LDS        BX,[BP].SKIPB      ;BX=ADDR(SKIPB)
           MUL        WORD PTR [BX]      ;AX=TYPEB*SKIPB
           PUSHTEMP   AX,B_ELEMENT_DISTANCE;USE STACK AS A TEMPORARY
           LDS        BX,[BP].TYPEA      ;DS:BX=ADDR(TYPEA)
           MOV        AX,[BX]            ;AX=TYPEA
           LDS        BX,[BP].SKIPA      ;DS:BX=ADDR(SKIPA)
           MUL        WORD PTR [BX]      ;AX=A ELEMENT DISTANCE
           JCXZ       DONE
GINP_LOOP:
           LDS        BX,[BP].TYPEA
           CMP        WORD PTR [BX],4    ;IS A SINGLE?
           JNE        A_DOUBLE
           MOV        DS,[BP].A+2        ;DS=SEGMENT(A)
           FLD        DWORD PTR [SI]     ;LOAD SINGLE A(I)
           JMP        MULT_B
A_DOUBLE:  MOV        DS,[BP].A+2        ;DS=SEGMENT(A)
           FLD        QWORD PTR [SI]     ;LOAD DOUBLE A(I)

MULT_B:    LDS        BX,[BP].TYPEB      ;DS:BX=ADDR(TYPEB)
           CMP        WORD PTR [BX],4    ;IS B SINGLE?
           JNE        B_DOUBLE
           MOV        DS,[BP].B+2        ;DS=SEGMENT(B)
           FMUL       DWORD PTR [DI]     ;MULTIPLY SINGLE B(I)
           JMP        NEXT_ELEMENT
B_DOUBLE:  MOV        DS,[BP].B+2        ;DS=SEGMENT(B)
           FMUL       QWORD PTR [DI]     ;MULTIPLY DOUBLE B(I)

NEXT_ELEMENT:
```

```
            ADD       SI,AX                 ;READY FOR NEXT ELEMENT
            ADD       DI,[BP].B_ELEMENT_DISTANCE
            FADDP     ST(1),ST              ;SUM=SUM+A(I)*B(I)
            LOOP      GINP_LOOP

DONE:
            LDS       BX,[BP].C             ;DS:BX=ADDR(C)
            FSTP      QWORD PTR [BX]        ;STORE
            POPTEMP   1
            POP       DI
            POP       SI
            POP       DX
            POP       CX
            POP       BX
            POP       AX
            TEMP_COUNT=TEMP_COUNT-6
            RETURN    GINPROD
            END
```

GINPROD leads immediately to a fast BASIC routine for matrix multiplication.

```
DEFINT   I-N
DEFDBL   S
REDIM A(L-1,M-1),B(M-1,N-1),C(L-1,N-1)
IONE=1:    ITYPE=4
   FOR   IROW=0 TO L-1
   FOR   JCOL=0 TO N-1
 CALL GINPROD(A(IROW,0),B(0,JCOL),SUM,ITYPE,ITYPE,M)IONE,M
  REM FIND  INNER   PRODUCT OF ROW IROW OF A WITH
  REM COLUMN JCOL   OF B RETURNING THE ANSWER IN SUM
  REM NOTE  ITYPE=4 INDICATES SINGLE PRECISION
        REM SUM=0
        REM FOR   K=0 TO M-1
        REM SUM=SUM+A(IROW,K)*B(K,JCOL)
        REM NEXT  K
    C(IROW,JCOL)=SUM
    NEXT JCOL
  NEXT IROW
```

For convenient comparison, we have adapted the earlier BASIC program for matrix multiplication by adding the CALL GINPROD statement. This program directly takes the inner product of each row of A with each column of B.

GINPROD allows us to easily create many variants of matrix multiplication. Suppose we want to multiply the transpose of a matrix A by a matrix B, as in

C=A'B, where A is l by m and B is m by n. Row i of A' is column i of A, so we can use GINPROD specifying a "skip" of m for A to specify a row of A'.

```
DEFINT I-N
DEFDBL S
REDIM A(M-1,L-1),B(M-1,N-1),C(L-1,N-1)
I1=1 : ITYPE=4
  FOR IROW=0 TO L-1
    FOR JCOL=0 TO N-1
CALL GINPROD(A(0,IROW),B(0,JCOL),SUM,ITYPE,ITYPE,M,I1,M)
          REM SUM=0
          REM     FOR K=0 TO M-1
          REM     SUM=SUM+A(K,IROW)*B(K,JCOL)
          REM     NEXT K
     C(IROW,JCOL)=SUM
     NEXT JCOL
  NEXT IROW
```

Notice that we essentially "tricked" GINPROD into using a column rather than a row by changing the SKIP parameter. This same trick can be used for accessing matrices stored in column-order, as is done by FORTRAN. For a row-order matrix, SKIP=1 moves across a row and SKIP=number of columns moves down a column. Just reverse these for a column-order matrix. (Actually, the Microsoft FORTRAN compiler (Version 4.0 and later) generates such good code that GINPROD doesn't gain you anything.)

Convenience suggests a pure 8087 routine for matrix multiplication. Routine MATMULT essentially imitates the BASIC code above.

```
INCLUDE   SUBROUT.MAC
          EXTERNAL  <GINPROD>
          SUBROUTINE MATMULT,<A,B,C,L,M,N>
;  ASSUMPTIONS: A,B ARE SINGLE PRECISION MATRICES
;               A IS L BY M
;               B IS M BY N
;               C IS DOUBLE PRECISION MATRIX
;               C IS L BY N
;               L,M,N ARE INTEGERS
;
;    THIS SUBROUTINE PERFORMS THE MATRIX MULTIPLICATION C=AB
;    SUCCESSIVE ROWS OF A ARE MULTIPLIED BY THE FIRST COLUMN OF B
;    THEN REPEAT FOR SECOND COLUMN, ETC.
;    THE MATRICES ARE ASSUMED TO BE IN ROW MAJOR ORDER
;    IF WE ARE USING TURBOPASCAL, ALL REFERENCES TO "4"
;    REALLY NEED TO BE "8"
;  TO CALL GINPROD WE MUST PUSH ONTO THE STACK:
```

```
;     A(I,0)
;     B(0,J)
;     C(I,J)
;     4
;     4
;     1
;     N
;     M
;
;         WE WILL TEMPORARILY STORE ON THE STACK 16 BYTES FOR
;         ARGUMENTS TO GINPROD + 4 BYTES FOR RETURN ADDRESS
;         WE'LL ALSO NEED 4 BYTES TO STORE A 4 AND A 1
          CHKSTCK   16+4
;         ELEMENT (I,J) OF A MATRIX WITH M COLUMNS IS FOUND AT
;         (0,0)+4*(I*M+J) (SINGLE) OR (0,0)+8*(I*M+J) (DOUBLE)
;         USE SI FOR I, CX FOR J, AND DI FOR M
;         DO EQUIVALENT OF
;         FOR I=L-1 TO 0 STEP -1:FOR J=N-1 TO 0 STEP -1
;         CALL GINPROD(A(I,0),B(0,J),C(I,J),4,4,1,N,M)
          MOV       AX,RealLength
          PUSHTEMP  AX,FOUR
          MOV       AX,1
          PUSHTEMP  AX,ONE
          LDS       BX,[BP].M           ;DS:BX=ADDR(M)
          MOV       DI,[BX]             ;DI=M
          LDS       BX,[BP].L           ;DS:BX=ADDR(L)
          MOV       SI,[BX]             ;SI=L
ILOOP:    DEC       SI                  ;L=L-1
          LDS       BX,[BP].N           ;DS:BX=ADDR(N)
          MOV       CX,[BX]             ;CX=N
JLOOP:    DEC       CX                  ;N=N-1
          MOV       AX,[BP].A+2
          PUSH      AX                  ;PUSH SEG(A)
          MOV       AX,SI               ;AX=I
          MUL       DI
          ADD       AX,AX
          ADD       AX,AX               ;AX=4*I*M (THE HARD WAY)
IFDEF     TPASCAL
          ADD       AX,AX
ENDIF
          ADD       AX,[BP].A
          PUSH      AX                  ;ADDR(A(I,0))
          MOV       AX,[BP].B+2
          PUSH      AX                  ;PUSH SEG(B)
          MOV       AX,CX               ;AX=J
          ADD       AX,AX
```

```
        ADD     AX,AX               ;AX=4*J
IFDEF   TPASCAL
        ADD     AX,AX
ENDIF
        ADD     AX,[BP].B
        PUSH    AX                  ;ADDR(B(0,J))
        MOV     AX,[BP].C+2
        PUSH    AX                  ;PUSH SEG(C)
        MOV     AX,SI               ;AX=I
        LDS     BX,[BP].N           ;DS:BX=ADDR(N)
        MUL     WORD PTR [BX]       ;AX=I*N
        ADD     AX,CX
        ADD     AX,AX
        ADD     AX,AX
        ADD     AX,AX               ;AX=8*(I*N+J)
        ADD     AX,[BP].C
        PUSH    AX                  ;ADDR(C(I,J))
        PUSH    SS                  ;PUSH SEG(4)
        LEA     AX,[BP].FOUR
        PUSH    AX                  ;PUSH OFFSET(4)
        PUSH    SS
        PUSH    AX                  ;AGAIN
        PUSH    SS                  ;PUSH SEG(1)
        LEA     AX,[BP].ONE
        PUSH    AX                  ;PUSH OFFSET(1)
        PUSH    [BP].N+2
        PUSH    [BP].N              ;PUSH ADDR(N)
        PUSH    [BP].M+2
        PUSH    [BP].M              ;PUSH ADDR(M)

        CALL    GINPROD
        CMP     CX,0
        JG      JLOOP
        CMP     SI,0
        JG      ILOOP

        POPTEMP 2
        RETURN  MATMULT
        END
```

Solving Systems of Linear Equations

This is a good place to pause in your reading. We spend the rest of this chapter on linear algebra and in writing BASIC programs for solving systems of linear equations and inverting matrices. Our next 8087 program doesn't appear until Chapter 11. If your main interest is the 8087 aspect of these problems, you should just quickly skim the rest of this chapter.

The next few pages move very fast. You can spend most of a course in college learning about linear equations. The next few pages are really more of a quick review than a proper introduction to the subject. If you're new to the topic—or if it's been a long time since you last saw the subject—spend some time playing with the BASIC programs. One of the nice things about exploring with a personal computer is that your "study" can be as fast or as slow as you please.

Equation Manipulation

Return now to our example of two linear equations in two unknowns. The equations to be satisfied are:

$$\begin{aligned} 18 &= 4x_1 + 2x_2 \\ 9 &= 2x_1 - 2x_2 \end{aligned}$$

which can also be written

$$y = Ax$$

For a given y, what value of x makes both equations true simultaneously? We solve for x by making judicious use of the following theorems.

1. *If we multiply both sides of a true equation by a constant, the resulting equation is also true.*
2. *If we add one true equation to another, the resulting equation is also true.*
3. *We can always exchange the position of two equations.*

Clever application of these principles allows us to easily solve systems of linear equations. Consider applying the following transformations to our example system.

1. Multiply the top equation by $-1/2$ and add the result to the second equation. The transformed system looks like this:

$$\begin{aligned} 18 &= 4x_1 + 2x_2 \\ 0 &= 0x_1 - 3x_2 \end{aligned}$$

2. By inspecting the bottom equation, we see that x_2 equals 0. Solving backwards, we set x_2 to zero in the top equation and see immediately that x_1 equals $^{18}/_4$, or 4.5.

Matrix Manipulation

These steps generalize to a two-step procedure for solving systems of linear equations in terms of matrices.

1. *Reduce* the system to triangular form. Multiply the first equation by a constant and add the result to the second equation so as to produce a zero in column 1, row 2. Multiply the first equation by a (different) constant and add the result to the third equation so as to produce a zero in column 1, row 3. Continue in this manner until the first column is all zeros below the diagonal.
   Now take the second equation, multiply it by a constant and add it to the third equation so as to produce a zero in column 2, row 3. Continue until the entire second column is zero below the diagonal. Apply this procedure repeatedly until the entire area below the diagonal equals zero. This sort of matrix, with all zeros below the diagonal is called *upper triangular.*
2. *Back substitute.* Take the transformed version of A and y and solve for x by

$$x_n = y_n/A_{n,n}$$
$$x_{n-1} = (Y_{n-1} - A_{n-1,n}x_n)/A_{n-1}$$

and so forth.

Let's look at what our sample system looks like in terms of matrices. We start with the original A and y.

$$A = \begin{bmatrix} 4 & 2 \\ 2 & -2 \end{bmatrix} \qquad y = \begin{bmatrix} 18 \\ 9 \end{bmatrix}$$

Now we begin the reduction process. Our first step multiplies the top row of A and y by $-\frac{1}{2}$ and adds the result to the second row giving us new values of A and y.

$$A = \begin{bmatrix} 4 & 2 \\ 0 & -3 \end{bmatrix} \qquad y = \begin{bmatrix} 18 \\ 0 \end{bmatrix}$$

You can see why A is said to be in "triangular form." The non-zero entries form a triangle on and above the diagonal.

Notice that A and y are changed. If you want to keep the original data intact, be certain to perform the reduction on a copy of the original matrices.

The second step is to back-substitute. The matrix equation $y=Ax$ still applies to the new versions of A and y. Starting at the bottom and working up we have

$$0 = (0)x_1 + (-3)x_2$$

so $x_2 = 0$. Now we can substitute this into the first equation.

$$18 = (4)x_1 + (2)0$$

X_1 equals (18−0)/4, or 4.5.

In theory, only one thing can go wrong with this procedure. Suppose that at some step the equation we are using to produce zeros below the diagonal has a zero as its own diagonal element. (This diagonal element is called the *pivot* element.) In this case, the equation cannot be used to eliminate the elements below it and the program stops. The solution to this problem is to exchange the offending equation with another so as to obtain a non-zero pivot. (Implementation of this solution is deferred until the next chapter.) If the entire column equals zero, the system of equations and the matrix A are said to be *singular.* The system of equations does not have a unique solution.

This method of solving linear systems is called *Gaussian elimination.* While not the best computational method (better ones are introduced in the next chapter), it is the most straightforward. The following BASIC program implements Gaussian elimination. Notice that the original contents of A and y are replaced by transformed values.

```
REM PROGRAM GAUSS
DEFINT I-N
REDIM  A(N-1,N-1),Y(N-1),X(N-1)
  REM BE SURE A,Y AND N ARE DEFINED
   FOR IEQ=0 TO N-1
   IF  A(IEQ,IEQ)=0 THEN PRINT"ZERO PIVOT AT",IEQ:STOP
       FOR JROW=IEQ+1 TO  N-1
       FACTOR=-A(JROW,IEQ)/A(IEQ,IEQ)
       Y(JROW)=Y(JROW)+FACTOR*Y(IEQ)
          FOR  K=IEQ TO N-1
          A(JROW,K)=A(JROW,K)+FACTOR*A(IEQ,K)
           NEXT K
        NEXT JROW
     NEXT IEQ
 REM
 REM A IS NOW UPPER TRIANGULAR
 REM
 X(N-1)=Y(N-1)/A(N-1,N-1)
    FOR IEQ=(N-1)-1  TO 0 STEP -1
    SUM=0
     FOR K=IEQ+1 TO N-1
     SUM=SUM+A(IEQ,K)*X(K)
     NEXT K
   X(IEQ)=(Y(IEQ)-SUM)/A(IEQ,IEQ)
   NEXT IEQ
```

How long does it take to solve a system using Gaussian elimination? The outermost loop, the IEQ loop, is executed N − 1 times. The next loop, the JROW loop, is done N − 1 times for the first IEQ, N −2 for the second, and so forth. So the JROW loop is executed approximately $n^2/2$ times. The innermost loop, K, executes N times per JROW for the first IEQ, N - 1 times per JROW for the second IEQ, for a total of about $n^3/3$ operations. In total, the time required to solve a system of n equations is proportional to $n^3/3$, plus a small factor proportional to $n^2/2$.

The logical next step would be to prepare 8087 routines to speed up the program. Since better solution methods are proposed in the next chapter, introduction of more 8087 routines will be postponed until that point. However, here are a couple of suggestions in case you'd like to experiment.

Almost the entire execution time is spent in the IEQ loop. These lines multiply a row vector by a scalar and then add two row vectors. The routines prepared in Chapter 7 could be used here. In addition, GINPROD could be used for the last loop in the program.

Solving Multiple Linear Systems

We frequently want to solve a number of linear systems, sharing a common A matrix but having different y vectors. In place of a single n by 1 column vector y, we can arrange m column vectors into an n by m matrix Y. The solutions can be placed in an n by m matrix X. The entire set of linear equations are represented in this way by the matrix equation

$$Y = AX$$

Examination of the Gaussian elimination routine shows that all the hard work, that is the order n^3 work, involves only the A matrix. If we blindly apply the program above, execution time will be of order mn^3. The revision below keeps the transformation of y and backsolving for x out of the innermost loop.

```
DEFINT I-N
REDIM A(N-1,N-1),Y(N-1,M),X(N-1,M)
  REM BE SURE A,Y,N, AND M ARE DEFINED
   FOR IEQ=0 TO N-1
   IF A(IEQ,IEQ)=0 THEN PRINT"ZERO  PIVOT AT",IEQ:STOP
    FOR  JROW=IEQ+1 TO N-1
    FACTOR=-A(JROW,IEQ)/A(IEQ,IEQ)
     FOR LEQ=0 TO M-1
     Y(JROW,LEQ)=Y(JROW,LEQ)+FACTOR*Y(IEQ,LEQ)
     NEXT LEQ
     FOR K=IEQ TO N-1
     A(JROW,K)=A(JROW,K)+FACTOR*A(IEQ,K)
```

```
      NEXT K
    NEXT JROW
  NEXT IEQ
REM
REM A IS NOW UPPER TRIANGULAR
REM
  FOR LEQ=0 TO M-1
  X(N-1,LEQ)=Y(N-1,LEQ)/A(N-1,N-1)
    FOR IEQ=(N-1)-1 TO 0 STEP -1
    SUM=0
      FOR  K=IEQ+1 TO N-1
      SUM=SUM+A(IEQ,K)*X(K,LEQ)
      NEXT K
    X(IEQ,LEQ)=(Y(IEQ,LEQ)-SUM)/A(IEQ,IEQ)
    NEXT IEQ
  NEXT LEQ
```

This version of Gaussian elimination executes in time proportional to n^3 plus mn^2. For moderately large m and n, this means an improvement factor of roughly m over repeated Gaussian elimination!

Space Efficient Gaussian Elimination

The Gaussian elimination program above solves multiple linear systems quickly, but requires a great deal of storage, since 2*m*n locations are allocated for Y and X. We frequently want to solve systems sequentially, so that only a single y and x need be stored.

Gaussian elimination transforms y. As you can see in lines 70-90 above, the same factors are used to transform every column of Y. If we save the factors, we can, at a later stage, transform as many different y's as we like.

At each step in the reduction, all the (lower) elements of y are transformed. Suppose we save all the factors, labeling the factors from the first step f_{00}, f_{10}, f_{20}, and so forth. The second step produces one less factor. We label these f_{11}, f_{21}, f_{31}, and so forth. Arranging the columns of factors into a matrix, we get

$$F = \begin{bmatrix} 1 & 0 & 0 & 0 & 0 & 0 \\ f_{10} & 1 & 0 & 0 & 0 & 0 \\ f_{20} & f_{21} & 1 & 0 & 0 & 0 \\ . & . & . & 1 & 0 & 0 \\ . & . & . & . & 1 & 0 \\ . & . & . & . & . & 1 \end{bmatrix}$$

The matrix of factors is *lower triangular* with ones along the diagonal. We need a convenient place to store F for later use. As we reduce A, the area below the diagonal fills with zeros. Since this lower part of A would otherwise go to waste, we'll use it to store the part of F below the diagonal, and remember that the remaining part of F is ones and zeros.

Suppose we label the transformed vector y, "y*." The reduction process transforms y according to the following rules:

$$y^*_0 = y_0$$
$$y^*_1 = y_1 + f_{10}y^*_0$$
$$y^*_2 = y_2 + f_{20}y^*_0 + f_{21}y^*_1$$
$$y^*_3 = y_3 + f_{30}y^*_0 + f_{31}y^*_1 + f_{32}y^*_2$$

and so forth.

The first step of our space efficient program is to reduce A to upper triangular form and store the factors in A's lower triangle. Then, each time we want to find x for a new y, we generate a new y* from the stored factors and back substitute. The next set of BASIC code takes this approach.

```
REM PROGRAM GAUSS-SE (SPACE EFFICIENT)
DEFINT I-N
REDIM A(N-1,N-1),Y(N-1),X(N-1),YSTAR(N-1)
 REM BE SURE A,Y, AND N ARE DEFINED
  FOR IEQ=0 TO N-1
  IF A(IEQ,IEQ)=0 THEN PRINT"ZERO PIVOT AT",IEQ:STOP
   FOR JROW=IEQ+1 TO N-1
   FACTOR= -A(JROW,IEQ)/A(IEQ,IEQ)
    FOR K=IEQ TO N-1
    A(JROW,K)=A(JROW,K)+FACTOR*A(IEQ,K)
    NEXT K
  A(JROW,IEQ)=FACTOR
  NEXT JROW
 NEXT IEQ
REM
REM A IS NOW UPPER TRIANGULAR
REM
YSTAR(0)=Y(0)
   FOR IEQ=0 TO (N-1)-1
   SUM=0
    FOR K=0 TO IEQ-1
    SUM=SUM+A(IEQ+1,K)*YSTAR(K)
    NEXT K
   YSTAR(IEQ+1)=Y(IEQ+1)+SUM
   NEXT IEQ
X(N-1)=YSTAR(N-1)/A(N-1,N-1)
   FOR IEQ=(N-1)-1 TO 0 STEP -1
```

```
   SUM=0
    FOR K=IEQ+1 TO  N-1
    SUM=SUM+A(IEQ,K)*X(K)
    NEXT K
  X(IEQ)=(YSTAR(IEQ)-SUM)/A(IEQ,IEQ)
  NEXT IEQ
```

The lines below the comments can be repeated for other y vectors as needed.

In the next chapter, we will discuss more advanced methods of solving linear systems.

Matrix Inversion

Suppose we were faced with the scalar equation

$$y = Ax$$

and were asked to solve for x given y. We might write the answer as $x = y/A$ or as

$$x = A^{-1}y$$

For a scalar equation, A^{-1}, pronounced "A inverse," is just $^1/_A$. The question arises as to whether there is not a matrix we could label "A^{-1}," such that $x = A^{-1}y$. There is indeed such a matrix. (With the technical exception of A being "singular.")

First, define the *identity matrix* as a square matrix with ones along the diagonal and zeros off the diagonal. For example, if I is the 3 by 3 identity matrix, then

$$I = \begin{bmatrix} 1 & 0 & 0 \\ 0 & 1 & 0 \\ 0 & 0 & 1 \end{bmatrix}$$

The identity matrix is analogous to a one in scalar multiplication. The identities $IX = X$ and $XI = I$ hold for the identity matrix and any conformable matrix X. For scalars, we say that A^{-1} is the inverse of A if $AA^{-1} = I$. Analogously, for matrices we say

A^{-1} is the matrix inverse of A if $AA^{-1} = I$.

(Note we are restricting our attention to square matrices. For a square matrix, not only does $AA^{-1} = I$, so does $A^{-1}A$.)

How do we "invert" a matrix? The equation $I = AA^{-1}$ has precisely the same form as the matrix equation $Y = AX$, where I is Y and A^{-1} is X. We can use our BASIC program above to reduce A to upper triangular form and then back substitute for each column of the identity matrix. Because of the special form of the identity matrix we can calculate y* without creating each y.

Assume we have created the reduction part of the previous program. The code below replaces the lines below the comment, to calculate A^{-1} in AINV.

```
REDIM AINV(N-1,N-1)
 FOR LEQ=0 TO N-1
  FOR IEQ=0 TO LEQ-1
  YSTAR(IEQ)=0
  NEXT IEQ
 YSTAR(LEQ)=1
 FOR IEQ=LEQ TO (N-1)-1
 SUM=0
  FOR K=0 TO IEQ
  SUM=SUM+A(IEQ+1,K)*YSTAR(K)
  NEXT K
YSTAR(IEQ+1)=SUM
NEXT IEQ
AINV(N-1,LEQ)=YSTAR(N-1)/A(N-1,N-1)
 FOR IEQ=(N-1)-1 TO 0 STEP -1
 SUM=0
  FOR K=IEQ+1 TO  N-1
  SUM=SUM+A(IEQ,K)*AINV(K,LEQ)
  NEXT  K
 AINV(IEQ,LEQ)=(YSTAR(IEQ)-SUM)/A(IEQ,IEQ)
 NEXT IEQ
NEXT LEQ
```

We now have a "complete" set of routines to solve systems of linear equations and invert matrices. But these routines still leave a few things to be desired.

- They stop if they hit a zero pivot.
- They would be a lot faster if written in 8087 code.
- They would be more accurate if higher precision arithmetic were used, but we do not want to sacrifice too much storage space.

In the next chapter, we remedy these faults . . . and learn a few new tricks.

9

Linear Systems and Matrix Inversion: More Advanced Computational Techniques

By the end of the last chapter, we had created a set of procedures for solving systems of linear equations and for handling the related operation of matrix inversion. These methods followed the logic of "school room" techniques. The methods we develop in this chapter are perhaps less familiar, but they lend themselves well to highly accurate and highly efficient 8087 implementation.

Our goals for this chapter are:

- Fix the "zero pivot" problem.
- Express the solution to a system of linear equations in terms of inner products, in order to take full advantage of the 8087's design.
- Move our procedures from BASIC to 8087 code.

The Cookbook—Chapter 9

Program: **GAUSS-PP**

Purpose: Solve linear equations by Gaussian elimination with partial pivoting.

Input:
A—N by N coefficient matrix.
Y—N vector.
YSTAR—N vector; scratch space.
N—number of rows and columns of A.

Output:
X—N vector; X solves equations Y = AX.
A—A replaced with permuted Gaussian reduction.
INDEX—N vector showing row swaps.

Language: BASIC.

Program: **CROUT-PP**

Purpose: Perform Crout decomposition with partial pivoting.

Input:
A—N by N coefficient matrix.
N—number of rows and columns of A.

Output:
A—A replaced with permuted Gaussian reduction.
INDEX—N vector showing row swaps.

Language: BASIC.

Program: **XINPROD**

Purpose: Inner product with permuted column.

Call: CALL XINPROD(A(I,0), A(0, K), SUM,INDEX, TYPE,SKIPA,N).

Input:
A—N vector.
B—permuted N vector.
INDEX—integer N vector of row permutations for B.
TYPE—integer giving length of element of A,B.

	SKIPA—integer "skip factor" (see text) for A. N—integer number of elements of A,B.
Output:	SUM—double precision scalar; sum = inner product A,B.
Language:	8087/8088 assembly language.
Program:	**PIVOT**
Purpose:	Perform pivot step in Crout decomposition.
Call:	CALL PIVOT(A(0,K),INDEX,TYPE,K,N).
Input:	A—N by N coefficient matrix. INDEX—integer N vector of row permutations. TYPE—integer giving length of element of A. K—integer index of column to be searched. N—integer number of rows and columns of A.
Output:	INDEX—updated to reflect new pivot.
Language:	8087/8088 assembly language.
Program:	**REDUCE**
Purpose:	Perform Crout decomposition with partial pivoting.
Call:	CALL REDUCE(A(0,0),INDEX,TYPE,IER,N).
Input:	A—N by N coefficient matrix. TYPE—integer giving length of element of A. N—integer number of rows and columns of A.
Output:	INDEX—integer N vector of row permutations. IER—integer error flag, IER = − 1 if A singular.
Language:	8087/8088 assembly language.
Note:	Requires procedures XINPROD and PIVOT.
Program:	**SOLP**

Purpose:	Solve system of linear equations after Crout decomposition with partial pivoting.
Input:	A—N by N matrix reduced by CROUTP with partial pivoting. Y—N vector. N—number of rows and columns of A. INDEX—N vector showing row swaps.
Output:	X—N vector; X solves equations Y = AX.
Language:	BASIC.
Program:	**SOLVE**
Purpose:	Solve system of linear equations after Crout decomposition with partial pivoting.
Call:	CALL SOLVE(A,Y,X,INDEX,TYPEA,TYPEY,TYPEX,N).
Input:	A—N by N matrix reduced by CROUTP with partial pivoting. Y—N vector. INDEX—N vector showing row swaps. TYPEA—integer giving length of element of A. TYPEY—integer giving length of element of Y. TYPEX—integer giving length of element of X. N—integer number of rows and columns of A.
Output:	X—N vector; X solves equations Y=AX.
Language:	8087/8088 assembly language.
Note:	Requires procedure GINPROD.
Program:	**INV**
Purpose:	Invert matrix.
Call:	CALL INV (A),AINV,SCRATCH, INDEX,IER,TYPEA,N).
Input:	A—N by N matrix.

	SCRATCH—single precision N vector of scratch space. TYPEA—integer giving length of element of A,AINV. N—integer number of rows and columns of A.
Output:	AINV—N by N matrix; inverse of A. A—A replaced by Crout reduction. INDEX—integer N vector, prermutations of reduced A. IER—integer error flag, IER= − 1 if A singular.
Language:	8087/8088 assembly language.
Note:	Requires procedures REDUCE and SOLVE.

Our original program for Gaussian elimination stops if it hits a zero diagonal, or "pivot," element. A zero pivot may indicate a "mathematical," not "just a computational," problem, because the system of equations may not have a unique solution. Consider the following linear system as an example.

$$Y_1 = 2x_1 + 4x_2$$
$$Y_2 = 4x_1 + 8x_2$$

The "A" matrix is originally

$$\begin{matrix} 2 & 4 \\ 4 & 8 \end{matrix}$$

After one step of Gaussian elimination, the reduced matrix looks like this:

$$\begin{matrix} 2 & 4 \\ 0 & 0 \end{matrix}$$

In addition, we have saved the FACTOR, −2.

At the next attempted step of Gaussian elimination, the programs finds that A_{22} equals zero, and therefore stops with the error message "ZERO PIVOT AT 2." The problem is a mathematical one. The matrix A is *singular,* so the pair of equations does not have a unique solution. In fact, an infinite set of combinations of x_1 and x_2 solve the system if y_2 is twice y_1. No solution exists if y_2 isn't exactly twice y_1.

Consider the following rather different pair of equations.

$$y_1 = 0x_1 + 1x_2$$
$$y_2 = 1x_1 + 0x_2$$

The "A" matrix is originally

$$\begin{matrix} 0 & 1 \\ 1 & 0 \end{matrix}$$

Our Gaussian elimination routine hits a zero pivot—and stops—on the very first step. This example demonstrates a computational, rather than a mathematical, problem. By inspection, the solution to the system is $x_1 = y_2$ and $x_2 = y_1$. The solution to the computational problem is simple. We just reorder the equations so that the diagonal elements aren't zero. Instead of solving the system as originally specified, we work on

$$y_2 = 1x_1 + 0x_2$$
$$y_1 = 0x_1 + 1x_2$$

with the "A" matrix

$$\begin{matrix} 1 & 0 \\ 0 & 1 \end{matrix}$$

Gaussian elimination proceeds smoothly as long as we keep track of the order in which the equations are solved.

These two examples illustrate the general rules for dealing with zero pivot elements.

1. *If a zero pivot is encountered in equation i, exchange the equation i with an equation below it that does not have a zero in column i.*
2. *If all the remaining equations have a zero in column i, the matrix is singular.*
3. *Keep a record of all equation exchanges, so that we can later "unswap" the equations, if desired.*

In practice, we add two further steps.

4. *Rather than actually exchanging the equations, create an array INDEX such that INDEX(I) is the original number of the equation that now belongs in row i.*

Just as a zero pivot stops the program by creating an infinite FACTOR, so too, a very small pivot creates a very large FACTOR and tends to generate sizable round-off error. Accuracy can be considerably enhanced by using the largest possible pivot.

5. *Instead of exchanging equations only when a zero pivot is encountered (as required by rule 1), search the remainder of column i for the element, A(J,I), with the largest absolute value and exchange rows i and j.*

The implementation of Gaussian elimination with rules 2 through 5 is called *Gaussian elimination with partial pivoting*. The BASIC code below rewrites the Gaussian elimination program of the previous chapter to include partial pivoting. Notice that instead of row I, we now reference row INDEX(I), but column j remains column j.

```
REM PROGRAM GAUSS-PP
DEFINT I-N
REDIM A(N-1,N-1),Y(N-1),X(N-1),YSTAR(N-1),INDEX(N-1)
  FOR IEQ=0 TO N-1
  INDEX(IEQ)=IEQ
  NEXT IEQ
  FOR IEQ=0 TO N-1
  REM NOW SWAP ROWS
  CALL FINDPIVOT(A,INDEX,IBIGGEST,N)
  SWAP INDEX(IEQ),INDEX(IBIGGEST)
  IEQX=INDEX(IEQ)
  IF A(IEQX,IEQ)=0 THEN PRINT "SINGULAR MATRIX",IEQ:STOP
    FOR JROW=IEQ+1 TO N-1
    JROWX=INDEX(JROW)
    FACTOR= -A(JROWX,IEQ)/A(IEQX,IEQ)
      FOR K=IEQ TO N-1
      A(JROWX,K)=A(JROWX,K)+FACTOR*A(IEQX,K)
      NEXT K
   A(JROWX,IEQ)=FACTOR
   NEXT JROW
 NEXT IEQ
REM
REM A IS NOW UPPER TRIANGULAR
REM
YSTAR(0)=Y(INDEX(0))
  FOR IEQ=1 TO N-1
  IEQX=INDEX(IEQ)
  SUM=0
    FOR K=0 TO IEQ-1
    SUM=SUM+A(IEQX,K)*YSTAR(K)
    NEXT K
  YSTAR(IEQ)=Y(IEQX)+SUM
  NEXT IEQ
  IN=INDEX(N-1)
  X(N-1)=YSTAR(N-1)/A(IN,N-1)
    FOR IEQ=(N-1)-1 TO 0 STEP -1
    IEQX=INDEX(IEQ)
    SUM=0
    FOR K=IEQ+1 TO N-1
    SUM=SUM+A(IEQX,K)*X(K)
    NEXT K
    X(IEQ)=(YSTAR(IEQ)-SUM)/A(IEQX,IEQ)
```

```
  NEXT IEQ
STOP
END
REM SUBROUTINE TO FIND LARGEST ELEMENT IN COLUMN
SUB FINDPIVOT(A(2),INDEX(1),IBIGGEST,N) STATIC
DEFINT I-N
BIGGEST=ABS(A(INDEX(IEQ),IEQ))
IBIGGEST=IEQ
  FOR I=IEQ+1 TO N-1
  PIV=ABS(A(INDEX(I),IEQ))
  IF PIV>BIGGEST THEN BIGGEST=PIV:IBIGGEST=I
  NEXT I
RETURN
END SUB
```

This program performs the same number of multiplications and additions as simple Gaussian elimination, but will run a little more slowly due to increased overhead. The time spent selecting pivot rows is an order n^2 operation, and is therefore negligible compared to the basic reduction operation.

We've fixed the "zero pivot" problem. Before moving on to the chapter's other goals, we need to discuss some more mathematics. If you're more interested in "how" than "why," skip ahead to the programs. It will help to look at the BASIC programs before the 8087 programs, since the former are easier to follow.

The Theory of the "LU Decomposition"

A number of advanced methods of solving systems of linear equations, and consequently of matrix inversion, rely on the principle of "LU decomposition." This principle states that a square matrix A can be factored into a lower triangular matrix L and an upper triangular matrix U such that L times U equals A. There are many such decompositions. A particular method is arrived at by our choice of restrictions on the contents of L or U.

LU methods all work in three steps. Suppose the initial problem is

$$y = Ax$$

1. Factor A into L and U. This decomposition is an order n^3 operation. Now we have

   $$y = (LU)x = L(Ux)$$

   While LU is a square matrix, Ux is a column vector.

2. Solve the following system of equations for y*. Solution of an upper (or lower) triangular system of equations is an order n^2 operation.

$$y = Ly^*$$

Since $y^* = L^{-1}y$, we next

3. Solve, the order n^2 problem

$$y^* = Ux$$

Does this look like a roundabout method? It really isn't, it only seems that way. For example, the reduction process of Gaussian elimination leaves us with an upper triangular matrix that we might call U. If we add a diagonal with all ones to the set of factors we store along the way, we have a lower triangular matrix that we might call L. A bit of calculation will show you that LU indeed equals A. Further, solving for y* and x in the Gaussian elimination programs are exactly steps 2 and 3 above. So Gaussian elimination is actually a particular example of using an LU decomposition.

The Crout Decomposition

The most useful LU method for the 8087 is called the *Crout decomposition.* (The Crout decomposition is a member of the family called "compact" methods.) The defining characteristic of the Crout decomposition is that U has all ones along the diagonal. So this LU decomposition looks like this:

$$L = \begin{bmatrix} L_{0,0} & 0 & 0 & \cdot & \cdot & 0 \\ L_{1,0} & L_{1,1} & 0 & & & \cdot \\ L_{2,0} & L_{2,1} & L_{2,2} & & & \cdot \\ \cdot & \cdot & \cdot & & & \\ \cdot & \cdot & \cdot & & & \\ \cdot & \cdot & \cdot & & & 0 \\ L_{N-1,0} & L_{N-1,1} & \cdot & \cdot & \cdot & L_{N1,N-1} \end{bmatrix}$$

$$U = \begin{bmatrix} 1 & U_{0,1} & U_{0,2} & \cdot & \cdot & \cdot & U_{0,N-1} \\ 0 & 1 & U_{1,2} & & & & U_{1,N-1} \\ 0 & 0 & 1 & & & & \cdot \\ \cdot & & & & & & \cdot \\ \cdot & & & & & & \cdot \\ \cdot & & & & & & U_{N-2,N-1} \\ 0 & 0 & \cdot & \cdot & \cdot & 0 & 1 \end{bmatrix}$$

Notice the special pattern in which the rows of L match up with the columns of U. The inner product of row 0 of L and column 0 of U, which equals $A_{0,0}$ is just $L_{0,0}$. Moving down to the second row of L we see that $L_{1,0}$ equals $A_{1,0}$, and so forth. In this way, the entire first column of L is defined.

Now multiply the first row of L with the second column of U. We find $L_{0,0}$ times $U_{0,1}$ equals $A_{0,1}$. Since we already know $L_{0,0}$, we can solve for $U_{0,1}$ directly. Moving on to the third column of U gets us $U_{0,2}$ in the same manner. In this way the entire first row of U is defined.

Having defined the first column of L and the first row of U, we move on to the second column of L and the first row of U. In effect, the Crout procedure marches down the diagonal of the matrix. At each step, the portion of the column of L hanging down from the diagonal and the portion of the row of U sticking out to the right, are defined. To conserve space, we reuse A to store L and U. The following BASIC program performs a CROUT decomposition.

```
       DEFINT I-N
       DEFDBL S
       REDIM A(N-1,N-1)
        FOR K=0 TO N-1
        IF A(K,K)=0 THEN PRINT "ZERO PIVOT",K:STOP
        REM FILL IN COLUMN OF L
         FOR I=K TO N-1
80       SUM=0
90        FOR L=0 TO K-1
100       SUM=SUM+A(I,L)*A(L,K)
110       NEXT L
        A(I,K)=A(I,K)-SUM
        NEXT I
       REM FILL IN ROW OF U
        FOR J=K+1 TO N-1
160     SUM=0
170      FOR L=0 TO K-1
180      SUM=SUM+A(K,L)*A(L,J)
190     NEXT L
        A(K,J)=(A(K,J)-SUM)/A(K,K)
        NEXT J
       NEXT K
```

Do you see why the Crout decomposition is so well suited to the 8087? Lines 80-110 and 160-190 form inner products between a portion of a column of L and a portion of a row of U! By using INPROD or GINPROD we take full advantage of the 8087's speed. Of probably greater importance, since the inner products are accumulated in temporary real precision, we can store a matrix in single or double precision and still get almost all the accuracy of 80-bit storage.

If you'd like to get a better handle on the logic of the Crout decomposition, you might try reducing the following 2 by 2 matrix into upper and lower triangular matrices.

$$A = \begin{bmatrix} 3 & 6 \\ 4 & 2 \end{bmatrix}$$

You should end up with these two matrices:

$$L = \begin{bmatrix} 3 & 0 \\ 4 & -6 \end{bmatrix} \quad U = \begin{bmatrix} 1 & 2 \\ 0 & 1 \end{bmatrix}$$

Note that our program stores both L and U in place of A.

$$A \text{ reduced } = \begin{bmatrix} 3 & 2 \\ 4 & -6 \end{bmatrix}$$

The "zero pivot" problem has returned with this version of Crout decomposition. We adapt this program to include partial pivoting by exchanging rows just before filling each row of U. The next BASIC program illustrates Crout decomposition with partial pivoting.

```
REM PROGRAM CROUT-PP
DEFINT I-N
DEFDBL S
REDIM A(N-1,N-1),INDEX(N-1),Y(N-1)
  FOR I=0 TO N-1
  INDEX(I)=I
  NEXT I
  FOR K= 0 TO N-1
  REM FILL IN COLUMN OF L
    FOR I=K TO N-1
    IX=INDEX(I)
    SUM=0
      FOR L=0 TO K-1
      LX=INDEX(L)
      SUM=SUM+A(IX,L)*A(LX,K)
      NEXT L
    A(IX,K)=A(IX,K)-SUM
    NEXT I
  REM SWAP ROWS
  CALL FINDPIVOT(A,INDEX,KBIGGEST,N)
  SWAP INDEX(K),INDEX(KBIGGEST)
```

```
    REM FILL IN ROW OF U
    KX=INDEX(K)
    IF A(KX,K)=0 THEN PRINT "SINGULAR MATRIX ",K:STOP
      FOR J= K+1 TO N-1
      SUM=0
        FOR L=0 TO K-1
        LX=INDEX(L)
        SUM=SUM+A(KX,L)*A(LX,J)
        NEXT L
      A(KX,J)=(A(KX,J)-SUM)/A(KX,K)
      NEXT J
    NEXT K
  STOP

  REM SUBROUTINE TO FIND LARGEST ELEMENT IN COLUMN
    SUB FINDPIVOT(A(2),INDEX(1),KBIGGEST,N) STATIC
    BIGGEST=ABS(A(INDEX(K),K))
    KBIGGEST=K
      FOR I=K+1 TO N-1
      PIV=ABS(A(INDEX(I),K))
      IF PIV>BIGGEST THEN BIGGEST=PIV:KBIGGEST=I
      NEXT I
    RETURN
  END SUB
```

This program effectively takes the original A, permutes A by swapping rows as indicated in INDEX, and then replaces A with the Crout decomposition of the permuted A. In the solution phase, we'll have to undo the row swaps.

8087 Routines for Solving Systems of Linear Equations

The time has finally arrived to prepare high-speed 8087 routines for solving systems of linear equations and for matrix inversion. Three routines based on the Crout decomposition with partial pivoting appear below. REDUCE reduces a matrix to its LU decomposition. Given the reduced matrix and the vector y, SOLVE calculates x, as in y = Ax. INV inverts a matrix in one step.

All the hard work in these routines consists of taking inner products. We can't use GINPROD because the rows of each column are permuted by the decomposition. We present a new inner product routine, XINPROD, which allows for such scrambling. We also present PIVOT, which conducts the search for the appropriate pivot element. In reducing a matrix, PIVOT is only called n times, where XINPROD is called n^2 times, so using it doesn't really save much time. However, it's easier to write REDUCE in a modular way and it also gives us a good excuse to present some code in which 8087 comparisons are made.

```
INCLUDE   SUBROUT.MAC
          SUBROUTINE XINPROD,<A,B,DSUM,INDEX,ARRAY_TYPE,SKIPB,N>
;  ASSUMPTIONS:     A,B ARE ARRAYS
;                   DSUM IS DOUBLE PRECISION
;                   INDEX IS THE ADDRESS OF INTEGER ARRAY INDEX
;                   ARRAY_TYPE,SKIPA,N ARE INTEGERS
;
;                   XINPROD RETURNS THE INNER PRODUCT OF THE FIRST N
;                   ELEMENTS OF A (ONE ROW)
;                   WITH B (PERMUTED BY INDEX)
;                   ELEMENTS OF B ARE ARRAY_TYPE*SKIPB APART
;         Save 6 registers since this routine is called from others
;         Also leave room for one word of temporary storage
;
          CHKSTCK   12+2
          PUSHTEMP  AX
          PUSHTEMP  BX
          PUSHTEMP  CX
          PUSHTEMP  DX
          PUSHTEMP  SI
          PUSHTEMP  DI
          FLDZ                          ;SET RUNNING SUM=0
          LDS       BX,[BP].N           ;DS:BX=ADDR(N)
          CMP       WORD PTR [BX],0     ;COUNT LE 0?
          JLE       DONE_RIGHT_AWAY
          PUSHTEMP  [BX],COUNT
;USE CX FOR SHIFTING AS AN EXAMPLE
;IF TYPE IS SINGLE PRECISION SET CX=2 ELSE SET CX=3
          MOV       CX,3                ;ASSUME TYPE DOUBLE
          LDS       BX,[BP].ARRAY_TYPE  ;DS:BX=ADDR(ARRAY_TYPE)
          CMP       WORD PTR [BX],4     ;IS ARRAY_TYPE SINGLE?
          JNE       NOT_SINGLE
          MOV       CX,2                ;YES, TYPE IS SINGLE
NOT_SINGLE:
          MOV       SI,[BP].A           ;SI=OFFSET(A)
          LDS       BX,[BP].SKIPB       ;DS:BX=ADDR(SKIPB)
          MOV       AX,[BX]             ;AX=SKIPB
          SHL       AX,CL               ;AX=ARRAY_TYPE*SKIPB
          PUSHTEMP  AX,B_DISTANCE
          MOV       DI,[BP].INDEX       ;DI=OFFSET(INDEX(0))
```

```
XINP_LOOP:
          MOV      DS,[BP].A+2         ;DS:SI=ADDR(A)
          CMP      CL,2                ;IS A SINGLE?
          JNE      A_DOUBLE
          FLD      DWORD PTR [SI]      ;LOAD SINGLE A ELEMENT
          ADD      SI,4                ;READY FOR NEXT A
          JMP      MULT_B
A_DOUBLE: FLD      QWORD PTR [SI]      ;LOAD DOUBLE A ELEMENT
          ADD      SI,8                ;READY FOR NEXT A
MULT_B:
          MOV      DS,[BP].INDEX+2     ;DS=SEG(INDEX)
          MOV      AX,[DI]             ;AX=INDEX(I)
          MUL      WORD PTR [BP].B_DISTANCE
;AX=ARRAY_TYPE*SKIPB*INDEX(I)
          LDS      BX,[BP].B           ;DS:BX=ADDR(B(0))
          ADD      BX,AX               ;DS:BX=ADDR(B(INDEX(I)))
          CMP      CL,2                ;IS B SINGLE?
          JNE      B_DOUBLE
          FMUL     DWORD PTR [BX]      ;MULTIPLY SINGLE
          JMP      NEXT_BELEMENT
B_DOUBLE: FMUL     QWORD PTR [BX]      ;MULTIPLY DOUBLE


NEXT_BELEMENT:
          ADD      DI,2                ;NEXT INDEX
          DEC      WORD PTR [BP].COUNT ;DECREMENT COUNT
          CMP      WORD PTR [BP].COUNT,0
          FADDP    ST(1),ST            ;SUM=SUM+A(I)*B(INDEX(I))
; WE PUT FADDP HERE TO ALLOW AS MUCH PARALLEL EXECUTION AS POSSIBLE
          JG       XINP_LOOP


DONE:
          POPTEMP  2
DONE_RIGHT_AWAY:                       ;AVOID POPTEMP IF N=0
          LDS      BX,[BP].DSUM        ;DS:BX=ADDR(DSUM)
          FSTP     QWORD PTR [BX]      ;STORE DSUM
          POP      DI
          POP      SI
          POP      DX
          POP      CX
          POP      BX
          POP      AX
          TEMP_COUNT=TEMP_COUNT-6
          RETURN   XINPROD
          END
```

XINPROD takes about 66 microseconds per element. This is a little slower than the best possible speed, because full parallel execution between the cpu and the 8087 isn't achieved between the FLD and the FMUL. In other words, the 8087 finishes executing FLD before the cpu has set up the addresses for the FMUL. One could rewrite the program and increase speed by a few percent, but the resulting code would be harder to follow.

```
INCLUDE   SUBROUT.MAC
          SUBROUTINE PIVOT,<A,INDEX,TYPEA,SKIPA,DIAG,N>
;  ASSUMPTIONS: A IS ADDRESS OF N-ARRAY OF DATA
;               INDEX IS AN INTEGER N-ARRAY
;               TYPEA,DIAG,N ARE INTEGERS
;
;               PIVOT SEARCHES A FROM DIAG
;               TO THE BOTTOM FOR THE ELEMENT LARGEST IN
;               ABSOLUTE VALUE.  PIVOT EXCHANGES THE INDEXES OF
;               DIAG AND THIS ELEMENT
;
;               A IS AN N-VECTOR PERMUTED ACCORDING TO INDEX
;         Save 6 registers since this routine is called from others
;         Also leave room for three words of temporary storage
          CHKSTCK   12+6
          PUSHTEMP  AX
          PUSHTEMP  BX
          PUSHTEMP  CX
          PUSHTEMP  DX
          PUSHTEMP  SI
          PUSHTEMP  DI
          PUSHTEMP  AX,STATUS_WORD
          LDS       BX,[BP].DIAG        ;DS:BX=ADDR(DIAG)
          MOV       AX,[BX]             ;AX=DIAG
          LDS       DI,[BP].INDEX       ;DS:DI=ADDR(INDEX)
          ADD       DI,AX
          ADD       DI,AX               ;DS:DI=ADDR(INDEX(DIAG))
          PUSHTEMP  DS                  ;PUT ADDRESS OF INDEX OF BIGGEST
          PUSHTEMP  DI,KBIGGEST         ;FOUND ON STACK
                                        ;INITIALLY ASSUME FIRST IS BIGGEST
          LDS       BX,[BP].N           ;DS:BX=ADDR(N)
          MOV       CX,[BX]             ;CX=N
          SUB       CX,AX               ;CX=N-DIAG,
          DEC       CX                  ; # OF ELEMENTS TO CHECK


          MOV       SI,[BP]+12          ;SI=ADDR(A)

          LDS       BX,[BP].SKIPA       ;DS:BX=ADDR(SKIPA)
```

```
          MOV     AX,[BX]               ;AX=SKIPA
          LDS     BX,[BP].TYPEA         ;DS:BX=ADDR(TYPEA)
          MUL     WORD PTR [BX]         ;AX=ELEMENT DISTANCE
          MOV     DS,[BP].INDEX+2       ;BE SURE DS=SEG(INDEX)
          MUL     WORD PTR [DI]         ;AX=ELEMENT DISTANCE*INDEX(DIAG)
          MOV     BX,AX                 ;OFFSET OF INDEX(DIAG) FROM A(0)
          LDS     SI,[BP].TYPEA         ;DS:SI=ADDR(TYPEA)
          CMP     WORD PTR [SI],4       ;IS A SINGLE?
          LDS     SI,[BP].A             ;DS:SI=ADDR(A(0))
          JNE     A_DOUBLE
          FLD     DWORD PTR [SI][BX]    ;LOAD SINGLE
          JMP     LOADED_ONE
A_DOUBLE: FLD     QWORD PTR [SI][BX]    ;LOAD DOUBLE
LOADED_ONE:
          FABS
          JCXZ    DONE
COMP_LOOP:
          ADD     DI,2                  ;NEXT INDEX
          LDS     BX,[BP].SKIPA         ;DS:BX=ADDR(SKIPA)
          MOV     AX,[BX]               ;AX=SKIPA
          LDS     BX,[BP].TYPEA         ;DS:BX=ADDR(TYPEA)
          MUL     WORD PTR [BX]         ;AX=ELEMENT DISTANCE
          MOV     DS,[BP].INDEX+2       ;BE SURE DS=SEG(INDEX)
          MUL     WORD PTR [DI]         ;AX=ELEMENT DISTANCE*INDEX(DIAG)
          MOV     BX,AX                 ;OFFSET OF INDEX(DIAG) FROM A(0)
          LDS     SI,[BP].TYPEA         ;DS:SI=ADDR(TYPEA)
          CMP     WORD PTR [SI],4       ;IS A SINGLE?
          LDS     SI,[BP].A             ;DS:SI=ADDR(A(0))
          JNE     AI_DOUBLE
          FLD     DWORD PTR [SI][BX]    ;LOAD SINGLE
          JMP     COMPARE
AI_DOUBLE:FLD     QWORD PTR [SI][BX]    ;LOAD DOUBLE
COMPARE:
          FABS
          FCOM                          ;COMPARE NEW TO BIGGEST
          FSTSW   [BP].STATUS_WORD
          FWAIT
          MOV     AH,BYTE PTR [BP].STATUS_WORD+1
          SAHF
          JB      LESS_OR_NONCOMPARABLE
;HERE IF NEW IS GREATER THAN OR EQUAL TO BIGGEST
          FSTP    ST(1)                 ;MOVE NEW DOWN STACK
          MOV     [BP].KBIGGEST,DI
          JMP     NEXT_ELEMENT
LESS_OR_NONCOMPARABLE:                  ;BIGGEST IS STILL CHAMP
          FSTP    ST(0)
```

```
NEXT_ELEMENT:
          LOOP       COMP_LOOP
;SWAP INDEX(DIAG) AND INDEX(KBIGGEST)
          LDS        BX,[BP].DIAG         ;DS:BX=ADDR(DIAG)
          MOV        DX,[BX]              ;DX=DIAG
          LDS        DI,[BP].INDEX        ;DS:DI=ADDR(INDEX)
          ADD        DI,DX
          ADD        DI,DX                ;DS:DI=ADDR(INDEX(DIAG))
          MOV        AX,[DI]              ;AX=INDEX(DIAG)
          MOV        BX,[BP].KBIGGEST     ;BX=ADDR(INDEX(KBIGGEST))
          XCHG       AX,[BX]
          XCHG       AX,[DI]
DONE:
          FSTP       ST(0)                ;CLEAR ELEMENT OFF STACK
          POPTEMP    3
          POP        DI
          POP        SI
          POP        DX
          POP        CX
          POP        BX
          POP        AX
          TEMP_COUNT=TEMP_COUNT-6
          RETURN     PIVOT
          END
```

With XINPROD and PIVOT in hand, we need only replace the appropriate lines of the BASIC program with CALL statements. The new version of the BASIC program appears below.

```
DEFINT I-N
DEFDBL S
REDIM A(N-1,N-1),INDEX(N-1)
 FOR I=0 TO N-1
 INDEX(I)=I
 NEXT I
 ITYPE=4
 FOR K=0 TO N-1
 REM FILL IN COLUMN OF L
  FOR I=K TO N-1
  IX=INDEX(I)
  SUM=0
   REM FOR L=0 TO K-1
   REM LX=INDEX(L)
   REM SUM=SUM+A(IX,L)*A(LX,K)
   REM NEXT L
  CALL XINPROD(A(IX,0),A(0,K),SUM,INDEX(0),ITYPE,N,K)
```

```
    A(IX,K)=A(IX,K)-SUM
    NEXT I
  REM SWAP ROWS
  REM CALL FINDPIVOT(A,INDEX,KBIGGEST)
  REM SWAP INDEX(K),INDEX(KBIGGEST)
  CALL PIVOT(A(0,K),INDEX(I),TYPE,K,N)
  REM FILL IN ROW OF U
  KX=INDEX(K)
  IF A(KX,K)=0 THEN PRINT "SINGULAR MATRIX",K:STOP
   FOR J=K+1 TO N-1
   SUM=0
    REM FOR L=0 TO K-1
    REM LX=INDEX(L)
    REM SUM=SUM+A(KX,L)*A(LX,J)
    REM NEXT L
   CALL XINPROD(A(KX,0),A(0,J),SUM,INDEX(0),ITYPE,N,K)
   A(KX,J)=(A(KX,J)-SUM)/A(KX,K)
   NEXT J
  NEXT K
  REM SUBROUTINE TO FIND LARGEST ELEMENT IN COLUMN
  REM BIGGEST=ABS(A(INDEX(K),K))
  REM KBIGGEST=K
   REM FOR I=K+1 TO N-1
  REM PIV=ABS(A(INDEX(I),K))
   REM IF PIV>BIGGEST THEN BIGGEST=PIV:KBIGGEST=I
   REM NEXT I
  REM RETURN
```

All we need now is a procedure to call XINPROD and PIVOT from BASIC. We'll call this procedure REDUCE. Procedure REDUCE is called by

```
CALL REDUCE(A,INDEX,TYPE,IER,N)
```

where A is the N by N matrix of coefficients. INDEX is an integer array returning the row permutations. TYPE, IER, and N are integers. TYPE indicates whether A is single or double precision. IER returns 0 if the matrix is nonsingular and -1 if the matrix is singular. REDUCE replaces A with its Crout reduction with partial pivoting.

```
INCLUDE    SUBROUT.MAC
           EXTERNAL  <XINPROD,PIVOT>
           SUBROUTINE REDUCE,<A,INDEX,IER,ARRAY_TYPE,N>
;  ASSUMPTIONS: A IS THE ADDRESS OF AN N BY N MATRIX
;               INDEX IS THE ADDRESS OF AN INTEGER N-ARRAY
;               IER IS THE ADDRESS OF AN INTEGER
;               ARRAY_TYPE,N ARE ADDRESSES OF INTEGERS
```

```
;
;               AT EXIT IER=-1 IF MATRIX IS SINGULAR, ELSE IER=0;
;
;         Save 6 registers since this routine is called from others
;         Also leave room seven words of temporary storage
;         and 9 words for call to XINPROD
;
          CHKSTCK    12+14+18
          PUSHTEMP   AX
          PUSHTEMP   BX
          PUSHTEMP   CX
          PUSHTEMP   DX
          PUSHTEMP   SI
          PUSHTEMP   DI
          PUSHTEMP   AX,STATUS_WORD
          PUSHTEMP   AX,K
          PUSHTEMP   AX,COUNT              ;ESTABLISH TEMPORARY
          PUSHTEMP   AX
          PUSHTEMP   AX
          PUSHTEMP   AX
          PUSHTEMP   AX,DSUM               ;TEMPORARY DOUBLE PRECISION
          LDS        BX,[BP].IER           ;DS:BX=ADDR(IER)
          MOV        WORD PTR [BX],0       ;IER=0
;FIRST SET INDEX(I)=I
          LDS        BX,[BP].N             ;DS:BX=ADDR(N)
          MOV        CX,[BX]               ;CX=N
          LDS        DI,[BP].INDEX         ;DS:DI=ADDR(INDEX)
          MOV        AX,0
INDEX_LOOP:
          MOV        [DI],AX               ;INDEX(I)=I
          INC        AX
          ADD        DI,2
          LOOP       INDEX_LOOP
;
;IF TYPE IS SINGLE PRECISION SET CX=2 ELSE SET CX=3
;  USE CX FOR SHIFTING BELOW
          MOV        CX,3                  ;ASSUME TYPE DOUBLE
          LDS        BX,[BP].ARRAY_TYPE    ;DS:BX=ADDR(ARRAY_TYPE)
          CMP        WORD PTR [BX],4       ;IS ARRAY_TYPE SINGLE?
          JNE        NOT_SINGLE
          MOV        CX,2                  ;YES, ARRAY_TYPE IS SINGLE
NOT_SINGLE:
;OUTERMOST LOOP IS FOR K=0 TO N-1
          MOV        SI,0                  ;KEEP K IN SI
;
MAJOR_LOOP:
```

```
        MOV     [BP].K,SI           ;STORE K FOR LATER REFERENCE
        MOV     AX,SI               ;AX=K
        SHL     AX,CL               ;AX=ARRAY_TYPE*K
        MOV     DX,AX
        ADD     DX,[BP].A           ;DX=OFFSET(A(0,K))
;FILL IN COLUMN OF L
;MOVE THROUGH INDEX(I) FOR I=K TO N-1
;
        LDS     BX,[BP].N           ;DS:BX=ADDR(N)
        MOV     AX,[BX]             ;AX=N
        SUB     AX,SI               ;AX=N-K
        MOV     [BP].COUNT,AX       ;COUNT=N-K
;
        MOV     DI,[BP].INDEX       ;DI=OFFSET(INDEX(0))
        ADD     DI,SI
        ADD     DI,SI               ;DI=OFFSET(INDEX(I))
L_LOOP:
;CALL XINPROD(A(INDEX(I),0),A(0,K),DSUM,INDEX,ARRAY_TYPE,N,K)
;
        PUSH    [BP].A+2            ;PUSH SEG(A)
        MOV     DS,[BP].INDEX+2     ;DS:SEG(INDEX)
        MOV     AX,[DI]             ;AX=INDEX(I)
        SHL     AX,CL               ;AX=ARRAY_TYPE*INDEX(I)
        LDS     BX,[BP].N           ;DS:BX=ADDR(N)
        MUL     BYTE PTR [BX]       ;AX=N*ARRAY_TYPE*INDEX(I)
;NOTICE SNEAKY USE OF MUL BYTE PTR!!
;THIS IS SAFE BECAUSE N MUST BE 255 OR LESS AND N*ARRAY_TYPE*INDEX(I)
;                       MUST BE UNDER 64k
;WE DID THIS TO AVOID MESSING UP CONTENTS OF DX REGISTER
        ADD     AX,[BP].A           ;AX=OFFSET(A(INDEX(I),0))
        PUSH    AX
        PUSH    [BP].A+2            ;PUSH SEG(A)
        PUSH    DX                  ;OFFSET(A(0,K))
        PUSH    SS                  ;SEG(DSUM)
        LEA     BX,[BP].DSUM        ;BX=OFFSET(DSUM)
        PUSH    BX
        PUSH    [BP].INDEX+2        ;SEG(INDEX)
        PUSH    [BP].INDEX          ;OFFSET(INDEX)
        PUSH    [BP].ARRAY_TYPE+2   ;SEG(ARRAY_TYPE)
        PUSH    [BP].ARRAY_TYPE     ;OFFSET(ARRAY_TYPE)
        PUSH    [BP].N+2            ;SEG(N)
        PUSH    [BP].N              ;OFFSET(N)
        PUSH    SS                  ;SEG(K)
        LEA     BX,[BP].K           ;OFFSET(K)
        PUSH    BX
        CALL    XINPROD
```

```
;
          FLD       QWORD PTR [BP].DSUM ;ST=DSUM
;GET ADDRESS OF A(INDEX(I),K))
          MOV       DS,[BP].A+2         ;DS=SEG(A)
;AX HAS OFFSET(A(INDEX(I),0)
          MOV       BX,SI               ;BX=K
          SHL       BX,CL               ;BX=ARRAY_TYPE*K
          ADD       BX,AX               ;BX=OFF(A(INDEX(I),K))
;CALCULATE A(INDEX(I),K)-SUM FOR SINGLE OR DOUBLE PRECISION
          CMP       CX,2                ;SINGLE?
          JNE       A_DOUBLE
          FSUBR     DWORD PTR [BX]      ;ST=A(INDEX(I),K)-DSUM
          FSTP      DWORD PTR [BX]      ;A(INDEX(I),K)=ST
          JMP       NEXT_COL_ELEMENT
;
A_DOUBLE: FSUBR     QWORD PTR [BX]      ;ST=A(INDEX(I),K)-DSUM
          FSTP      QWORD PTR [BX]      ;A(INDEX(I),K)=ST
          JMP       NEXT_COL_ELEMENT
;
NEXT_COL_ELEMENT:
          ADD       DI,2                ;NEXT INDEX(I)
          DEC       WORD PTR [BP].COUNT
          CMP       WORD PTR [BP].COUNT,0
          JG        L_LOOP
;
;
;CALL PIVOT(A(0,K),INDEX,ARRAY_TYPE,N,K,N)
          PUSH      DS                  ;DS STILL HAS SEG(A)
          PUSH      DX                  ;OFFSET(A(0,K))
          PUSH      [BP].INDEX+2        ;SEG(INDEX)
          PUSH      [BP].INDEX          ;OFFSET(INDEX)
          PUSH      [BP].ARRAY_TYPE+2   ;SEG(ARRAY_TYPE)
          PUSH      [BP].ARRAY_TYPE     ;OFFSET(ARRAY_TYPE)
          PUSH      [BP].N+2            ;SEG(N)
          PUSH      [BP].N              ;OFFSET(N)
          PUSH      SS                  ;SEG(K)
          LEA       BX,[BP].K           ;OFFSET(K)
          PUSH      BX
          PUSH      [BP].N+2            ;SEG(N)
          PUSH      [BP].N              ;OFFSET(N)
          CALL      PIVOT
;********CHECK FOR SINGULAR MATRIX
;IS A(INDEX(K),K)=0???
;
          LDS       DI,[BP].INDEX       ;DS:DI=ADDR(INDEX(0))
          ADD       DI,SI
```

```
          ADD       DI,SI                 ;DS:DI=ADDR(INDEX(K))
          MOV       AX,[DI]               ;AX=INDEX(K)
          SHL       AX,CL                 ;AX=ARRAY_TYPE*INDEX(K)
          LDS       BX,[BP].N             ;DS:BX=ADDR(N)
          MUL       BYTE PTR [BX]         ;AX=N*ARRAY_TYPE*INDEX(K)
          MOV       DS,[BP].A+2           ;DS:SEG(A)
          ADD       AX,DX                 ;DS:DI=ADDR(A(INDEX(K),K)
          MOV       DI,AX
;
          CMP       CX,2                  ;SINGLE?
          JNE       A_DOUBLE2
          FLD       DWORD PTR [DI]        ;LOAD A(INDEX(K),K)
                                          ;AND LEAVE IT ON STACK
          JMP       TEST_FOR_ZERO
A_DOUBLE2:FLD       QWORD PTR [DI]
TEST_FOR_ZERO:
          FXAM
          FSTSW     [BP].STATUS_WORD
          FWAIT
          MOV       AH,BYTE PTR [BP].STATUS_WORD+1
          SAHF

;THE STATUS BITS SHOULD BE  C3 C2 C1 C0
;         POSITIVE NORMAL   0  1  0  0
;         NEGATIVE NORMAL   0  1  1  0
;ASSUME ANYTHING ELSE, INCLUDING UNDERFLOW, IS ERROR
          JBE       SINGULAR              ;JUMP IF (C3 OR C0)=1
          JNP       SINGULAR              ;JUMP IF C2=0
          JMP       NOT_SINGULAR
SINGULAR:
;SINGULAR MATRIX
          LDS       BX,[BP].IER           ;DS:BX=ADDR(IER)
          MOV       WORD PTR [BX],-1      ;IER=-1
          FSTP      ST(0)
          NEARJMP   DONE

NOT_SINGULAR:
;FILL IN ROW OF U
;MOVE J THROUGH K+1 TO N-1
          LDS       DI,[BP].INDEX         ;DS:DI=ADDR(INDEX(0))
          ADD       DI,SI
          ADD       DI,SI                 ;DS:DI=ADDR(INDEX(K))
          MOV       AX,[DI]               ;AX=INDEX(K)
          SHL       AX,CL                 ;DI=ARRAY_TYPE*INDEX(K)
          LDS       BX,[BP].N             ;DS:BX=ADDR(N)
          MUL       WORD PTR [BX]         ;AX=N*ARRAY_TYPE*INDEX(K)
```

```
        MOV     DI,[BP].A               ;DI=OFFSET(A(0,0))
        ADD     DI,AX                   ;DI=OFFSET(A(INDEX(K),0))
;
        MOV     AX,SI                   ;KEEP "J" IN AX
        SHL     AX,CL
        MOV     DX,[BX]                 ;DX=N
        SUB     DX,SI                   ;DX=N-K
        MOV     [BP].COUNT,DX
U_LOOP: DEC     WORD PTR [BP].COUNT     ;COUNT=COUNT-1
        CMP     WORD PTR [BP].COUNT,0
        JLE     END_U_LOOP
;
        MOV     BX,1
        SHL     BX,CL                   ;BX=ARRAY_TYPE
        ADD     AX,BX                   ;AX=NEXT J
;
;CALL XINPROD(A(INDEX(K),0),A(0,J),DSUM,INDEX,ARRAY_TYPE,N,K)
        PUSH    [BP].A+2
        PUSH    DI                      ;ADDR(A(INDEX(K),0))
        LDS     BX,[BP].A               ;DS:BX=ADDR(A(0,0))
        ADD     BX,AX                   ;BX=OFFSET(A(0,J))
        PUSH    DS
        PUSH    BX                      ;ADDR A(0,J)
        PUSH    SS                      ;SEG DSUM
        LEA     BX,[BP].DSUM
        PUSH    BX                      ;OFFSET DSUM
        PUSH    [BP].INDEX+2            ;
        PUSH    [BP].INDEX              ;ADDR INDEX
        PUSH    [BP].ARRAY_TYPE+2
        PUSH    [BP].ARRAY_TYPE         ;ADDR ARRAY_TYPE
        PUSH    [BP].N+2
        PUSH    [BP].N                  ;ADDR N
        PUSH    SS                      ;SEG(K)
        LEA     BX,[BP].K               ;OFFSET(K)
        PUSH    BX
        CALL    XINPROD
;CALCULATE A(INDEX(K),J) = (A(INDEX(K),J)-DSUM)/A(INDEX(K),K)
; FOR SINGLE OR DOUBLE PRECISION
        FLD     QWORD PTR [BP].DSUM     ;PUT DSUM BACK IN ST
                                        ;AND A(INDEX(K),K) IN ST(1)
        MOV     BX,DI                   ;DS:BX=ADDR(A(INDEX(K),0)
        ADD     BX,AX                   ;DS:BX=ADDR(A(INDEX(K),J)
        CMP     CX,2                    ;SINGLE?
        JNE     A_DOUBLE3
        FSUBR   DWORD PTR [BX]          ;ST=A(INDEX(K),J)-DSUM
        FDIV    ST,ST(1)                ;ST=ST/A(INDEX(K),K)
```

```
          FSTP      DWORD PTR [BX]      ;A(INDEX(K),J)=ST
          JMP       NEXT_ROW_ELEMENT
;
A_DOUBLE3:
          FSUBR     QWORD PTR [BX]      ;ST=A(INDEX(K),J)-DSUM
          FDIV      ST,ST(1)            ;ST=ST/A(INDEX(K),K)
          FSTP      QWORD PTR [BX]      ;A(INDEX(K),J)=ST
;
NEXT_ROW_ELEMENT:
          JMP       U_LOOP
;
END_U_LOOP:
          FSTP      ST(0)               ;CLEAR ST
;READY FOR NEXT K
          INC       SI
          LDS       BX,[BP].N           ;DS:BX=ADDR(N)
          CMP       SI,WORD PTR [BX]    ;K=N?
          JGE       DONE
          JMP       MAJOR_LOOP
;
DONE:
          POPTEMP   7
          POP       DI
          POP       SI
          POP       DX
          POP       CX
          POP       BX
          POP       AX
          TEMP_COUNT=TEMP_COUNT-6
          RETURN    REDUCE
          END
```

REDUCE reduces an n by n metrix in about $25n^3$ microseconds, or about three seconds for a 50 by 50 matrix.

Back Substitution After a Crout Reduction

REDUCE leaves the LU decomposition in A and the order of row permutation in INDEX. Temporarily setting aside the question of INDEXing, we face a computationally straightforward problem of solving $y = LUx$ for x. We do this in two steps. First, solve $y = Ly^*$ for y^*. Second, solve $y^* = Ux$ for x.

Examination of the triangular matrices above shows the simple form for solving triangular systems of equations. For a lower triangular system,

$$y_0 = L_{0,0}y^*_0$$
$$y_1 = L_{1,0}y^*_0 + L_{1,1}y^*_1$$
$$y_2 = L_{2,0}y^*_0 + L_{2,1}y^*_1 + L_{2,2}y^*_2$$

and so forth.

Turning these equations around we can solve directly for y*.

$$y^*_0 = y_0/L_{0,0}$$
$$y^*_1 = (y_1 - L_{1,0}y^*_0)/L_{1,1}$$
$$y^*_2 = (y_2 - (L_{2,0}y^*_0 + L_{2,1}\ y^*_1))/L_{2,2}$$

and so forth.

For an upper triangular system we have:

$$y^*_{n-1} = U_{n-1,n-1}x_{n-1}$$
$$y^*_{n-2} = U_{n-2,n-2}x_{n-2} + U_{n-2,n-1}x_{n-1}$$
$$y^*_{n-3} = U_{n-3,n-3}x_{n-3} + U_{n-3,n-2}x_{n-2} + U_{n-3,n-1}x_{n-1}$$

and so forth.

As we turn these equations around to solve for x, remember that $U_{i,i}$ equals 1 after the Crout reduction.

$$x_{n-1} = y^*_{n-1}$$
$$x_{n-2} = (y^*_{n-2} - U_{n-2,n-1}x_{n-1})$$
$$x_{n-3} = (y^*_{n-3} - (U_{n-3,n-2}x_{n-2} + U_{n-3,n-1}x_{n-1}))$$

and so forth.

The following BASIC code takes a Crout reduced matrix A and a column vector X and solves for X.

```
DEFINT I-N
DEFDBL S
REDIM A(N-1,N-1),YSTAR(N-1),Y(N-1),X(N-1)
REM SOLVE LOWER TRIANGULAR SYSTEM FOR YSTAR
 FOR I=0 TO N-1
 SUM=0
  FOR J=0 TO I-1
  SUM=SUM+A(I,J)*YSTAR(J)
  NEXT J
 YSTAR(I)=(Y(I)-SUM)/A(I,I)
 NEXT I
REM SOLVE UPPER TRIANGULAR SYSTEM FOR X
 FOR I=N-1 TO 0 STEP -1
 SUM=0
  FOR J=I+1 TO N-1
  SUM=SUM+A(I,J)*X(J)
  NEXT J
 X(I)=YSTAR(I)-SUM
NEXT I
```

Notice that solving the lower triangular and upper triangular system are both order n^2 operations. Once order n^3 operations have been performed to reduce A, each new y can be solved for x at the expense of only order n^2 additional operations.

REDUCE performs row permutations in the process of generating a triangular form. Our next set of BASIC code "undoes" the INDEXing and also makes explicit use of GINPROD.

```
 REM PROGRAM SOLP
 ITYPE=4
 I1=1
 REM USE X FOR SCRATCH SPACE, RATHER THAN "Y*"
 REM SOLVE LOWER TRIANGULAR SYSTEM FOR YSTAR
   FOR I=0 TO N-1
   NUM=I
   CALL GINPROD(A(INDEX(I),0),X(0),SUM,ITYPE,ITYPE,I1,N,
NUM)
  X(I)=(Y(INDEX(I))-SUM)/A(INDEX(I),I)
NEXT I
REM SOLVE UPPER TRIANGULAR SYSTEM FOR X
  FOR I=N-1 TO 0 STEP -1
  IP=I+1
  NUM=N-IP
CALL GINPROD(A(INDEX(I),IP),X(IP),SUM,
ITYPE,ITYPE,1I,N,NUM)
X(I)=X(I)-SUM NEXT I
```

The BASIC program is easily recoded into an assembly language procedure, SOLVE.

```
INCLUDE   SUBROUT.MAC
          EXTERNAL   <GINPROD>
          SUBROUTINE SOLVE,<A,Y,X,INDEX,TYPEA,TYPEY,TYPEX,SKIPX,N>
;  ASSUMPTIONS: A IS AN N BY N MATRIX
;               Y,X,INDEX ARE N ARRAYS
;               TYPEA,TYPEY,TYPEX,N ARE INTEGERS
;
;               SOL SOLVES Y=AX FOR X, WHERE A AND INDEX RESULT
;               FROM A CROUT DECOMPOSITION WITH PARTIAL PIVOTING
;
;         Save 6 registers since this routine is called from others
;         Also leave room seven words of temporary storage
;         and 16 words for call to GINPROD
;
          CHKSTCK   12+14+32
```

```
         PUSHTEMP  AX
         PUSHTEMP  BX
         PUSHTEMP  CX
         PUSHTEMP  DX
         PUSHTEMP  SI
         PUSHTEMP  DI
         PUSHTEMP  AX
         PUSHTEMP  AX
         PUSHTEMP  AX
         PUSHTEMP  AX,DSUM
         MOV       AX,1
         PUSHTEMP  AX,ONE
         PUSHTEMP  AX,I
         PUSHTEMP  AX,ANOTHER_WORD
;TAKE CARE OF LOWER TRIANGLE
;FOR I=0 TO N-1
         LDS       BX,[BP].N           ;DS:BX=ADDR(N)
         MOV       CX,[BX]             ;CX=N
         CMP       CX,0
         JG        AROUND
         NEARJMP   DONE
AROUND:  MOV       SI,0                ;KEEP I IN SI
         MOV       DI,[BP].INDEX       ;DI=OFFSET(INDEX(0))
L_LOOP:
         MOV       [BP].I,SI           ;STORE I IN MEMORY
;CALL GINPROD(A(INDEX(I),0),X(0),DSUM,TYPEA,TYPEX,1,SKIPX,I)
         MOV       DS,[BP].INDEX+2     ;DS=SEG(INDEX)
         MOV       AX,[DI]             ;AX=INDEX(I)
         LDS       BX,[BP].TYPEA       ;DS:BX=ADDR(TYPEA)
         MUL       WORD PTR [BX]       ;AX=TYPEA*INDEX(I)
         LDS       BX,[BP].N           ;DS:BX=ADDR(N)
         MUL       WORD PTR [BX]       ;AX=N*TYPEA*INDEX(I)
         ADD       AX,[BP].A           ;AX=OFFSET(A(INDEX(I),0))
         PUSH      [BP].A+2
         PUSH      AX                  ;ADDR(A(INDEX(I),0))
         PUSH      [BP].X+2
         PUSH      [BP]+X              ;ADDR(X(0))
         PUSH      SS
         LEA       BX,[BP].DSUM
         PUSH      BX                  ;ADDR(DSUM)
         PUSH      [BP].TYPEA+2
         PUSH      [BP].TYPEA          ;ADDR(TYPEA)
         PUSH      [BP].TYPEX+2
         PUSH      [BP].TYPEX          ;TYPEX
         PUSH      SS
         LEA       BX,[BP].ONE
```

```
          PUSH      BX                    ;ONE
          PUSH      [BP].SKIPX+2
          PUSH      [BP].SKIPX            ;SKIPX
          PUSH      SS
          LEA       BX,[BP].I
          PUSH      BX                    ;I
          CALL      GINPROD
          FLD       QWORD PTR [BP].DSUM ;DSUM IS NOW IN ST
;X(I)=(Y(INDEX(I))-DSUM)/A(INDEX(I),I)
          MOV       DS,[BP].INDEX+2       ;DS=SEG(INDEX)
          MOV       BX,[DI]               ;BX=INDEX(I)
          SHL       BX,1
          SHL       BX,1                  ;BX=4*INDEX(I)
          MOV       DX,BX                 ;SAVE BX TEMPORARILY
          LDS       BX,[BP].TYPEY         ;DS:BX=ADDR(TYPEY)
          CMP       WORD PTR [BX],4       ;IS Y SINGLE?
          MOV       BX,DX                 ;RESTORE BX
          MOV       DS,[BP].Y+2           ;DS=SEG(Y)
          JNE       Y_DOUBLE
          ADD       BX,[BP].Y             ;DS:BX=ADDR(Y(INDEX(I)))
          FSUBR     DWORD PTR [BX]        ;ST=Y(INDEX(I))-DSUM
          JMP       DO_DIV
Y_DOUBLE: SHL       BX,1                  ;BX=8*INDEX(I)
          ADD       BX,[BP].Y             ;BX=ADDR(Y(INDEX(I)))
          FSUBR     QWORD PTR [BX]        ;ST=Y(INDEX(I))-DSUM
;
DO_DIV:
;AX HAS OFFSET(A(INDEX(I),0)), SO ADD TYPEA*I
          MOV       BX,AX                 ;BX=OFFSET(A(INDEX(I),0))
          MOV       AX,SI                 ;AX=I
          SHL       AX,1
          SHL       AX,1                  ;AX=4*I


          MOV       DX,BX                 ;SAVE BX TEMPORARILY
          LDS       BX,[BP].TYPEA         ;DS:BX=ADDR(TYPEA)
          CMP       WORD PTR [BX],4       ;IS A SINGLE?
          MOV       BX,DX                 ;RESTORE BX
          MOV       DS,[BP].A+2           ;DS=SEG(A)
          JNE       A_DOUBLE
          ADD       BX,AX                 ;BX=ADDR(A(INDEX(I),I))
          FDIV      DWORD PTR [BX]        ;(Y(I)-DSUM)/A(INDEX(I),I)
          JMP       DO_STORE
A_DOUBLE: SHL       AX,1                  ;AX=8*I
          ADD       BX,AX                 ;BX=ADDR(A(INDEX(I),I))
          FDIV      QWORD PTR [BX]        ;(Y(I)-DSUM)/A(INDEX(I),I)
;
```

```
DO_STORE: MOV       AX,SI                 ;AX=I
          LDS       BX,[BP].SKIPX         ;BX=ADDR(SKIPX)
          MUL       WORD PTR [BX]         ;AX=I*SKIPX
          SHL       AX,1
          SHL       AX,1                  ;BX=4*I
          LDS       BX,[BP].TYPEX         ;DS:BX=ADDR(TYPEX)
          CMP       WORD PTR [BX],4       ;IS X SINGLE?
          MOV       BX,AX                 ;BX=4*I
          MOV       DS,[BP].X+2           ;DS=SEG(X)
          JNE       X_DOUBLE
          ADD       BX,[BP].X             ;BX=ADDR(X(I))
          FSTP      DWORD PTR [BX]        ;STORE X(I)
          JMP       L_BOTTOM
X_DOUBLE: SHL       BX,1                  ;BX=8*I
          ADD       BX,[BP].X             ;BX=ADDR(X(I))
          FSTP      QWORD PTR [BX]        ;STORE X(I)
L_BOTTOM:
          INC       SI                    ;I=I+1
          ADD       DI,2                  ;NEXT INDEX
          LOOP      GOTO_L_LOOP
          JMP       U_TOP
GOTO_L_LOOP: JMP L_LOOP
;
U_TOP:
;TAKE CARE OF UPPER TRIANGLE
;FOR I=N-1 TO 0 STEP -1
          LDS       BX,[BP].N             ;DS:BX=ADDR(N)
          MOV       SI,[BX]               ;KEEP I IN SI
          MOV       DI,[BP].INDEX         ;DI=OFFSET(INDEX(0))
          ADD       DI,SI
          ADD       DI,SI                 ;DI=OFFSET(INDEX(N))
U_LOOP:
          DEC       SI                    ;I=I-1
          MOV       [BP].I,SI             ;STORE IN MEMORY
          SUB       DI,2                  ;NEXT INDEX
;CALL GINPROD(A(INDEX(I),I+1),X(I+1),DSUM,TYPEA,TYPEX,1,SKIPX,N-I-1)
          MOV       DS,[BP].INDEX+2       ;DS=SEG(INDEX)
          MOV       AX,[DI]               ;AX=INDEX(I)
          LDS       BX,[BP].N             ;DS:BX=ADDR(N)
          MUL       WORD PTR [BX]         ;AX=N*INDEX(I)
          ADD       AX,SI                 ;
          INC       AX                    ;AX=N*INDEX+(I+1)
          SHL       AX,1
          SHL       AX,1                  ;AX=4*AX
          LDS       BX,[BP].TYPEA         ;DS:BX=ADDR(TYPEA)
          CMP       WORD PTR [BX],4       ;IS A SINGLE?
```

```
            JE      A_SINGLE
            SHL     AX,1                 ;AX=8*(...)
A_SINGLE:   ADD     AX,[BP].A            ;AX=ADDR(A(INDEX(I),I+1))
            PUSH    [BP].A+2             ;
            PUSH    AX                   ;A(INDEX(I),I+1)
            MOV     AX,SI                ;AX=I
            INC     AX                   ;AX=I+1
            SHL     AX,1
            SHL     AX,1                 ;AX=4*(I+1)
            LDS     BX,[BP].SKIPX
            MUL     WORD PTR [BX]        ;AX=SKIPX*4*(I+1)
            LDS     BX,[BP].TYPEX        ;DS:BX=TYPEX
            CMP     WORD PTR [BX],4      ;IS X SINGLE?
            JE      X_SINGLE
            SHL     AX,1                 ;AX=SKIPX*8*(I+1)
X_SINGLE:   ADD     AX,[BP].X            ;AX=ADDR(X(I+1))
            PUSH    [BP].X+2
            PUSH    AX                   ;X(I+1) NOTE: LEAVE ADDR IN AX
            PUSH    SS
            LEA     BX,[BP].DSUM
            PUSH    BX                   ;ADDR(DSUM)
            PUSH    [BP].TYPEA+2
            PUSH    [BP].TYPEA           ;TYPEA
            PUSH    [BP].TYPEX+2
            PUSH    [BP].TYPEX           ;TYPEX
            PUSH    SS
            LEA     BX,[BP].ONE
            PUSH    BX                   ;ONE
            PUSH    [BP].SKIPX+2
            PUSH    [BP].SKIPX           ;SKIPX
            LDS     BX,[BP].N            ;DS:BX=ADDR(N)
            MOV     DX,[BX]              ;DX=N
            SUB     DX,SI
            DEC     DX                   ;DX=N-(I+1)
            MOV     [BP].ANOTHER_WORD,DX
            LEA     BX,[BP].ANOTHER_WORD
            PUSH    SS
            PUSH    BX                   ;N-(I+1)
            CALL    GINPROD
;
;X(I)=X(I)-DSUM
            FLD     QWORD PTR [BP].DSUM ;ST=DSUM
;NOTE AX STILL POINTS TO X(I+1)
            MOV     DX,AX                ;SAVE AX TEMPORARILY
            LDS     BX,[BP].TYPEX        ;DS:BX=ADDR(TYPEX)
            MOV     AX,[BX]              ;BX=TYPEX
```

```
          LDS       BX,[BP].SKIPX       ;DS:BX=ADDR(SKIPX)
          MUL       BYTE PTR [BX]       ;AX=SKIPX*TYPEX (DX UNCHANGED)
          XCHG      AX,DX               ;AX HAS ADDRESS AGAIN
          SUB       AX,DX               ;AX=OFFSET(X(I))
          LDS       BX,[BP].TYPEX       ;BX=ADDR(TYPEX)
          CMP       WORD PTR [BX],4     ;ONCE AGAIN, IS X SINGLE?
          JNE       X_DOUBLE2
          XCHG      AX,BX               ;SWAP SO WE CAN USE BX AS INDEX
          MOV       DS,[BP].X+2         ;DS:BX=ADDR(X(I))
          FSUBR     DWORD PTR [BX]      ;ST=X(I)-DSUM
          FSTP      DWORD PTR [BX]      ;STORE X(I)
          JMP       U_BOTTOM
X_DOUBLE2:
          XCHG      AX,BX               ;SWAP SO WE CAN USE BX AS INDEX
          MOV       DS,[BP].X+2         ;DS:BX=ADDR(X(I))
          FSUBR     QWORD PTR [BX]      ;ST=X(I)-DSUM
          FSTP      QWORD PTR [BX]      ;STORE X(I)
U_BOTTOM:
          CMP       SI,0                ;DONE YET?
          JLE       DONE
          JMP       U_LOOP
;
DONE:
          POPTEMP   7
          POP       DI
          POP       SI
          POP       DX
          POP       CX
          POP       BX
          POP       AX
          TEMP_COUNT=TEMP_COUNT-6
          RETURN    SOLVE
          END
```

Matrix Inversion

One good reason for creating procedures from modular programs is the ease with which the subroutines may be rearranged. It is now quite easy to prepare a matrix inversion subroutine. Since matrix inversion is equivalent to solving a system of equations n times (first for a "y vector" 1,0,0 . . ., then for 0,1,0,0 . . ., and so forth), we can use SOLVE and REDUCE to create a new subroutine INV.

INV is called by

```
CALL INV(A,AINV,SCRATCH,INDEX,IER,TYPEA,N)
```

A initially contains the n by n matrix to be inverted. When INV returns, A contains the Crout decomposition, with permutation index in INDEX; AINV contains A^{-1}. IER equals 0 if A is nonsingular and -1 otherwise. INV calls REDUCE to reduce A. It then sets up a "y column," in vector SCRATCH, n times, and calls SOLVE to fill in the columns of the inverse matrix, AINV.

```
INCLUDE   SUBROUT.MAC
          EXTERNAL  <REDUCE,SOLVE>
          SUBROUTINE INV,<A,AINV,SCRATCH,INDEX,IER,TYPEA,N>
;    ASSUMPTIONS:  A,AINV ARE N BY N MATRICES OF TYPE TYPEA
;                  SCRATCH IS SINGLE PRECISION N LONG
;                  INDEX IS INTEGER ARRAY N LONG
;                  IER,TYPEA,N ARE INTEGERS
;
;    INV INVERTS A INTO AINV
;
;         Leave room for one word of temporary storage
;         and eight words for call to SOLVE
;
          CHKSTCK   2+16
          MOV       AX,4
          PUSHTEMP  AX,FOUR

          LDS       BX,[BP].N            ;DS:BX=ADDR(N)
          MOV       CX,[BX]              ;CX=N
          CMP       CX,0
          JG        AROUND
          NEARJMP   DONE
AROUND:
;CALL REDUCE(A,INDEX,IER,TYPEA,N)
;SET UP CALL PARAMETERS
          PUSH      [BP].A+2
          PUSH      [BP].A               ;A(0,0)
          PUSH      [BP].INDEX+2
          PUSH      [BP].INDEX           ;INDEX(0)
          PUSH      [BP].IER+2
          PUSH      [BP].IER             ;IER
          PUSH      [BP].TYPEA+2
          PUSH      [BP].TYPEA           ;TYPEA
          PUSH      [BP].N+2
          PUSH      [BP].N               ;N
          CALL      REDUCE
;WAS IT SINGULAR
          LDS       BX,[BP].IER          ;DS:BX=ADDR(IER)
```

```
        CMP     WORD PTR [BX],0     ;IER=0?
        JE      AROUNDB
        JMP     DONE
AROUNDB:
;
;SOLVE FOR COLUMNS I=0 TO N-1
        MOV     SI,0                ;KEEP I IN SI
INV_LOOP:
;CLEAR SCRATCH
        LDS     BX,[BP].N           ;DS:BX=ADDR(N)
        MOV     CX,[BX]             ;CX=N
        LDS     BX,[BP].SCRATCH     ;DS:BX=ADDR(SCRATCH)
ZERO_LOOP:
        MOV     WORD PTR [BX],0
        MOV     WORD PTR [BX]+2,0   ;SCRATCH(J)=0
        ADD     BX,4                ;J=J+1
        LOOP    ZERO_LOOP
;NOW FILL IN APPROPRIATE 1
        MOV     BX,SI               ;BX=I
        SHL     BX,1
        SHL     BX,1                ;BX=4*I
        ADD     BX,[BP].SCRATCH     ;BX=ADDR(SCRATCH(I))
        FLD1                        ;PUSH 1.0 ONTO STACK
        FSTP    DWORD PTR [BX]      ;STORE INTO MEMORY
;
;CALL SOLVE(A,SCRATCH,AINV(0,I),INDEX,TYPEA,4,TYPEA,N,N)
        PUSH    [BP].A+2
        PUSH    [BP].A              ;A
        PUSH    [BP].SCRATCH+2
        PUSH    [BP].SCRATCH        ;SCRATCH
        PUSH    [BP].AINV+2
;GET OFFSET OF AINV(0,I)
        MOV     AX,SI               ;AX=I
        LDS     BX,[BP].TYPEA       ;DS:BX=ADDR(TYPEA)
        MUL     WORD PTR [BX]       ;AX=TYPEA*I
        ADD     AX,[BP].AINV        ;AX=OFFSET(AINV(0,I))
;
        PUSH    AX                  ;AINV(0,I))
        PUSH    [BP].INDEX+2
        PUSH    [BP].INDEX          ;INDEX
        PUSH    [BP].TYPEA+2
        PUSH    [BP].TYPEA          ;TYPEA
        PUSH    SS
        LEA     BX,[BP].FOUR
        PUSH    BX                  ;FOUR
        PUSH    [BP].TYPEA+2
```

```
            PUSH      [BP].TYPEA          ;TYPEA
            PUSH      [BP].N+2
            PUSH      [BP].N
            PUSH      [BP].N+2
            PUSH      [BP].N
;
            CALL      SOLVE
;
            INC       SI                  ;I=I+1
            LDS       BX,[BP].N           ;BX=ADDR(N)
            CMP       SI,[BX]             ;SI>N?
            JGE       DONE
            JMP       INV_LOOP
;
DONE:
            POPTEMP   1
            RETURN    INV
            END
```

Of Linear Things Not Covered Above

Two chapters and hundreds of lines of code will have to suffice as an introduction to matrix methods. Before moving on, it's worth listing a few of the things not covered here. This is also a good point to pause for a review of some general themes in programming the 8087.

The routines in these two chapters will do just about every ordinary thing you usually need to do with a matrix. However, if you have really large problems, you may soon develop an interest in extraordinary procedures. Everything you need to know about the 8087 is included here, but there are many sophisticated algorithms that we haven't even touched upon. These algorithms appear in many excellent books on numerical computation. Two exceptional books are:

Elementary Numerical Analysis, by S. D. Conte, McGraw-Hill.

Introduction to Matrix Computations, by G. W. Stewart, Academic Press.

Another excellent (but advanced) book is *Matrix Computations*, by G. Golum and C.f. van Loan, The Johns Hopkins University Press, 1983.

One of the best ways to learn more about the "tricks" of numerical programming is to browse through the documentation of a large numerical programming subroutine library. Such a "library collection" can usually be found at your local college computer center. The *IMSL* library is particularly good. You will find an excellent applied discussion of numerical methods and the IMSL library in (this book is moderately advanced):

Numerical Methods, Software, and Analysis, by John R. Rice, McGraw-Hill.

An excellent, and easily found, source of algorithms for both linear and nonlinear algorithms is

Numerical Recipes by W.H. Press, B.P. Flannery, S.A. Teuksolsky, and W.T. Vettering, Cambridge University Press, 1986.

Numerical Recipes includes source code in both Fortran and Pascal.

The procedures in this and the last chapter provide the basic foundation for matrix programming. Some advanced topic areas not covered here include:

- *Matrices with a lot of zeros.* Problems in the natural sciences often give rise to special forms of matrices. For example, if we know a matrix is triangular, we can avoid processing the zeros. That would double the speed of matrix multiplication. As we've seen, taking advantage of the shape of a triangular matrix can improve the speed of matrix inversion or solving a system of equations by a factor of n. Other special forms include the "diagonal matrix," in which all off-diagonal elements are zero; the "band matrix," which is zero except for elements close to the diagonal; and the general designation of a "sparse matrix." Sparse matrices, which often arise from solving systems of differential equations, may be 99 percent zeros. Special storage techniques, in which only the nonzero elements are stored, must be used to work with sparse matrices.
- *Matrices with special mathematical properties.* Sometimes the mathematics of a problem supply special information about the structure of the numbers stored in a matrix. For example, many problems give rise to a *symmetric* matrix, one in which $A_{i,j}$ equals $A_{j,i}$. You can double the speed of many matrix operations by taking advantage of symmetry. Symmetric matrices are especially common in statistical work.
- *Super-high accuracy methods.* One of the lessons of numerical programming is that mathematically correct procedures don't always give the mathematically correct answer when executed on a computer with finite precision. One place this lesson is often learned is in the reduction of a matrix to triangular form. We picked the Crout reduction with partial pivoting because it is particularly well suited to the 8087's high-precision, temporary real format internal registers. Nonetheless, you may eventually want to learn about other methods, including *iterative* techniques, which are much slower, but which can be much more accurate.
- *Advanced numerical methods for special problems.* Scientists use so much computer time solving matrix problems that special matrix algorithms have been developed for a number of different problems. These algorithms are more accurate and/or faster than the general purpose matrix routines presented in this chapter. If much of your computing

concentrates in a narrow area, then it's probably worth investigating these special algorithms. (The references given above should get you started.) It is frequently true that the bulk of the computation in such algorithms lies in forming inner products. Therefore, you may find that you can easily code an appropriate algorithm in a high level language while using INPROD or GINPROD from Chapter 8, or XINPROD from this Chapter, to drive the 8087.

8087 Matrix Program Review

1. Expect assembly language programs to be 10 times as long as their BASIC counterparts. Writing large programs in assembler is time consuming and error prone. In fact, the expense in programming time may be prohibitive. (Even if the time is "free," because it's your own.)
2. *Optimize the inner-most loop.* Worry about optimizing, for speed and for accuracy, the equivalent of the inner-most FOR/NEXT loop. For matrix operations, this usually means having an inner product routine carefully hand-coded for the 8087. We chose Crout decomposition over Gaussian elimination for two reasons. First, the inner product specification allowed accumulation in a high-precision register even if the overall operation is only single precision. Second, this specification allows us, if we wish, to code just the inner product routine in assembler and leave the shell of the program in BASIC.
3. Never invert a matrix when you really need only solve a system of equations. Reducing a matrix is an order n^3 operation. Inverting a reduced matrix requires an additional order n^3 operations, while solving a system of equations only requires an additional order n^2 operations. A series of solutions is best obtained with one call to REDUCE and several calls to SOLVE, not one call of INV and several MATMULTs. The principle exception to this rule occurs when the inverse matrix itself has an important interpretation, as it frequently does in statistical applications.
4. The cpu can do most bookkeeping faster than the 8087 can do floating point arithmetic, so most cpu operations run in parallel with the 8087's speed as the limiting factor. An exception is the integer multiply used in addressing matrix elements. It pays to keep integer multiplication out of inner-most loops. Sometimes multiplication can be avoided by adding to a location counter at each loop. At other times, a "left shift" can be substituted for each multiply-by-2. (Not coincidentally, Intel made

the multiply instruction on its newer processors, the 188 and 186, and the 286 three times as fast as on the original 8088 and 8086.)

5. Counter testing can be done at either the top or the bottom of a loop. The choice is largely a matter of style. (Loops which use the cpu LOOP instruction test more naturally at the bottom.) Some of the programs in the last two chapters test at the top and some test at the bottom, so that you can see both methods. Ordinarily, it's good programming practice to choose one style or the other and stick to it.
6. To conserve storage, the routines here reduce a matrix "in place." If you need to save the original matrix, make a copy first using GCOPY from Chapter 7.

Onward Non-Linearly

We set aside matrix operations here, and move on to non-linear operations in Chapter 10. If you'd like some practical applications of our matrix routines, skip ahead to the discussion of statistical computing in Chapter 12.

10

Advanced Instruction Set

In this chapter, we pick up and complete the task laid aside at the end of Chapter 4, our description of the 8087 instruction set.

The Cookbook—Chapter 10

Program:	**ADVANCED.MAC**
Purpose:	Macros for loading arguments onto and popping them off 8087 stack.
Language	8087/8088 assembly language
Program:	**VLN**
Purpose:	Natural logarithm (base e).
Call:	Call VLN(X,Y,ARRAY_TYPE. ARRAY_TYPE,N integers.
Input:	X — N long array of type ARRAY_TYPE. ARRAY_TYPE,N integer.
Output:	Y — N long array of type ARRAY_TYPE. Y=ln(X)

Language:	8087/8088 assembly language
Program:	**VLOG10**
Purpose:	Common logarithm (base 10).
Call:	Call VLOG10(X,Y,ARRAY_TYPE,N).
Input:X—	N long array of type ARRAY_TYPE. ARRAY_TYPE,N integers.
Output:	Y — N long array of type ARRAY_TYPE. Y=log10(X)
Language:	8087/8088 assembly language
Program:	**TWO2THEZ**
Purpose:	Raises 2 to the power Z.
Call:	Call TWO2THEZ.
Input:	Z in 8087 register ST.
Output:	$ST=2^Z$
Language	8087/8088 assembly language
Program:	**TWO2THEX**
Purpose:	Raises 2 to the power X.
Call:	Call TWO2THEX(X,Y,ARRAY_TYPE,N).
Input:	X — N long array of type array_TYPE. ARRAY_TYPE,N–integers.
Output:	Y — N long array of type ARRAY_TYPE. $Y=2^X$.
Language:	8087/8088 assembly language
Program:	**VEXP**
Purpose:	Raises e to the power X.

Call: Call VEXP(X,Y,ARRAY_TYPE,N).

Input: X — N long array of type ARRAY_TYPE.
ARRAY_TYPE,N–integers.

Output: Y — N long array of type ARRAY_TYPE. $Y=e^X$.

Language: 8087/8088 assembly language

Program: TEN2THEX

Purpose: Raises 10 to the power X.

Call: Call TEN2THEX(X,Y,ARRAY_TYPE,N).

Input: X — N long array of type ARRAY_TYPE.
ARRAY_TYPE,N–integers.

Output: Y — N long array of type ARRAY_TYPE. $Y=10^X$.

Language: 8087/8088 assembly language

Program: Z2THEX

Purpose: Raises Z to the power X.

Call: Call Z2THEX(X,Y,Z,ARRAY_TYPE,N).

Input: X — N long array of type ARRAY_TYPE
ARRAY_TYPE,N–integers.

Output: Y — N long array of type ARRAY_TYPE. $Y=Z^X$.

Language: 8087/8088 assembly language

Program: TANGENT

Purpose: Compute tangent.

Call: Call TANGENTX(X,Y,ARRAY_TYPE,N).

Input: X — N long array of type ARRAY_TYPE.
ARRAY_TYPE,N–integers.

Output:	Y — N long array of type ARRAY_TYPE. Y=tan(x).
Language:	8087/8088 assembly language
Program:	**SINCOS**
Purpose:	Compute sine or cosine.
Call:	Call SINCOS(IFCOS).
Input:	IFCOS integer, = 0 if sine, else cosine 8087 register ST.
Output:	new ST = sine (or cosine) ST.
Language:	8087/8088 assembly language
Program:	**SINE**
Purpose:	Compute sine.
Call:	Call SINE(X,Y,ARRAY_TYPE,N).
Input:	X — N long array of type ARRAY_TYPE. ARRAY_TYPE,N–integers.
Output:	Y — N long array of type ARRAY_TYPE. Y=sin(x).
Language:	8087/8088 assembly language
Program:	**COSINE**
Purpose:	Compute cosine.
Call:	Call COSINE(X,Y,ARRAY_TYPE,N).
Input:	X — N long array of type ARRAY_TYPE. ARRAY_TYPE,N–integers.
Output:	Y — N long array of type ARRAY_TYPE. Y=cos(x).
Language:	8087/8088 assembly language

Program:	**ARCTAN**
Purpose:	Compute arctangent.
Call:	Call ARCTAN(X,Y,ARRAY_TYPE,N).
Input:	X — N long array of type ARRAY_TYPE. ARRAY_TYPE,N–integers.
Output:	Y — N long array of type ARRAY_TYPE. Y=atan(x).
Language:	8087/8088 assembly language
Program:	**SINE387**
Purpose:	Compute sine (387 only).
Call:	Call SINE387(X,Y,ARRAY_TYPE,IER,N).
Input:	X — N long array of type ARRAY_TYPE. ARRAY_TYPE,IER,N–integers.
Output:	Y — N long array of type ARRAY_TYPE. Y=sin(x) IERO = 0 if all arguments in range, −1 otherwise.
Language:	387/386 assembly language
Program:	**DETECT87**
Purpose:	Detect coprocessor type.
Call:	Call DETECT87(TYPE_OF_87).
Output:	TYPE_OF_87 – integer.
Language:	8087/8088 assembly language

This chapter is divided into four sections. The first two sections finish describing the arithmetic and constant instructions. The last two sections present the *transcendental* and *processor control* instructions. A number of examples are included for the more intricate operations.

Arithmetic Instructions

Four arithmetic instructions remain to be discussed. Remember that the instruction timings shown below are for an IBM PC or equivalent and a 16 megahertz 387.

FRDINT {ST} 9 {5} microseconds

FRDINT (round to integer) rounds the element on top of the 8087 stack to an integer. (The number continues to be represented as a temporary real; after an FRDINT the temporary real number has an integer value.) The 8087 offers four rounding modes: *round to nearest, round down, round up,* and *chop* (round toward zero). Round to nearest is the default mode.

FSCALE {ST,ST(1)} 7 {5} microseconds

FSCALE (scale by powers of two) adds the value found in ST(1) to the exponent of ST. This effectively multiplies the top of stack element by 2 to the power contained in ST(1). Since the exponent field is an integer, the value in ST(1) should be an integer as well. If ST(1) is not an integer, the value is rounded toward zero before being added to the exponent in ST. The scale factor in ST(1) must be between −32768 and 32768 (2^{15}). If the scale factor is out of range or a non-integer value between −1 and +1, the result is undefined. For safety, load ST(1) from a word integer. Notice that FSCALE provides an extremely fast way to multiply or divide numbers by a power of 2.

FSCALE has been improved a bit on the 387. If ST(1) is between −1 and +1, zero is used as a scaling factor. (On the 8087 and 287 the result is undefined.) In addition, the range of ST(1) is unlimited.

FPREM {ST,ST(1)} 25 {8} microseconds

FPREM (partial remainder) divides the stack top by ST(1) and places the *remainder* back in the stack top. (We explain use of the name "partial" below.) The result is exact with no loss of precision. FPREM (in effect) repeatedly subtracts ST(1) from ST and leaves the remainder in ST. When no more subtractions can be done without getting a negative difference, FPREM quits. Thus, if ST initially holds X, at completion of FPREM ST holds X−(q x ST(1)), where q is an integer.

FPREM will, however, only reduce the difference in magnitude between ST and ST(1) by 2^{64}. If the difference is greater than this, repeated executions are necessary. (The 8087 doesn't allow itself to be interrupted in the middle of an instruction. Some programs might want to interrupt the 8087 in a bit of a hurry, so FPREM was designed to work part way through a modular division problem at each execution.) At each step, the "partial remainder" is left in ST. At the end of each execution, three possible comparisons exist between ST and ST(1). If ST <ST(1), the remainder is in ST. If ST = ST(1), the remainder is 0. If ST >ST(1), then ST has only the partial remainder and FPREM should be repeated. FPREM sets bit C2 of the status word when it needs to be repeated and clears the bit when it has completed. FPREM also places the least-significant three bits of the quotient, q, in bits C0, C3, and C1, which is quite useful in analyzing periodic functions, such as sine, cosine, and tangent. For example, if all C0, C3, and C0 equal zero, then the quotient is a multiple of eight. If C1 alone equals one, then the quotient is one greater than a multiple of eight. (Why eight? Because trigonometric calculations are based on dividing a circle into eight parts.) Table 10.1 describes the possible bit patterns.

Table 10-1. Condition code bits after FPREM.

Least Significant Bits of Quotient	*C0*	*C3*	*C1*
0	0	0	0
1	0	0	1
2	0	1	0
3	0	1	1
4	1	0	0
5	1	0	1
6	1	1	0
7	1	1	1

The most important use of FPREM is in bringing arguments into the valid range for the transcendental instructions. Examples using FPREM are given in the section "Trigonometric Functions", below.

There is a bug in the FPREM instruction on the 8087 and 287. If the reduction is incomplete, the quotient bits are set incorrectly when performing a reduction of $64^N + M$ when N is positive and M = 1 or 2. Fortunately, we generally only check the quotient bits after a complete reduction. The bug has been fixed on the 387.

FPREM1 {ST,ST(1)} **(387 only)** {9} microseconds

FPREM1 is almost, but not quite, identical to FPREM. The number of subtractions done by FPREM1 may differ by 1 from the number done by FPREM. FPREM chooses the number of subtractions by dividing ST by ST(1) and chopping toward zero. In contrast, FPREM1 rounds to the nearest integer. In rare circumstances, using FPREM1 rather than FPREM will make the calculation of trigonometric functions more consistent across a range of arguments.

- *The initial release of Microsoft's MASM assembler 5. generates the wrong code for FPREM1. You can work around the but by supplying your own hexadecimal code.* For FPREM1 use "DB 0D9H,0F9H."

FXTRACT {ST} 10 {5} microseconds

FXTRACT (extract exponent and significand) separates out the exponent and significand of the top of stack element. The exponent replaces the top of stack element and the significand is then *pushed* onto the stack. (Both are represented as temporary reals.) If ST originally held zero, both exponent and significand are zero, on the 8087 and 287. On the 387, the exponent is set to $-\infty$ and a zero divide exception occurs. If the original argument was $+\infty$, the 8087 and 287 raise an invalid operation exception. The 387 gives an exponent of $+\infty$ and does not generate an error. (The changes make FXTRACT compatible with the IEEE floating point standard.) Note that FXTRACT is the logical inverse of FSCALE.

Constant Instructions

The 8087 has seven useful constants "hardwired in." These constants have full temporary real accuracy (over 19 decimal digits). Use of a constant instruction saves considerable nuisance as compared to retrieving data from memory.

The constants are zero, one, pi, and four logarithmic values.

FLDZ {ST} 3 {1} microseconds

FLDZ (load zero) *pushes* 0.0 onto the stack.

FLD1 {ST} 4 {1} microseconds

FLD1 (load one) *pushes* 1.0 onto the stack.

FLDPI {ST} 4 {1} microseconds

FLDPI (load pi) *pushes* pi onto the stack.

FLDL2T {ST} 4 {2} microseconds

FLDL2T (load $\log_2 10$) *pushes* $\log_2 10$ onto the stack.

FLDL2E {ST} 4 {2} microseconds

FLDL2E (load $\log_2 e$) *pushes* $\log_2 e$ onto the stack. (e is the base of the natural logarithms.)

FLDLG2 {ST} 4 {3} microseconds

FLDLG2 (load common logarithm of 2) *pushes* $\log_{10} 2$ onto the stack.

FLDLN2 {ST} 4 {3} microseconds

FLDLN2 (load natural logarithm of 2) *pushes* $\log_e 2$ onto the stack.

It is interesting to note that the clock count for the constant instructions increased considerably on the 387.

Transcendental Instructions

Five transcendental instructions are provided on the 8087. Two of these instructions are used for logarithmic calculations, one for exponentiation, and two for trigonometric calculations. The five instructions provide *core calculations* for a much larger set of transcendental operations. We have written this section in two parts. In the first part we describe the five instructions. In the second part we present a series of 8087 NEAR procedures that can be used for the most common transcendental functions.

The transcendental instructions require valid (normalized) arguments and require that the arguments be within range. Further, the *transcendental instructions do not check their arguments. Invalid arguments may produce erroneous results.* (The 387 does check for denormals.)

F2XM1 {ST} 100 {21} microseconds

F2XM1 (2 to the X, minus 1) takes the stack top as X, calculates 2^x-1, and places the answer back in the stack top. X must be between 0 and ½, inclusive, on the 8087 and 287. For the 387, the range has been extended to -1 through $+1$, inclusive. While calculating 2^x-1 instead of 2^x seems peculiar at first, this method allows much more accuracy when X is small. For example, $2^{0.000001}$ is approximately 1.000000693. Subtracting one allows the 8087 to report, in this case, about seven extra significant digits.

Below, we show how to use F2XM1 to calculate exponents to bases other then two.

FYL2X {ST,ST(1)} 190 {20} microseconds

FYL2X (Y times $\log_2$ X) calculates Y x $\log_2$ X, where X is in ST and Y in ST(1). The stack is *popped,* eliminating X, and the answer then replaces Y in the new top of stack. X must be strictly positive.

Below, we show how to use FYL2X to calculate logarithms using bases other than two.

FYL2XP1 {ST,ST(1)} 170 {25} microseconds

FYL2XP1 (Y times $\log_2$ (X + 1)) takes X from the stack top, Y from ST(1), and calculates Y x $\log_2$ (1 + X). X is popped and the result replaces Y on the new stack top. The absolute value of X must be greater than zero and less than SQRT(2)/2. FYL2XP1 should be used in preference to FYL2X when the argument is very close to one.

FPTAN {ST} 90 {22} microseconds

FPTAN (partial tangent) calculates tan(theta), where theta is in the stack top. The argument theta is restricted to the range 0 < theta < pi/4. The answer is in the form of a ratio Y/X. Y replaces theta and X is *pushed* onto the stack.

The range of theta has been greatly expanded on the 387 to lie between $\pm 2^{63}$. This greatly reduces the need for use of the FPREM instruction. In addition, the Y value that replaces ST is actually the tangent and the X value is always 1.0.

We can translate from tangent to sine and cosine by use of standard trigonometric identities. (See "Trigonometric Functions", below.)

FPATAN {ST,ST(1)} 130 {25} microseconds

FPATAN (partial arctangent) calculates arctan (Y/X) where X is taken from ST and Y from ST(1). Y and X must observe the inequality 0 < Y < X < infinity. FPATAN *pops* the stack and then places the answer in the new stack top, replacing Y.

The range of Y and X is unrestricted on the 387.

FPATAN serves as a base for calculating all the inverse trigonometric functions.

An Advanced Macro

If you glance at the Cookbook section, you'll see that most of the routines in this chapter have the same basic form—take an array in, compute a log or a sine or whatever, and put an array out. The housekeeping details for these programs are pretty much identical. It would be, well, boring to see the same loops over and over. The fix is simple—we create two macros and store them in a file named ADVANCED.MAC. The macro TRANS_HEAD is the front end of a loop. It's responsible for loading the variable N into a loop counter and then pushing consecutive elements of the array X onto the 8087 stack. TRANS_HEAD uses ARRAY_TYPE to decide if X is single or double precision. If a variable Z is defined, it is also pushed onto the 8087 stack. (We use Z when the routine has two inputs, as the Z2THEX program does.)

After invoking TRANS_HEAD, we give the 8087 instruction to do the actual work of the routine. Finally, we invoke TRANS_TAIL, which pops the result off the stack into the output array and closes up the loop.

```
TRANS_HEAD MACRO
;;SUBROUTINE DECLARATION HAD BETTER BE OF FORM
;;          SUBROUTINE foo,<X,{Z},Y,ARRAY_TYPE,N>
;           X,Y ARE N LONG OF TYPE ARRAY_TYPE
;           Z IS OPTIONAL N LONG OF TYPE ARRAY_TYPE
;           ARRAY_TYPE,N ARE INTEGERS
          LDS       BX,[BP].N            ;DS:BX=ADDR(N)
          MOV       CX,[BX]              ;CX=N
          CMP       CX,0
          JG        AROUND
          NEARJMP   DONE
AROUND:
          LDS       BX,[BP].ARRAY_TYPE   ;DS:BX=ADDR(ARRAY_TYPE)
          MOV       DX,[BX]              ;DX=ARRAY_TYPE
          MOV       AX,0                 ;INDEX SOURCE IN AX
          LES       DI,[BP].Y            ;ES:DI=ADDR(Y)
V_LOOP:   CMP       DX,4                 ;IS IT SINGLE?
          JNE       DOUBLE
          LDS       SI,[BP].X            ;DS:SI=ADDR(X(0))
          ADD       SI,AX                ;DS:SI=ADDR(X(I))
          FLD       DWORD PTR [SI]       ;LOAD X(I)
IFDEF     Z
          LDS       SI,[BP].Z            ;DS:SI=ADDR(Z)
          ADD       SI,AX                ;DS:SI=ADDR(Z(I))
          FLD       DWORD PTR [SI]       ;PUSH Z(I)
ENDIF
          JMP       DO_INSTRUCTION
DOUBLE:   LDS       SI,[BP].X            ;DS:SI=ADDR(X(0))
          ADD       SI,AX                ;DS:SI=ADDR(X(I))
          FLD       QWORD PTR [SI]       ;LOAD X(I)
;; X(I) IS LOADED IN ST NOW
IFDEF     Z
          LDS       SI,[BP].Z            ;DS:SI=ADDR(Z)
          ADD       SI,AX                ;DS:SI=ADDR(Z(I))
          FLD       QWORD PTR [SI]       ;PUSH Z(I)
ENDIF
DO_INSTRUCTION:
          PUSH      AX                   ;SAVE AX BEFORE STARTING
INSTRUCTION
          ENDM


TRANS_TAIL MACRO
```

```
          POP       AX                  ;RESTORE AX
          CMP       DX,4                ;IS IT SINGLE?
          JNE       DOUBLEB
          FSTP      DWORD PTR ES:[DI]   ;STORE RESULT
          JMP       NEXT_ELEMENT
DOUBLEB:  FSTP      QWORD PTR ES:[DI]   ;STORE RESULT
NEXT_ELEMENT:
          ADD       AX,DX               ;NEXT X{,Z}
          ADD       DI,DX               ;NEXT Y
          LOOP      GOTO_V_LOOP
          JMP       SHORT DONE
GOTO_V_LOOP: JMP    V_LOOP
DONE:
          ENDM
```

Logarithms

The 8087 hardware calculates logarithms for log base two. Most mathematical applications require natural logarithms, log base e, or common logarithms, log base 10. These are easily calculated using the fundamental identity for changing the base of a logarithm. Suppose we want the log of X base n, and only know how to calculate logarithms using base two.

$$\log_n X = \log_n 2 \times \log_2 X$$

In this case, n is e or 10. Typical execution times to take the log are 197 microseconds (8087/287) and 24 microseconds (387).

```
INCLUDE   SUBROUT.MAC
INCLUDE   ADVANCED.MAC
          SUBROUTINE VLN,<X,Y,ARRAY_TYPE,N>
;         Y=LN(X) (NATURAL LOG)
          TRANS_HEAD
          FLDLN2                     ;push log base e of 2
          FXCH                       ;swap ST,ST(1)
          FYL2X                      ;pop and replace ST with natural log
          TRANS_TAIL
          RETURN    VLN
          END
```

```
INCLUDE   SUBROUT.MAC
INCLUDE   ADVANCED.MAC
```

```
        SUBROUTINE VLOG10,<X,Y,ARRAY_TYPE,N>
;       Y=LOG10(X) (LOG BASE 10, COMMON LOG)
        TRANS_HEAD
        FLDLG2          ;push log base e of 10
        FXCH            ;swap ST,ST(1)
        FYL2X           ;pop and replace ST with natural log
        TRANS_TAIL
        RETURN    VLOG10
        END
```

Exponentiation

The 8087 hardware provides the instruction F2XM1 for raising 2 to the power X. Mathematical calculations often require e^x, 10^x, and y^x. These are easily calculated using the fundamental identity for changing the base of an exponent. Suppose we want y^x and only know how to calculate 2^x.

$$y^x = 2^{(X \times \log_2 y)}$$

Exponentiation routines would be simple if we had an instruction to raise 2 to an arbitrary power. Since F2XM1 only accepts arguments in a limited range, we need a procedure to perform the operation 2^z for an arbitrary Z. The 8087 instruction set is organized to make this a relatively easy operation, though a bit of planning is required. We actually have two hardware operations for taking a power of two. F2XM1 accepts exponents between 0 and ½. FSCALE accepts any integer exponent. We'll pick Z_1 and Z_2 such that Z_1 is an integer and Z_2 is a positive fraction. If Z_2 is greater than ½, we'll subtract ½ from Z_2 and then multiply the answer by $2^{1/2}$. (This is all easier than it sounds.) The algorithm works as follows:

1. Let Z_1 equal the greatest integer less than or equal to Z. This is a little messy since we need to *round down* Z. In order to accomplish this, we need to change the 8087 rounding control by using the load control word, FLDCW, and store control word, FSTCW instructions; instructions we don't officially meet until the next section.
2. Let $Z_2 = Z - Z_1$. Note that Z_2 is guaranteed to be positive.
3. Is $Z_2 > 1/2$? If so, subtract ½ and make note of the fact.
4. Raise 2 to the Z_2 and scale by Z_1.
5. If we subtracted ½ from Z_2 above, now multiply the result by $2^{1/2}$.

Subroutine TWO2THEZ finds its argument in ST and leaves the result there as well. This makes it easy for other routines to call it.

```
INCLUDE  SUBROUT.MAC
         SUBROUTINE TWO2THEZ
;        ST=2^ST
;        Z IS IN STACK TOP
;SET ASIDE SOME TEMPORARY LOCATIONS
         CHKSTCK   2*4                ;TEMPORARY STORAGE
         PUSHTEMP  AX                 ;SAVE AX
         PUSHTEMP  AX,STATUS_WORD
         PUSHTEMP  AX,CONTROL_WORD
         PUSHTEMP  AX,CONTROL_WORD_TEMP
         FSTCW     [BP].CONTROL_WORD  ;save control word so we can
                                      ;restore it later
         FSTCW     [BP].CONTROL_WORD_TEMP;use TEMP to change
                                      ;rounding control(RC)
         FWAIT
         AND       [BP].CONTROL_WORD_TEMP,0F3FFH ;clear out RC bits
         OR        [BP].CONTROL_WORD_TEMP,00400H ;RC = round-down
         FLDCW     [BP].CONTROL_WORD_TEMP ; set to round down
         FLD       ST(0)              ;push copy of Z onto ST
         FRNDINT                      ;ok, ST=Z1, ST(1)=Z
         FLDCW     [BP].CONTROL_WORD  ;return things to normal
         FSUB      ST(1),ST           ;ST(1)(Z2) = Z-Z1
         FXCH                         ;ST=Z2, ST(1)=Z1
                                      ;now put a 1/2 onto stack top
         FLD1                         ;ST=1
         FCHS                         ;ST=-1
         FLD1                         ;ST=1 ST(1)= -1
         FSCALE                       ;ST=1/2 ST(1)=-1
         FXCH                         ;ST(1)=1/2
         FSTP      ST(0)              ;ST=1/2
                                      ;1/2 IN ST!!

         FXCH                         ;ST=Z2 ST(1)=1/2
         FPREM                        ;ST has Z2 or Z2-1/2
                                      ;C1=1 in the latter case
         FSTSW     [BP].STATUS_WORD
         FWAIT
                                      ;NOW WE'VE GOT FLAGS SET
         FSTP      ST(1)              ;GET RID OF THE 1/2
         F2XM1                        ;ST=(2 to the ST)-1
         FLD1
         FADDP     ST(1),ST
         TEST      BYTE PTR [BP].STATUS_WORD+1,00000010B
                                      ;ST HAS Z2 IF BIT 1 ON
         JZ        WAS_Z2             ;OTHERWISE IT WAS Z2-1/2
         FLD1                         ;SO,
         FADD      ST,ST(0)           ;MULTIPLY BY THE
```

```
         FSQRT                             ;SQUARE ROOT OF 2
         FMULP     ST(1),ST
;
WAS_Z2:                                    ; WE JUST NEED TO SCALE
         FSCALE                            ;NOTICE WE DIDN'T CHECK
                                           ;FOR OVER OR UNDERFLOW
         FSTP      ST(1)
         POPTEMP   3
         POP       AX
         TEMP_COUNT = TEMP_COUNT - 1
         RETURN    TWO2THEZ
         END
```

TWO2THEZ needs to find its argument in ST. Subroutine TWO2THEX uses ADVANCED.MAC to connect up TWO2THEZ with memory. Typical times for TWO2THEX are 295 microseconds for 8087/287 and 71 microseconds for the 387.

```
INCLUDE    SUBROUT.MAC
INCLUDE    ADVANCED.MAC
           EXTERNAL  <TWO2THEZ>
           SUBROUTINE TWO2THEX,<X,Y,ARRAY_TYPE,N>
;          Y=2^X
           TRANS_HEAD
           CALL      TWO2THEZ
           TRANS_TAIL
           RETURN    TWO2THEX
           END
```

Of course, we aren't actually interested in raising two to some power all that often. With the TWO2THEZ firmly in hand, it's easy to provide routines for e^x, 10^x, and y^x. Typical times for the first two are 322 {77} microseconds for e^x and 10^x and 482 {92} microseconds for y^x.

```
INCLUDE    SUBROUT.MAC
INCLUDE    ADVANCED.MAC
           EXTERNAL  <TWO2THEZ>
           SUBROUTINE VEXP,<X,Y,ARRAY_TYPE,N>
;          Y=EXP(X)
           TRANS_HEAD
           FLDL2E                     ;push log e base 2
           FMULP     ST(1),ST         ;ST=X times log e base 2
           CALL      TWO2THEZ         ;ST=exp(X)
           TRANS_TAIL
           RETURN    VEXP
           END
```

```
INCLUDE    SUBROUT.MAC
INCLUDE    ADVANCED.MAC
           EXTERNAL  <TWO2THEZ>
           SUBROUTINE TEN2THEX,<X,Y,ARRAY_TYPE,N>
;          Y=10^X
           TRANS_HEAD
           FLDL2T                        ;push log 10 base 2
           FMULP     ST(1),ST            ;ST=X times log 10 base 2
           CALL      TWO2THEZ            ;ST=10 to the X
           TRANS_TAIL
           RETURN    TEN2THEX
           END
```

```
INCLUDE    SUBROUT.MAC
INCLUDE    ADVANCED.MAC
           EXTERNAL  <TWO2THEZ>
           SUBROUTINE Z2THEX,<X,Z,Y,ARRAY_TYPE,N>
;          Y=Z^X  (ASSUMES THAT Z IS POSITIVE)
           TRANS_HEAD
           FYL2X                         ;ST=Z times log X base 2
           CALL      TWO2THEZ            ;ST=Z to the X
           TRANS_TAIL
           RETURN    Z2THEX
           END
```

Trigonometric Functions

The tangent function provides the base for calculating all the common trigonometric functions. FPTAN calculates the tangent for arguments between 0 and pi/4. Computation of a trigonometric function involves three broad steps. First, prologue code is used to bring the argument within range of the FPTAN instruction. Second, the FPTAN instruction is applied. Third, epilogue code is used to correct the result of FPTAN. The trigonometric identities used are described in the code below. Tangent typically takes 370 {45} microseconds.

```
INCLUDE   SUBROUT.MAC
INCLUDE   ADVANCED.MAC
          SUBROUTINE TANGENT,<X,Y,ARRAY_TYPE,N>
;         Y=TAN(X) (TANGENT) X IS ASSUMED TO BE A VALID NUMBER
          CHKSTCK   4+4
```

```
        PUSHTEMP  AX
        PUSHTEMP  BX
        PUSHTEMP  AX,STATUS_WORD
        PUSHTEMP  AX,SIGN_STORE
        TRANS_HEAD
;First check for a negative argument
; Note TAN(-X) = - TAN(X)
        MOV       BYTE PTR [BP].SIGN_STORE,0 ;ASSUME POSITIVE
        FTST
        FSTSW     [BP].STATUS_WORD
        FWAIT
        MOV       AH,BYTE PTR [BP].STATUS_WORD+1
        SAHF
        JNC       NON_NEGATIVE
        MOV       BYTE PTR [BP].SIGN_STORE,-1 ;ITS NEGATIVE
        FABS                          ;NOW POSITIVE

NON_NEGATIVE:
;NOW GET ST BETWEEN 0 AND PI/4
                                      ;PUT -2 ON STACK
        FLD1                          ;ST=1
        FADD      ST,ST               ;ST=2
        FCHS                          ;ST=-2
        FLDPI                         ;LOAD PI
        FSCALE                        ;GOT PI/4
        FSTP      ST(1)               ;DUMP -2
        FXCH
; NOW X IS IN ST AND PI/4 IN ST(1)
RANGE:
        FPREM
        FSTSW     [BP].STATUS_WORD
        FWAIT
        MOV       AH,BYTE PTR [BP].STATUS_WORD+1
        SAHF
        JP        RANGE               ;THIS TESTS BIT C2
;AT THIS POINT AH HAS THE STATUS BITS
;NOW LETS SEE IF THE REMAINDER WAS EXACTLY ZERO
        FTST
        FSTSW     [BP].STATUS_WORD
        FWAIT
;IT WAS ZERO IF C3=1 AND C0=0
;IF ZERO, SET BX=-1, ELSE BX=0
        MOV       BX,0
        AND       BYTE PTR [BP].STATUS_WORD+1,01000001B
        CMP       BYTE PTR [BP].STATUS_WORD+1,01000001B
        JNE       NOT_ZERO
        MOV       BX,-1
```

```
NOT_ZERO:
;THERE ARE FOUR POSSIBILITIES GIVEN ST NOW HAS X MOD PI/4
;OCTANT   C3  C1        CALCULATE              IF ZERO
;0,4      0   0         FPTAN(ST)                0
;1,5      0   1         1/FPTAN(PI/4 - ST)       1
;2,6      1   0         -1/FPTAN(ST)          INFINITY
;3,7      1   1         -FPTAN(PI/4 - ST)        -1
;
;FIRST CHECK BIT C1 AND TAKE FPTAN
          TEST      AH,10B                  ;IS C1 ON
          JZ        C1ISOFF                 ;JUMP IF OFF
          CMP       BX,0                    ;ST EXACTLY ZERO?
          JNE       ST0ANDC1                ;JUMP IF YES
          FSUBP     ST(1),ST                ;NOW PI/4-ST
          FPTAN
          JMP       TANDONE
ST0ANDC1:
          FSTP      ST                      ;POP ST
          FSTP      ST                      ; AND PI/4
          FLD1                              ;LOAD RATIO 1 TO 1
          FLD1
          JMP       TANDONE

C1ISOFF:
          FSTP      ST(1)                   ;GET RID OF PI/4
          CMP       BX,0                    ;ST EXACTLY ZERO?
          JNE       ST0ANDNOC1              ;JUMP IF YES
          FPTAN
          JMP       TANDONE
ST0ANDNOC1:
          FSTP      ST                      ;DUMP ST
          FLDZ                              ;LOAD RATIO 0 TO 1
          FLD1
TANDONE:
;PUT C1 XOR C3 IN BX
          MOV       BX,0                    ;ASSUME C3 OFF

;IF C3 IS ON THEN CHANGE SIGNS
          TEST      AH,01000000B
          JZ        NOC3                    ;JUMP IF OFF
          FCHS
          MOV       BX,1                    ;NOTE C3 ON
NOC3:
;IS C1 ON ?
          TEST      AH,10B
          JZ        NOC1                    ;JUMP IF OFF
          XOR       BX,1
```

```
          JMP       RECIP
NOC1:     XOR       BX,0
RECIP:
;IF BX=1 THEN WE WANT RECIPROCAL OF RATIO
          CMP       BX,1
          JNE       NORECIP
          FXCH
NORECIP:  FDIVP     ST(1),ST            ;THAT'S IT
;DID WE ORIGINALLY CHANGE SIGN?
          CMP       BYTE PTR [BP].SIGN_STORE,0
          JE        LEAVE_POS
          FCHS
LEAVE_POS:
          TRANS_TAIL
          POPTEMP   2
          POP       BX
          POP       AX
          TEMP_COUNT = TEMP_COUNT-2
          RETURN    TANGENT
          END
```

Sine and cosine functions are also calculated using FPTAN. (But see the discussion below on 387 trigonometric instructions.) Since a cosine is just a sine rotated 90 degrees, we can calculate both sine and cosine with one routine if we adjust the argument a little. Routine SINCOS computes the sine of ST if its argument IFCOS equals 0 (IFCOS is false) and cosine otherwise. Routines SINE and COSINE are used to connect up SINCOS with memory. Typical execution times for SINE and COSINE are 473 {127} microseconds.

```
INCLUDE   SUBROUT.MAC
          SUBROUTINE SINCOS,<IFCOS>
;         IFCOS IS ADDRESS OF INTEGER
;         ST=SINE(ST) IF IFCOS=0
;         ST=COSINE(ST) IF IFCOS<>0
          CHKSTCK   6+4
          PUSHTEMP  AX
          PUSHTEMP  BX
          PUSHTEMP  SI
          PUSHTEMP  AX,STATUS_WORD
          PUSHTEMP  AX,SIGN_STORE
          LDS       SI,[BP].IFCOS       ;DS:SI=ADDR(IFCOS)
          CMP       WORD PTR [SI],0     ;USE DS:SI FOR IFCOS
          JNE       COS_ENTRY
;First check for a negative argument
; Note SIN(-X) = - SIN(X)
          MOV       WORD PTR [BP].SIGN_STORE,0   ;ASSUME POSITIVE
```

```
          FTST
          FSTSW     [BP].STATUS_WORD
          FWAIT
          MOV       AH,BYTE PTR [BP].STATUS_WORD+1
          SAHF
          JNC       NON_NEGATIVE
          MOV       WORD PTR [BP].SIGN_STORE,-1  ;ITS NEGATIVE
          FABS                                   ;NOW POSITIVE
          JMP       SHORT NON_NEGATIVE

COS_ENTRY:
          FABS
          MOV       WORD PTR [BP].SIGN_STORE,0    ;ITS POSITIVE NOW

NON_NEGATIVE:
;NOW GET ST BETWEEN 0 AND PI/4
                                         ;LOAD -2
          FLD1
          FLD1
          FADDP     ST(1),ST
          FCHS                           ;ST=-2
          FLDPI                          ;LOAD PI
          FSCALE                         ;GOT PI/4
          FSTP      ST(1)                ;DUMP -2
          FXCH
; NOW X IS IN ST AND PI/4 IN ST(1)
RANGE:
          FPREM
          FSTSW     [BP].STATUS_WORD
          FWAIT
          MOV       AH,BYTE PTR [BP].STATUS_WORD+1
          SAHF
          JP        RANGE                 ;THIS TESTS BIT C2
;AT THIS POINT AH HAS THE STATUS BITS


;IF WE ARE REALLY DOING COSINE, WE NEED TO ADD TWO TO THE OCTANT
          CMP       WORD PTR [SI],0
          JE        ITS_SINE
;ADD INTO C3 AND CARRY INTO C0
          XOR       AH,01000000B
          TEST      AH,01000000B
          JNZ       NOCARRY
          XOR       AH,1B
NOCARRY:
ITS_SINE:
;NOW LETS SEE IF THE REMAINDER WAS EXACTLY ZERO
```

```
          FTST
          FSTSW     [BP].STATUS_WORD
          FWAIT
;IT WAS ZERO IF C3=1 AND C0=0
;IF ZERO, SET BX=-1, ELSE BX=0
          MOV       BX,0
          AND       BYTE PTR [BP].STATUS_WORD+1,01000001B
          CMP       BYTE PTR [BP].STATUS_WORD+1,01000001B
          JNE       NOT_ZERO
          MOV       BX,-1
NOT_ZERO:
;THERE ARE FOUR POSSIBILITIES GIVEN ST NOW HAS X MOD PI/4
;OCTANT    C3  C1        CALCULATE           IF ZERO
;0         0   0         SIN(ST)                  0
;1         0   1         COS(PI/4 - ST)           SQRT(2)/2
;2         1   0         COS(ST)                  1
;3         1   1         SIN(PI/4 - ST)           SQRT(2)/2
;
; OCTANTS 4-7 ARE JUST LIKE 0-3 ONLY NEGATIVE
;NOTE:  IF TAN(THETA)=X/Y, THEN
;           SIN(THETA)=X/SQRT(X*X+Y*Y)
;           COS(THETA)=Y/SQRT(X*X+Y*Y)
;
;FIRST CHECK BIT C1 AND TAKE FPTAN
          TEST      AH,10B                   ;IS C1 ON
          JZ        C1ISOFF                  ;JUMP IF OFF
          CMP       BX,0                     ;ST EXACTLY ZERO?
          JNE       ST0ANDC1                 ;JUMP IF YES
          FSUBP     ST(1),ST                 ;NOW PI/4-ST
          FPTAN
          JMP       SINDONE
ST0ANDC1:
          FSTP      ST                       ;POP ST
          FSTP      ST                       ; AND PI/4
          FLD1                               ;LOAD RATIO 1 TO 1
          FLD1
          JMP       SINDONE


C1ISOFF:
          FSTP      ST(1)                    ;GET RID OF PI/4
          CMP       BX,0                     ;ST EXACTLY ZERO?
          JNE       ST0ANDNOC1               ;JUMP IF YES
          FPTAN
          JMP       SINDONE
ST0ANDNOC1:
          FSTP      ST                       ;DUMP ST
```

```
            FLDZ                                ;LOAD RATIO 0 TO 1
            FLD1
SINDONE:
;IS C1 XOR C3 TRUE?
            MOV         BX,0                    ;ASSUME C3 OFF


;IF C3 IS ON
            TEST        AH,01000000B
            JZ          NOC3                    ;JUMP IF OFF
            MOV         BX,1                    ;NOTE C3 ON
NOC3:
;IS C1 ON ?
            TEST        AH,10B
            JZ          NOC1                    ;JUMP IF OFF
            XOR         BX,1
            JMP         DOSINE
NOC1:       XOR         BX,0
DOSINE:
;IF BX=1 THEN WE WANT COSINE FUNCTION
            CMP         BX,1
            JNE         SINFUNC
            FXCH
SINFUNC:
;ST(1)=X, ST(0)=Y
;SIN(THETA)=X/SQRT(X*X+Y*Y)
            FMUL        ST(0),ST(0)             ;ST(0)=Y*Y
            FLD         ST(1)                   ;ST(0)=X
            FMUL        ST(0),ST(0)             ;ST(0)=X*X
            FADDP       ST(1),ST(0)             ;ST(0)=X*X+Y*Y
            FSQRT
            FDIVP       ST(1),ST(0)
;
;IS BIT C0 ON?
            TEST        AH,1B
            JZ          C0OFF
            NOT         WORD PTR [BP].SIGN_STORE
C0OFF:
;DO WE NEED TO CHANGE SIGN?


            CMP         WORD PTR [BP].SIGN_STORE,0
            JE          LEAVE_POS
            FCHS
LEAVE_POS:
            POPTEMP     2
            POP         SI
            POP         BX
```

```
        POP       AX
        TEMP_COUNT = TEMP_COUNT-3
        RETURN    SINCOS
        END



INCLUDE SUBROUT.MAC
INCLUDE ADVANCED.MAC
        EXTERNAL   <SINCOS>
        SUBROUTINE SINE,<X,Y,ARRAY_TYPE,N>
;       Y=SINE(X)
        CHKSTCK   2*4
        PUSHTEMP  AX,SINE_FLAG          ;0 SIGNALS WE WANT A SINE TAKEN
        MOV       WORD PTR [BP].SINE_FLAG,0
        TRANS_HEAD
        PUSH      BX
        LEA       BX,[BP].SINE_FLAG
        PUSH      SS
        PUSH      BX                    ;ADDR(SINE_FLAG) IS ON STACK
        CALL      SINCOS                ;ST=SIN(X)
        POP       BX
        TRANS_TAIL
        POPTEMP   1
        RETURN    SINE
        END



INCLUDE SUBROUT.MAC
INCLUDE ADVANCED.MAC
        EXTERNAL  <SINCOS>
        SUBROUTINE COSINE,<X,Y,ARRAY_TYPE,N>
;       Y=COSINE(X)
        CHKSTCK   2*4
        PUSHTEMP  AX,COSINE_FLAG        ;-1 SIGNALS WE WANT A COSINE
                                        ;TAKEN
        MOV       WORD PTR [BP].COSINE_FLAG,-1
        TRANS_HEAD
        PUSH      BX
        LEA       BX,[BP].COSINE_FLAG
        PUSH      SS
        PUSH      BX                    ;ADDR(COSINE_FLAG) IS ON STACK
        CALL      SINCOS                ;ST=COS(X)
```

```
        POP        BX
        TRANS_TAIL
        POPTEMP    1
        RETURN     COSINE
        END
```

For further explanation of trigonometric calculations and for programs which perform sophisticated error checking, see

Getting Started With the Numeric Data Processor, by Bill Rash, Intel Corporation, Application Note AP-113.

387 Trigonometric Instructions

The sine/cosine routine above is the most convoluted and thus the least pleasant routine to read in the entire book. It is one of the slowest as well. Intel introduced three new sine and cosine instructions on the 387. These instructions simplify programming and speed execution.

FCOS {ST} {48} microseconds

FCOS (cosine) replaces the number in ST with its cosine. The number must be less than 26^3 in absolute value, which is effectively unrestricted for most applications. If ST is in range, C2 is cleared. In the unlikely circumstance that ST is out of range, C2 is set to 1 and ST is unchanged. In this case, you can use FPREM or FPREM1 to bring the argument within range.

FSIN {ST} {48} microseconds

FSIN (sine) replaces the number in ST with its sine. Restrictions are the same as FCOS.

- *The initial release of Microsoft's MASM assembler 5.0 generates the wrong code for FCOS, and FSIN. You can work around the bug by supplying your own hexadecimal codes.*
  For FCOS use "DB 0D9H,OFFH."
  For FSIN use "DB 0D9H,OFEH."
  (Microsoft has fixed these bugs in Version 5.00A of the assembler.)

FSINCOS {ST} {48} microseconds

FSINCOS (sine and cosine) replaces the number in ST with its sine and then pushes the cosine onto the stack, so that the stack ends up with ST = cos, ST(1) = sin. Restrictions are the same as FCOS.

A single instruction to compute both sine and cosine seems a bit peculiar. It's present for two reasons. First, once one function is being computed it's pretty cheap to compute the other—so why not? Second, some trig problems call for using both the sine and the cosine of an angle and for these it is convenient to have both done at once.

To demonstrate the new 387 trig instructions, we provide the routine SINE387. Typical execution time on a 387 is {47} microseconds. You will notice that SINE387 INCLUDES SUBR387.MAC rather than SUBROUT.MAC. LINK requires that seqments that include the .386 directive have different segment names from 16-bit programs. In order to be able to link SINE387 with other programs, we made a copy of SUBROUT.MAC in which the code segment name is changed to CSEG387.

```
.386
INCLUDE    SUBR387.MAC
INCLUDE    ADVANCED.MAC
           SUBROUTINE SINE387,<X,Y,ARRAY_TYPE,IER,N>
;          Y=SIN(X) (SINE)
;          REQUIRES  387 TO OPERATE
;          IER=0 IF ALL ARGUMENTS IN RANGE -1 OTHERWISE
           LDS        BX,[BP].IER           ;DS:BX=ADDR(IER)
           MOV        WORD PTR [BX],0       ;ASSUME NO ERROR
           TRANS_HEAD
;           FSIN                             ;ST=SIN
           DB         0D9H,0FEH             ;FAKE A FSIN
           FSTSW      AX                    ;RETRIEVE CONDITION CODES
           SAHF                             ;STORE FLAGS
           JP         RANGE_ERR             ;JMP IF C2=1
           TRANS_TAIL
           JMP        ALLDONE
RANGE_ERR:
           LDS        BX,[BP].IER           ;DS:BX=ADDR(IER)
           MOV        WORD PTR [BX],-1      ;INDICATE ERROR
           FSTP       ST(0)                 ;CLEAR STACK
                                            ;AND BAIL OUT
ALLDONE:
           RETURN     SINE387
           END
```

Inverse Trigonometric Functions

The 8087 instruction FPATAN performs the core calculations for the inverse trigonometric functions: Arctan, Arcsin, Arccos, Arccot, Arccsc, and Arcsec. Just as FPTAN produces a result in the form Y/X, so FPATAN accepts an argument in the form Y/X. The inverse trigonometric functions require somewhat less programming, because the argument range is less restricted for

FPATAN than for FPTAN. (The direct trigonometric functions are periodic, where the inverse trigonometric functions aren't.) For FPATAN, we need only assure that the arguments obey the relation 0 < Y < X < infinity. Thus to compute Arctan(Z) we need to check seven cases: Z equal 0, Z positive or negative and ABS(Z) less than, equal to, or greater than 1. We bring Z into the proper range by using the identities:

$$\text{Arctan}(Z) = -\text{Arctan}(-Z)$$
$$\text{Arctan}(Z) = \text{pi}/2 - \text{Arctan}(1/Z)$$

ARCTAN typically uses 351 {41} microseconds.

```
INCLUDE    SUBROUT.MAC
INCLUDE    ADVANCED.MAC
           SUBROUTINE ARCTAN,<X,Y,ARRAY_TYPE,N>
;          Y=ARCTAN(X) (ARCTANGENT) X IS ASSUMED TO BE A VALID NUMBER
           CHKSTCK   2+4
           PUSHTEMP  AX
           PUSHTEMP  AX,STATUS_WORD
           PUSHTEMP  AX,SIGN_STORE
           TRANS_HEAD
;The first problem is to check for a zero or negative argument
           MOV       WORD PTR [BP].SIGN_STORE,0  ;ASSUME NON-NEGATIVE
           FTST
           FSTSW     [BP].STATUS_WORD
           FWAIT
           MOV       AH,BYTE PTR [BP].STATUS_WORD+1
           SAHF
           JA        POSITIVE
           JZ        ZERO                ;ASSUME ITS ZERO
           JMP       NEGATIVE
ZERO:
;ARCTAN(0)=0
           FSTP      ST(0)
           FLDZ
           JMP       ARCTAN_DONE
NEGATIVE: ;DEAL WITH A NEGATIVE ARGUMENT USING IDENTITY
;ARCTAN(-X)= - ARCTAN(X)
           FCHS
           MOV        WORD PTR [BP].SIGN_STORE,-1

POSITIVE:  ; HOW DOES 1 COMPARE TO X
           FLD1
           FCOM
           FSTSW     [BP].STATUS_WORD
           FWAIT
           MOV       AH,BYTE PTR [BP].STATUS_WORD+1
```

```
          SAHF
          JA        Z_LT_1
          JC        Z_GT_1
;EXACTLY 1 RETURN ARCTAN(1)=PI/4
          FCHS                          ;ST NOW = -1
          FADD      ST(0),ST(0)         ;ST=-2
          FLDPI
          FSCALE                   ;ST NOW PI/4
          FSTP      ST(1)
          JMP       RESTORE_SIGN
Z_GT_1:
;USE IDENTITY ATAN(X)= PI/2 - ATAN(1/X)
          FXCH                     ;ST=Z,ST(1)=1
          FPATAN
          FLD1                     ;NOW ADJUST BY PI/2
          FCHS
          FLDPI
          FSCALE
          FSTP      ST(1)
          FSUBRP    ST(1),ST
          JMP       RESTORE_SIGN
Z_LT_1:
          FPATAN                        ;ST=1,ST(1)=Z
RESTORE_SIGN:
          TEST      WORD PTR [BP].SIGN_STORE,0FFH
          JZ        ARCTAN_DONE
          FCHS
ARCTAN_DONE:
          TRANS_TAIL
          POPTEMP   2
          POP       AX
          TEMP_COUNT = TEMP_COUNT-1
          RETURN    ARCTAN
          END
```

Processor Control Instructions

Sixteen instructions are used to examine and control the internal status of the 8087. We make regular use of the instructions that manipulate the *status word* and the *control word*. In particular, these instructions are used for examining the results of comparisons and for setting the controls, such as for rounding, on the 8087. Most of the other instructions are needed for writing system programs. We discuss these briefly for completeness. The processor control instruction FSTSW (store status word) was discussed in Chapter 4.

- As we mentioned in Chapter 3, the 287 and 387 electronically synchronize most instructions (unlike the 8087, which requires a WAIT instruction). However, processor control instructions are not synchronized electronically. The assembler will automatically generate the necessary WAIT instructions for processor control instructions for both the 8087 and the 287/387. For system programming purposes, it is possible to prevent automatic generation of WAIT instructions by using the "no-wait" form of the processor control instructions. For example, FNSTCW rather than FSTCW.

FLDCW word-integer 4{1} microseconds

FLDCW (load control word) loads a word from a two-byte memory location into the 8087's internal control word register. FLDCW is used, for example, to change the 8087 rounding control.

- Microsoft's FORTRAN *User's Guide* instructs us "do not alter the 8087/80287 control word with the FLDCW instruction." This is because some of the error-handling routines need to keep track of the control word. Of course, sometimes we have to change the control word. So long as our assembly language program restores the control word before an error can occur, this is probably safe enough. For absolute safety while using FORTRAN, one could call the FORTRAN routine LCWRQQ instead of using FLDCW.

FSTCW word-integer 5 {1} microseconds

FSTCW (store control word) stores the 8087 control word at the two-byte destination location.

FWAIT

FWAIT is actually an 8088, not an 8087, instruction. (The FWAIT mnemonic generates the 8088 WAIT instruction.) FWAIT halts the 8088 until the 8087 completes its current instruction. FWAIT should be coded before any 8088 instruction that references a memory location being read from or written to by the 8087. During an FWAIT, the 8088 checks the 8087 once per microsecond, and resumes execution as soon as the 8087 is free.

The description of the remaining processor control instructions is included for completeness. None of these instructions are necessary for the programs in this book.

The following two instructions are useful in writing subroutines because they allow a subroutine to save a copy of the 8087's internal state and then restore it.

FSAVE memory 44 {23} microseconds

FSAVE (save state) copies all internal 8087 information into memory and then reinitializes the processor by the equivalent of executing an FINIT (see below). Thus FSAVE can be used to reset the 8087 to its "virgin" state before passing control over to another routine. The FRSTOR instruction can be used when control is regained to take up where work left off.

FSAVE stores the 8087 environment (control registers, etc.), and then the contents of the stack. Figure 10.1 shows the layout in memory. The layout is identical on a 287 running in real mode, but the environment is slightly different in protected mode (Figure 10.3). There are four possibilities for the memory layout for the 387. When running using a 16-bit address, the 387 environment is laid out just as with the real or protected mode of the 287. When using a 32-bit address, the environment occupies 28 bytes rather than 14 and the registers are saved starting at "memory + 38" rather than "memory + 14." Again, the environment layout is slightly different in real and protected mode, as in Figures 10-4 and 10-5.

FRSTOR memory 44 {19} microseconds

FRSTOR (restore state) reloads the 8087 state from memory, effectively "undoing" a previous FSAVE.

FINIT 1 microsecond

FINIT (initialize processor) resets the 8087. The initialized conditions are slightly different on the 8087/287 versus the 387. The only change likely to be of interest to an applications programmer is that the 387 always uses affine infinity (positive and negative infinity are far apart) where the earlier coprocessors are initialized to projective infinity (positive and negative infinity are equal). The initialized conditions are described in Figure 10-2.

FSETPM 1 microsecond

FSETPM (set Protected mode) is available only on the 287. FSETPM places the 287 in *Virtual Protected Address Mode.* The 287 can be returned to *Real Mode* only by a hardware reset. In particular, the FINIT instruction will not affect the address mode of the 287. FSETPM is not available on the 8087. On the 387, FSETPM is "ignored." (The 387 treats the instructions as a FNOP, a null operation.)

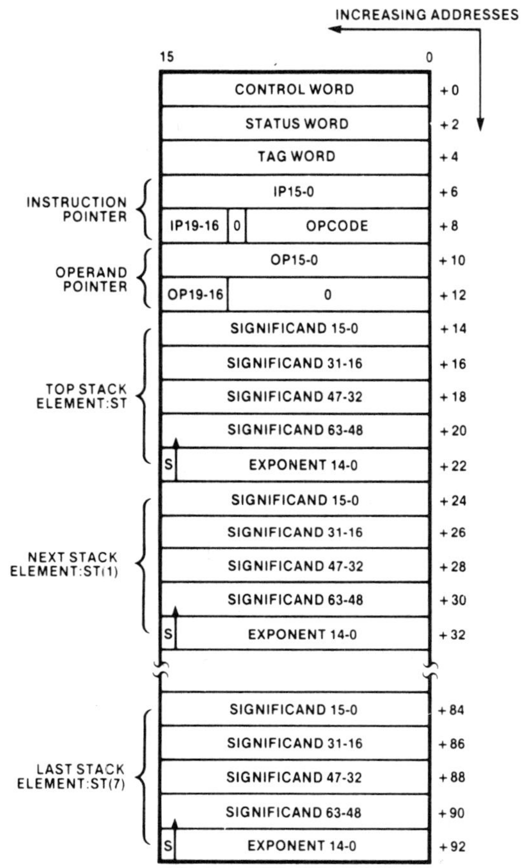

NOTES:
S = Sign
Bit 0 of each field is rightmost, least significant bit of corresponding register field.
Bit 63 of significand is integer bit (assumed binary point is immediately to the right).

Figure 10.1. Memory layout for 8087 internal state. (Used with permission of Intel Corporation.)

Interrupt and Exception-handling Instructions

Normally, we allow exceptions to be masked; that is, the 8087 hardware handles computational errors automatically. If a given exception type is unmasked, the 8087 will interrupt the 8088 when the exception occurs.

In this way, a computational error can be processed by user- or system-specified exception-handling software. If the 8088 is handling a task with higher priority than accepting 8087 "messages," 8087 interrupts can be disabled with the FDISI instruction.

FDISI — 1 {1} microsecond

FDISI (disable interrupts) disables interrupts on the 8087 by setting the interrupt enable mask bit in the control word. FDISI is ignored on the 287 and 387. 8087 programs that rely on FDISI almost certainly must be rewritten to function properly on a 287/387. Fortunately, FDISI is used almost exclusively by system programmers.

FENI — 1 {1} microsecond

FENI (enable interrupts) enables interrupts on the 8087 by clearing the interrupt enable mask bit in the control word. FENI is ignored on the 287 and 387. As with FDISI, 8087 programs that rely on FENI almost certainly must be rewritten to function properly on a 287/387. Fortunately, FENI too is used almost exclusively by system programmers.

FCLEX — 1 {1} microsecond

FCLEX (clear exceptions) clears the exception flags, the interrupt request flag, and the busy flag in the status word. FCLEX is principally used by exception-handling routines after an exception has been taken care of. If the exception were not cleared before returning control to the 8087, a second interrupt request would be issued immediately.

FSTENV memory — 11{7} microseconds

FSTENV (store environment) stores the control, status, and tag words, and the exception pointers in memory, so that these items may be examined by an exception handling routine. FSTENV stores a subset of the information stored by FSAVE and operates with considerably greater speed.

The memory layout for the environment on the 8087,287 real mode, and 387 16-bit real mode is shown in Figure 10.3. The layout for 287 protected mode and 387 16-bit protected mode apppears in Figure 10-4. Figures 10-5 and 10-6 show the 387 32-bit real and protected mode environment respectively.

FLDENV memory — 10 {5} microseconds

FLDENV (load environment) loads the control, status, and tag words, and the exception pointers from memory, as in Figures 10.3–10.6.

Table 10.2. 8087/287/387 initial conditions.

Field	*8087/287*	*387*
Control Word		
Infinity Control	Projective	Affine
Rounding Control	Nearest	Nearest
Precision Control	64 bits	64 bits
Interrupt-enable Mask	Disabled	Disabled
Exception Masks	Masked	Masked
Status Word		
Busy	Not busy	Not busy
Condition Code	Not changed	Zero
Stack Top	Empty stack	Empty stack
Interrupt Request	No interrupt	No interrupt
Exception Flags	No exceptions	No exceptions
Tag Word		
Tags	Empty	Empty
Registers	Not changed	Not changed
Exception Pointers		
Instruction Code	Not changed	Not changed
Instruction Address	Not changed	Not changed
Operand Address	Not changed	Not changed

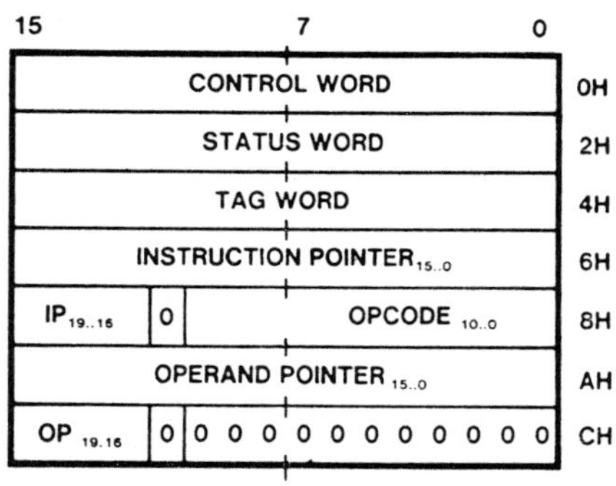

Figure 10.2. Memory layout for 16-bit Real Mode environment.

15 — 7 — 0	
CONTROL WORD	0H
STATUS WORD	2H
TAG WORD	4H
IP OFFSET	6H
CS SELECTOR	8H
OPERAND OFFSET	AH
OPERAND SELECTOR	CH

Figure 10.3. Memory layout for 16-bit Protected Mode environment.

31 — 23 — 16		15 — 7 — 0		
RESERVED		CONTROL WORD		0H
RESERVED		STATUS WORD		4H
RESERVED		TAG WORD		8H
RESERVED		INSTRUCTION POINTER $_{15..0}$		CH
0 0 0 0	INSTRUCTION POINTER $_{31..16}$	0	OPCODE $_{10..0}$	10H
RESERVED		OPERAND POINTER $_{15..0}$		14H
0 0 0 0	OPERAND POINTER $_{31..16}$	0 0 0 0 0 0 0 0 0 0 0 0		18H

Figure 10.4. Memory layout for 32-bit Real Mode environment.

31 — 23 — 16		15 — 7 — 0	
RESERVED		CONTROL WORD	0H
RESERVED		STATUS WORD	4H
RESERVED		TAG WORD	8H
IP OFFSET			CH
0 0 0 0 0	OPCODE $_{10..0}$	CS SELECTOR	10H
DATA OPERAND OFFSET			14H
RESERVED		OPERAND SELECTOR	18H

Figure 10.5. Memory layout for 32-bit Protected Mode environment.

FLDENV memory 10 {5} microseconds

FLDENV (load environment) loads the control, status, and tag words, and the exception pointers from memory, as in Figures 10.2–10.5.

FINCSTP 2 {1} microseconds

FINCSTP (increment stack pointer) increments the 8087 stack pointer. Do not use this instruction to pop the stack, since it does not mark ST as empty. Use FSTP ST(0) instead.

FDECSTP 2 {1} microseconds

FDECSTP (decrement stack pointer) decrements the 8087 stack pointer.

FFREE ST(i) 2 {1} microseconds

FFREE (free register) marks the indicated register as empty.

FNOP 3 {1} microseconds

FNOP (no operation) executes an FST ST,ST(0) in order to do nothing.

Detecting the Coprocessor Type

Routine DETECT87 checks coprocessor type, reporting a 0, 1, 2, or 3 for no coprocessor, 8087, 287, or 387 respectively. (If a 386 is emulating a 387 in software, DETECT87 reports 3.) Basically, three tests are done. First, we ask the coprocessor to store the control word in memory. If a coprocessor is present, a 3 is stored in the upper byte of the control word. Once we know a coprocessor is present, we need to decide between models. We use FDISI to set a bit in the control word. If the bit is set, the coprocessor must be an 8087. Finally, we choose between the 287 and 387 by putting a positive and negative infinity on the stack and checking if they are equal—which implies a 287. (You can find similar versions of this program in the *80387 Programmer's Reference Manual* and in an article by Ted Forgeron in the August 1987 issue of *PC Tech Journal.*)

The routine illustrates a couple of points about programming for all the coprocessors. First, we use the .286 directive so that we can use the FSTSW AX instruction. As a result, we would need to explicitly code FWAITs in the 8087 portion of the code if they were needed. Second, we have to be careful that neither the assembler nor the programmer puts a WAIT instruction in any part of the code that could be run on a machine without a coprocessor, since the WAIT would hang the machine. (Our RETURN macro usually includes an extra FWAIT, so this routine should be assembled with /DNOFWAIT on the assembler command line.)

```
.286C                                   ;ENABLES FSTSW AX, BUT REQUIRES
                                        ;EXPLICIT FWAITS
INCLUDE  SUBROUT.MAC
         SUBROUTINE DETECT87,<TYPE_OF_87>
```

```
;ON RETURN TYPE(AN INTEGER) EQUALS
;         0         NO COPROCESSOR
;         1         8087
;         2         80287
;         3         80387
          CHKSTCK   4                   ;ROOM FOR CONTROL WORDS
          MOV       AX,0
          PUSHTEMP  AX,CONTROL_WORD     ;INITIALLY CONTROL_WORD=0
          PUSHTEMP  AX,CONTROL_COPY
;ASSUME COPROCESSOR IS INITIALIZED IF PRESENT
          LDS       BX,[BP].TYPE_OF_87  ;DS:BX=ADDR(TYPE_OF_87)
          MOV       WORD PTR [BX],0     ;ASSUME NOTHING THERE
          FNSTCW    [BP].CONTROL_WORD   ;WORKS IF 80X87 PRESENT
          CMP       BYTE PTR [BP].CONTROL_WORD+1,03H
          JNE       ALLDONE             ;NO 03H STORED=>NO 80X87
          MOV       AX,[BP].CONTROL_WORD;
          MOV       [BP].CONTROL_COPY,AX;MAKE COPY OF CONTROL WORD
;SET INTERRUPT ENABLE BIT TO ZERO
          AND       [BP].CONTROL_COPY,0FF7FH
          FLDCW     [BP].CONTROL_COPY
          FDISI                         ;SET BIT BACK TO 1 ON 8087
                                        ; BUT NO EFFECT ON 287, 387
          FSTCW     [BP].CONTROL_COPY
          FWAIT
          TEST      WORD PTR [BP].CONTROL_COPY,0080H ;IF EQUAL THEN 8087
          MOV       WORD PTR [BX],1
          JNZ       DONE
;SET INFINITY CONTROL TO PROJECTIVE (IGNORED BY 387)
          AND       [BP].CONTROL_COPY,0EFFFH ; INFINITY BIT=0
          FLDCW     [BP].CONTROL_COPY
          FLD1                          ;ST=1
          FLDZ                          ;ST=0, ST(1)=1
          FDIVP     ST(1),ST            ;ST=INFINITY
          FLD       ST
          FCHS                          ;ST=-INFINITY ST(1)=INFINITY
          FCOMPP                        ;COMPARE AND CLEAR STACK
          FSTSW     AX                  ;THIS INSTRUCTION ONLY WORKS
                                        ; ON 287 OR 387, BUT THAT'S HOW
                                        ; WE GOT HERE
          SAHF
          JZ        ITS_287             ;MUST HAVE BEEN EQUAL
          MOV       WORD PTR [BX],3     ; FOUND 387
          JMP       DONE
ITS_287:  MOV       WORD PTR [BX],2
DONE:
          FLDCW     [BP].CONTROL_WORD   ;RESTORE CONTROL WORD
```

```
ALLDONE:  POPTEMP   2
          RETURN    DETECT87
          END
```

Advanced Instruction Set Summary

This chapter has seen much intricate detail. It took quite a few instructions to calculate a tangent even though the 8087 has a built-in "tangent" instruction. (If you think it took a lot of work this way, try writing a tangent instruction using only 8088 code!)

It is more difficult to build a small set of assembly language modules for non-linear problems than it is for linear problems. This is a place which really calls for an 8087-compatible language translator. The nonlinear programs in the next chapter are written in BASIC for this reason.

11

Non-Linear Methods

This chapter takes us on a bit of a digression. We present several of the basic algorithms for non-linear problems, but all the programs are in BASIC rather than assembler. The speed of the 8087 endows a personal computer with enough horsepower to make solution of non-linear problems feasible. However, coding such algorithms in assembler isn't likely to be cost effective because there isn't a short list of functions which dominate non-linear computation the way matrix multiplication and inversion dominate linear computation. Still, many of the same people who are interested in the 8087 are likely also to be interested in these kinds of problems. (So, if you only want pure 8087 information, you can safely skip this chapter.)

The COOKBOOK—Chapter 11

Program: **DIFFER**

Purpose: Demonstrate numerical differentiation

Language: BASIC

Program: **INTEGRAT**

Purpose: Demonstrate numerical intergration

Language: BASIC

Program: **ZERO**

Purpose:	Demonstrate solution of a non-linear equation
Language:	BASIC
Program:	**MAX**
Purpose:	Demonstrate maximization of a non-linear equation
Language:	BASIC

Given a non-linear function, y = f(x), how do we find the value of x that makes y equal to zero? The value that makes y equal one? What value of x gives the maximum possible value of the function? Answers to these and related questions are the subject of this chapter. BASIC's DEF FN statement makes it easy to define an algebraic formula as a function, f(x). For example, suppose we wish to explore the function

$$y = 17-(x-12)^2$$

We write this in BASIC as

```
DEFDBL Y,X
DEF FNY(X)=17-(X-12)^12
```

Of course, this particular function could be coded in assembly language in only a few minutes. A really complicated function might take some time. Worse, every time we need to work with a new function, we would need to write a new assembly language routine. Non-linear programs call for use of a high-level language. We use BASIC due to its widespread availability for personal computers.

In this chapter we discuss:

- Numerical differentiation
- Numerical integration
- Solving a non-linear equation
- Non-linear optimization

For many readers, the most interesting topic may be "solving a non-linear equation." As the first sections of the chapter provide useful background material for solving non-linear equations, you should probably work through these sections as well.

For a concrete focus of the discussion which follows, look now at the chart of the function y = f(x). Figure 11.1 shows the plot of our sample function.

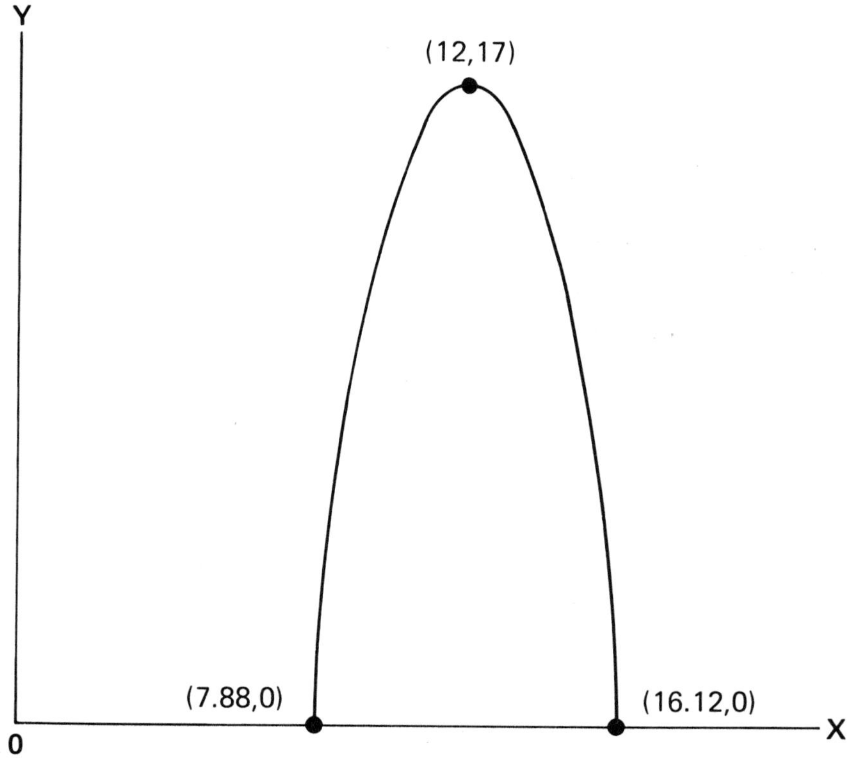

Figure 11.1. Graph of function $y = 17 - (x - 12)^2$.

This particular function equals zero at $x = 7.88$ and $x = 16.12$. It reaches its maximum value, 17.0, at $x = 12$.

Numerical Differentiation

The *derivative* of a function is the slope of the function at a particular point. To find the derivative graphically, draw a line tangent to the function at the point of interest and measure the ratio of the change in the vertical distance in the horizontal distance, as in Figure 11.2.

The computer can't very well draw such a line (at least, not unless it knows the slope). Since the computer can easily evaluate the function, we approximate the tangent line by picking another point close to the point of interest and having the computer effectively "draw" a line to connect these two points. Figure 11.3 shows an "enlargement" of a small part of the function with just such a line.

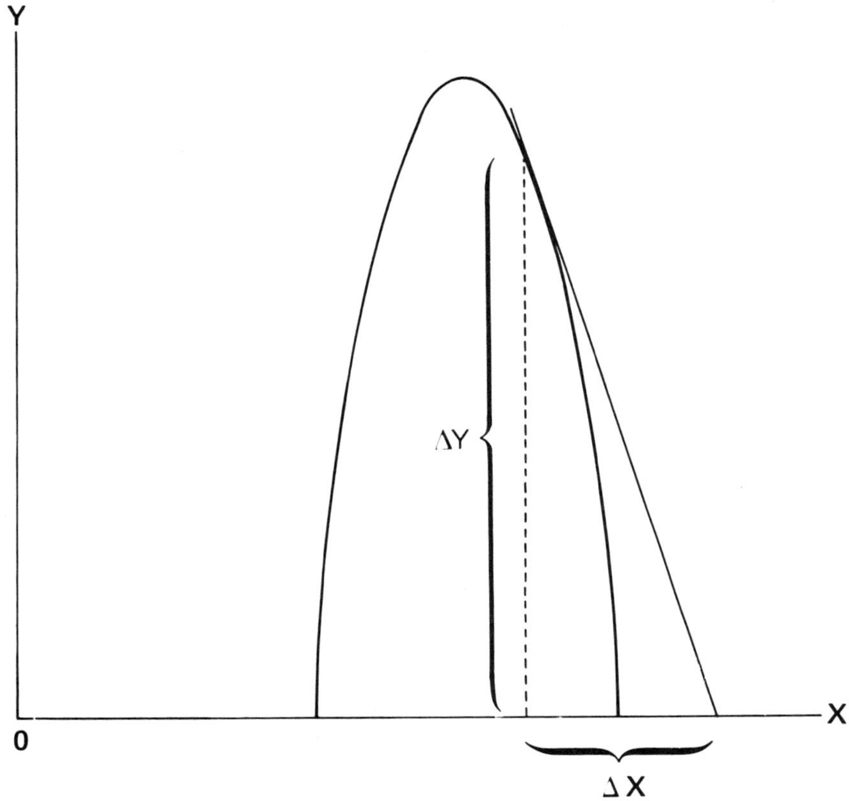

Figure 11.2. Tangent line.

The ratio of the vertical to the horizontal change is *approximately* the derivative of the function. If we pick the second point quite close to the first point, then the approximation will be quite accurate. How close do we need to be to assure some desired level of accuracy? The usual procedure is to evaluate the derivative once and then re-evaluate it with a closer second point. If the two answers lie within a distance "epsilon" of each other (that is, if they are no more than epsilon apart), then the answers are probably within epsilon of the true answer as well.

The following BASIC program evaluates the derivative of the function FNY at the point X0, assuming we require an answer accurate to within plus or minus EPS.

```
REM PROGRAM DIFFER
DEFDBL Y,X,F,E,D
DEF FNY(X)=17-(X-12)^2
REM SET X0 EPS ITLIM
```

```
XO=16
EPS=.001
ITLIM=100
DELTA=.01*XO
FXO=FNY(XO)
DIFOLD=(FNY(XO+DELTA)-FXO)/DELTA
IT=1
REM LOOP UNTIL CONVERGENCE OR ITERATION LIMIT REACHED
100  DELTA=DELTA/2
DIF=(FNY(XO+DELTA)-FXO)/DELTA
IF ABS(DIF-DIFOLD) < EPS THEN 200
IT=IT+1
IF IT>ITLIM THEN 300
DIFOLD=DIF
GO TO 100
200 REM CONVERGENCE ACHIEVED
PRINT "DERIVATIVE AT ";XO;" IS ";DIF
PRINT " AFTER ";IT;" ITERATIONS"
STOP
300 REM NO CONVERGENCE
PRINT "FAILED TO CONVERGE AFTER ";ITLIM;" ITERATIONS
PRINT "APPROXIMATE DERIVATE AT ";XO;" IS ";DIF
STOP
```

Always take the accuracy of this sort of numerical approximation with a grain of salt. It can happen that two successive approximations are close to one another without being equally close to the correct answer. Round-off error can also give results a false appearance of accuracy. The arithmetic operation at which computers are the least accurate is subtracting two numbers that are nearly equal in value, as in FNY(X0 + DELTA) − FNY(X0), for example.

By the way, you should always include an "iteration limit" in a program that otherwise relies on a mathematical condition to stop. Computer arithmetic is imperfect. With sufficient bad luck ("sufficient bad luck" means "sooner or later for sure"), your program will end up in an endless loop, if it doesn't have a guaranteed stopping mechanism.

The execution time for a non-linear program is roughly proportional to the number of function evaluations. That's why we evaluated FNY(X0) early in the program and saved the answer.

Numerical Integration

Integration is the inverse function of differentiation. Integration tells us the area under a curve between two points. The area under our sample function, from XLOWER to XUPPER, is shown in Figure 11.4.

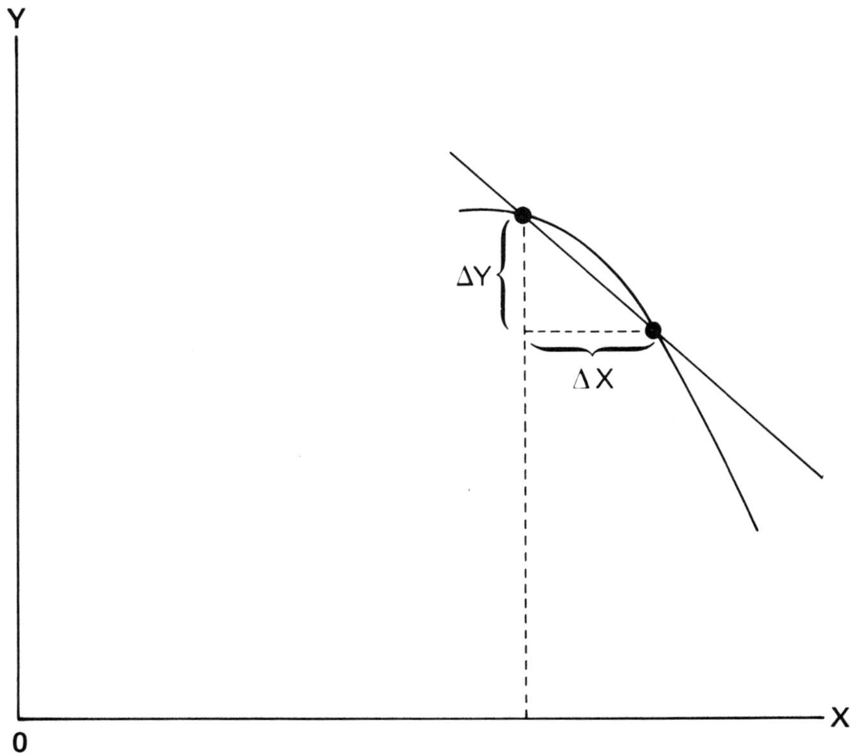

Figure 11.3. Enlarged view of tangent line.

We can approximate the area under the curve by drawing in rectangles as in Figure 11.5. The total area in all the rectangles is approximately the area under the curve. The more, and smaller, the rectangles we draw, the closer we come to the answer.

If we draw n rectangles, we make the width of each one one-nth of the distance between XLOWER and XUPPER. Since the area is just the height times the width, and since each of the n rectangles has the same width one-nth, we can find the area by just adding up the heights and multiplying the sum by the XUPPER-XLOWER. To obtain a more accurate answer, we cut each old rectangle in half and add new rectangles as in 11.6.

The following BASIC program integrates the function FNY.

```
REM PROGRAM INTEGRATE
DEFDBL Y,X,F,E,D,A
DEF FNY(X)=17-(X-12)^2
REM SET XLOWER XUPPER EPS ITLIM
XLOWER=9
XUPPER=13
```

```
EPS=.001
ITLIM=13
REM ADDING 1 TO ITLIM DOUBLES PROGRAM RUNNING TIME
XWIDTH=(XUPPER-XLOWER)/2
FSUM=FNY(XLOWER)+FNY(XUPPER)
AREAOLD=FSUM*(XUPPER-XLOWER)
IT=1
N=2
REM LOOP UNTIL CONVERGENCE OR ITERATION LIMIT REACHED
100 XWIDTH=XWIDTH/2
N=N*2
FSUM=0
  FOR I=1 TO N STEP 2
  X=XLOWER+XWIDTH*I
  FSUM=FSUM+FNY(X)
  NEXT I
AREA=FSUM*XWIDTH+(AREAOLD/2)
IF ABS(AREA-AREAOLD) < EPS THEN 200
IT=IT+1
IF IT>ITLIM THEN 300
AREAOLD=AREA
GOTO 100
200 REM CONVERGENCE ACHIEVED
PRINT "INTEGRAL FROM ";XLOWER;" TO";XUPPER;" IS ";AREA
PRINT " AFTER ";IT;" ITERATIONS"
STOP
300 REM NO CONVERGENCE
PRINT "FAILED TO CONVERGE AFTER ";ITLIM;" ITERATIONS
PRINT "APPROXIMATE INTEGRAL IS ";AREA
STOP
```

Notice that increasing the number of iterations by one doubles the running time of the program. By the way, after 13 iterations, INTEGRAT hasn't quite converged, reporting an area of 58.6715. (The mathematically correct answer is $58\frac{2}{3}$.)

Of course, one can usually use calculus in place of numerical computation. The formula for the derivative of our sample function is $24-2x$. The formula for the integral is $17x-(1/3)(x-12)^3$.

Derivatives can be found by applying the rules of calculus mechanically, so sometimes packaged programs actually figure out the formula for the derivative instead of using numerical methods. Integrals cannot be found by purely mechanical rules.

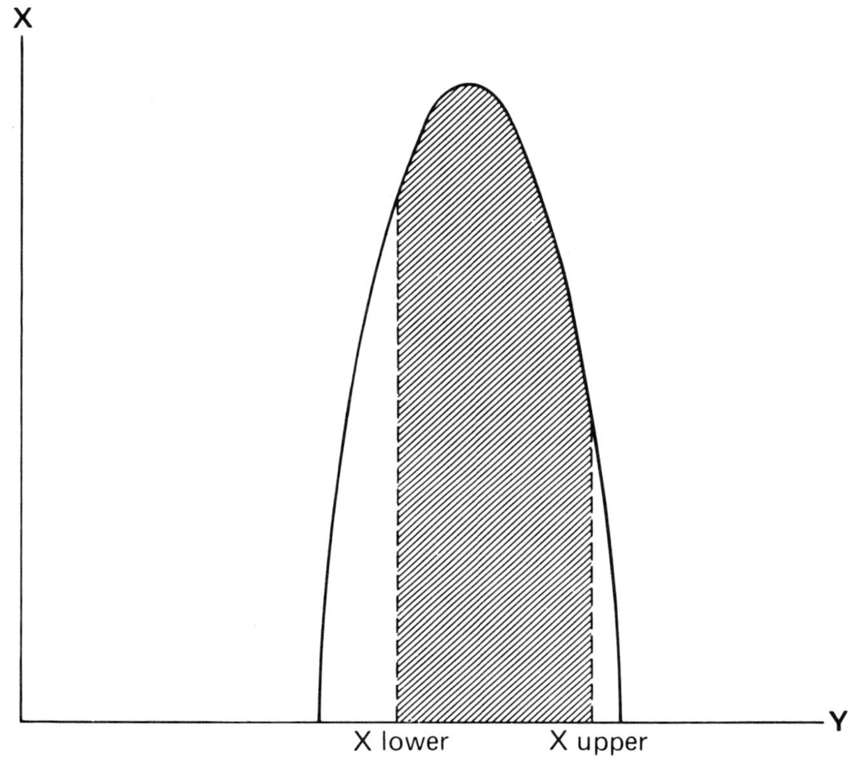

Figure 11.4. Area under function $y=17-(x-12)^2$.

Solving a Non-linear Equation

Suppose we have a function y= f(x) and know that the value of y is Y0. How can we find the value of x that produced Y0? Suppose that Y0=0 and look back at Figure 11.2. Start at the point (f(X0),X0). If the function f(x) was actually a straight line, we could just run our finger down the tangent line until we hit the x axis at (0,X1). Since f(x) is not a straight line, when we hit the x-axis we actually get (f(X1),X1) instead. Now draw a tangent line from the new point and try again.

If the function f(x) is sufficiently smooth, this "shooting method" will usually converge to the correct point fairly quickly. However, sometimes after we shoot down the tangent, we are even further from the correct answer than we were originally. We'll add another rule to the procedure to prevent this. If

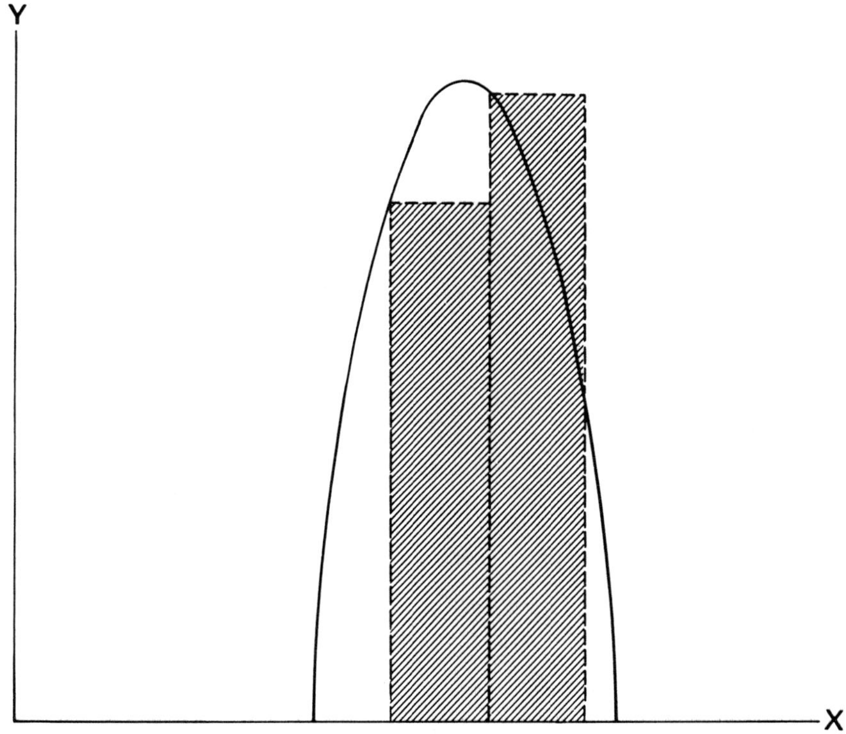

Figure 11.5. Approximation to area under function.

our new guess is even further from the right spot then the initial guess, we cut in half the size of the step we took and try again. The BASIC program below implements this modified shooting method.

```
REM PROGRAM ZERO
DEFDBL Y,X,F,E,D
DEF FNY(X)=17-(X-12)^2
DEF FNDIF(X)=(FNY((1+DEL)*X)-FNY(X))/(DEL*X)
REM SET YTARGET EPS DEL X0 ITLIM
YTARGET=0
DEL=.001
EPS=.01
X0=14
X=X0
ITLIM=20
STEPLIM=5
Y=FNY(X)
IT=1
```

```
100 ISTEP=0
STEPSIZE=1
200 XNEW=X+STEPSIZE*((YTARGET-Y)/FNDIF(X))
YNEW=FNY(XNEW)
IF ABS(YNEW-YTARGET)<EPS THEN 500
IF ABS(YNEW-YTARGET)>ABS(Y-YTARGET) THEN 400
Y=YNEW
X=XNEW
300 IT=IT+1
IF IT>ITLIM THEN 600
GOTO 100
400 REM reduce step size
ISTEP=ISTEP+1
IF ISTEP>STEPLIM THEN 300
STEPSIZE=STEPSIZE/2
GOTO 200
500 PRINT "SOLUTION IS ";XNEW;" AFTER ";IT;" ITERATIONS"
STOP
600 PRINT "FAILED TO CONVERGE AFTER ";ITLIM;" ITERATIONS"
PRINT "APPROXIMATE ANSWER ";XNEW
STOP
```

For the sample function, there are actually two correct answers for some values of YTARGET. This program only finds one, usually the closest to the initial starting point X0. In order to check for more than one solution, the program can be rerun with several different initial values.

Notice that the program uses DEF FNDIF to approximate the derivative. To increase the accuracy of the final solution, DEL should generally be reduced along with EPS. FNDIF could be redefined to give the exact derivative by using calculus. This would speed up the program a little by reducing the number of function evaluations and possibly also because of the greater accuracy of an exact derivative. On the other hand, figuring out analytic derivatives is more work for the user.

Non-linear Optimization

Suppose that y in our sample function described the profits of a small programming business as a function of the number of hours, x, spent typing on the keyboard of a personal computer. We would like to *maximize* this function, that is, find the value of x that gives us the highest possible value of y.

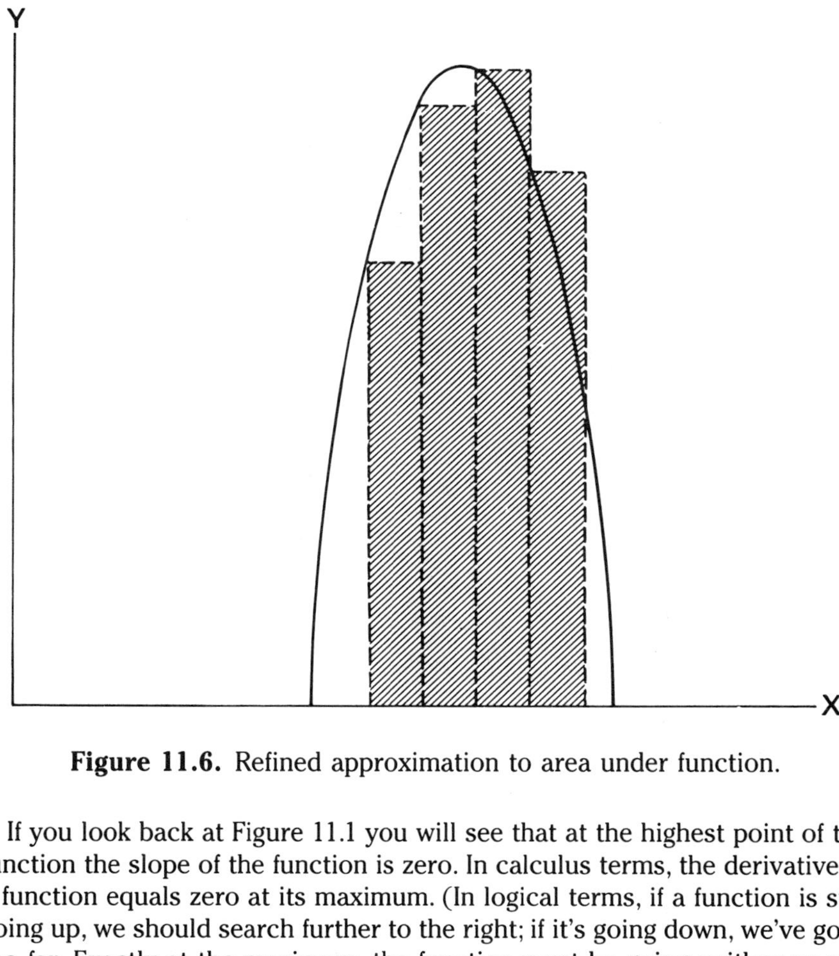

Figure 11.6. Refined approximation to area under function.

If you look back at Figure 11.1 you will see that at the highest point of the function the slope of the function is zero. In calculus terms, the derivative of a function equals zero at its maximum. (In logical terms, if a function is still going up, we should search further to the right; if it's going down, we've gone too far. Exactly at the maximum, the function must be going neither up nor down. Its slope must be zero.)

Finding the maximum of a function f(x) reduces to finding the point where the derivative of f(x) equals zero. The previous program will handle this quite nicely if we redefine the function calls to look at the derivative instead of the original function and the calls on the function for the derivative to look at the derivative of the derivative.

```
REM PROGRAM MAX
DEFDBL Y,X,F,E,D
DEF FNY(X)=17-(X-12)^2
DEF FNDIF(X)=(FNY((1+DEL)*X)-FNY(X))/(DEL*X)
```

```
DEF FNDDIF(X)=(FNDIF((1+DEL)*X)-FNDIF(X))/(DEL*X)
REM SET YTARGET EPS DEL X0 ITLIM
YTARGET=0
DEL=.001
EPS=.001
X0=14
X=X0
ITLIM=20
STEPLIM=5
Y=FNDIF(X)
IT=1
100 ISTEP=0
STEPSIZE=1
XNEW=X+STEPSIZE*((YTARGET-Y)/FNDDIF(X))
200 YNEW=FNDIF(XNEW)
IF ABS(YNEW-YTARGET)<EPS THEN 500
IF ABS(YNEW-YTARGET)>ABS(Y-YTARGET) THEN 400
Y=YNEW
X=XNEW
300 IT=IT+1
IF IT>ITLIM THEN 700
GOTO 100
400 REM reduce step size
ISTEP=ISTEP+1
IF ISTEP>STEPLIM THEN 300
STEPSIZE=STEPSIZE/2
GOTO 200
500 FM=FNY(XNEW)
IF FM>=FNY((1+DEL)*XNEW) AND FM>=FNY((1-DEL)*XNEW) THEN 600
PRINT "CAN'T FIND MAXIMUM"
PRINT "STOPPED AT ";XNEW; "AFTER ";IT;" ITERATIONS
STOP
600 PRINT "MAXIMUM IS AT ";XNEW;" AFTER ";IT;" ITERATIONS
PRINT "VALUE AT THE MAXIMUM IS ";FNY(XNEW)
STOP
700 PRINT "FAILED TO CONVERGE AFTER ";ITLIM;" ITERATIONS"
PRINT "APPROXIMATE ANSWER ";XNEW
STOP
```

Our BASIC program will find that the maximum, $y=17$, is found at $X= 12$. Just as a non-linear function can have exactly one solution, no solution, or many solutions, in the same way a function can have one maximum, no maximum, or many maxima. The code at line 500 checks for the possibility that the program located a point where the derivative equals zero, but which is not a maximum. Such a point might be a minimum or an "inflection point." Even with this check, care on the part of the user is still a good idea. The program has no way to check whether it has found only a "local maximum," that is, whether there might be a point elsewhere that has an even higher value than the point found by the program.

By the way, this program can also be used to find a minimum, by redefining the objective function, since minimizing F(x) is the same as maximizing −F(x).

Back to Linearity

In the next chapter, we build a small statistical analysis system and, in so doing, return to linear problems and to the use of assembly language modules.

12

Statistical Analysis and Program Canning

This chapter has two principle objectives: gaining an understanding of some of the basic techniques of programming for statistical analysis, and working through an example of how to make a "canned" program. This chapter will give you:

- Some basic methods for statistical analysis.
- Some practice in going from mathematical ideas to working programs.
- An adaptable "canned" program (which you can modify if you wish to add your own procedures).
- A complete, working multiple regression package.

The Cookbook—Chapter 12

Program:	**8087 Statistical Analysis Program**
Purpose:	"Canned" program for multiple regression and other statistical analysis.
Input:	Interactive.
Output:	Interactive.
Language:	BASIC with 8087/8088 assembly language modules.

Statistical Analysis

Three of the basic procedures used in statistical analysis are descriptive statistics, correlation, and multiple regression. These methods are used to summarize data, to examine the relation between different events, and to make tests of scientific hypotheses. We discuss the use of these methods, and how to perform the necessary calculations, below.

One caveat first. The combination of sophisticated statistical methods and high-speed computers has made it possible to draw incorrect conclusions far more easily than at any time in the past. Almost any statistical procedure can be applied to almost any body of data. Just because we can do so does not mean we should. Various important mathematical caveats and warnings are omitted from the discussion below, since a thorough job would occupy a PhD course. We hope that the reader experienced in statistical analysis will not be offended—and that the reader first encountering statistical analysis will be careful.

Descriptive Statistics

Given repeated observations on an "event," such as the number of cars passing a certain intersection between 8:00 AM and 8:05 AM, we begin a statistical analysis by looking for simple ways to characterize the observed data. Assume we have made n observations. Call a typical datum, "x."

The very first question usually asked is "What was the average value of the data?" Calculating an average is simple. The *mean* of the data is the sum of all the data points divided by the number of observations. The mean of x is often written $\bar{x}$.

$$\bar{x} = \frac{x_1 + x_2 + \ldots + x_n}{n}$$

Next we would like to determine whether the observed data all lie close to one another or whether they are spread out over a wide range. The most common measurement is called the *variance.* Variance is a measure of the dispersion of data around its mean. Essentially, the variance is the average of the squared value of the difference between x and the mean of x. The variance can be calculated by subtracting the mean off of each datum, squaring this difference, summing the results, and dividing by $n-1$. (It turns out that, under reasonable assumptions, dividing by $n-1$ rather than n gives a more accurate average answer.)

$$var(x) = \frac{(x_1 - \bar{x})^2 + (x_2 - \bar{x})^2 + \ldots (x_n - \bar{x})^2}{(n-1)}$$

Closely related to the variance is the *standard deviation.* The standard deviation is the square root of the variance. The standard deviation is frequently a more convenient measure than the variance because it has the same units of measurement as the original data. If you multiply every piece of data by, say, 16, you also multiply the mean and the standard deviation by 16, while the variance is multiplied by 256. Thus if the original data is measured in pounds, then both mean and standard deviation are measured in pounds (and 16 times either is measured in ounces), while the variance is measured in the less familiar units of "pounds-squared."

The following rule gives a feeling for the "spread" of your data: If the data is drawn from a Normal ("bell curve") distribution, then about two-thirds of the data should lie in the range from one standard deviation below the mean to one standard deviation above the mean.

While these three descriptive statistics are probably the most common, there are many others you might also look at. What are the highest and lowest values of the data? What's the middle value? Does the data cluster around certain values? We'll stop at three: mean, variance, and standard deviation.

Correlation

Given two sets of data, x and y, we are frequently interested in whether the two sets of data tend to move together, to move in opposite directions, or whether the two appear to be unassociated. Statisticians use the *correlation coefficient* as a measure of association between two variables. Two variables that are exactly proportional to one another have a correlation coefficient of one. Two variables that are exactly proportional but that move in opposite directions have a correlation coefficient of minus one. A zero correlation coefficient usually indicates that knowing x tells you nothing about y, and vice versa.

The correlation coefficient is constructed as a ratio. The numerator measures how much x and y move together. The denominator measures how much each moves separately. The numerator is calculated as the average of the product of x minus x's mean and y minus y's mean. The numerator is the product of the standard deviations of x and y. (However, in this context we use n rather than $n-1$ in calculating the standard deviations.)

Guess what's back! Our friend from linear algebra—the inner product. (We promised you it was good for more than playing with systems of linear equations.) Think about calculating the numerator of the correlation coefficient. We begin the calculation by preparing two vectors, the first made up of each observation of x minus x's mean and the second made up similarly from y. The inner product of these vectors is the sum of the product of the elements. So the required average is just the inner product divided by n.

Actually, the same calculation can be done in a more simple form by avoiding the construction of the two vectors of deviations from the means. A little algebra will show that the required average can also be calculated as the inner product of x and y divided by n, minus n times the quantity the mean of x times the mean of y.

A little exercise for the reader: what's the correlation coefficient between x and y if the observations of x are all the same? The answer is that it doesn't make much sense to ask whether x and y move together if x doesn't move at all. Both the numerator and denominator of the correlation coefficient equal zero. We'll want to watch for this situation when programming in order to avoid "Division by zero" error messages.

Multiple Regression

Multiple regression must be far and away the most common statistical technique for equation estimation and forecasting. Suppose we have a sequence of observations on a variable to be explained, the *dependent* variable, y, and observations made at the same time on several explanatory, or *independent,* variables, x_1, x_2 and so forth. We might look for a linear relationship between the dependent and independent variables of the form:

$$y = b_0 + b_1x_1 + b_2x_2 + \ldots + b_kx_k + u$$

where u is an unobservable *error term,* indicative of the fact that x variables will not explain y perfectly. Regression may be interpreted in two ways: as either a statistical procedure or as a technique for fitting an equation to data.

The term "multiple regression" arises out of the statistical interpretation. We might posit that the equation above is a "true" equation in nature and that while we have observed a set of y's and x's, we have been unable to observe the u's. Given a certain set of statistical assumptions, multiple regression produces optimal estimates of the coefficients b_0 through b_k in the above equation. (The assumptions are fairly reasonable, but require more mathematics than we want to go into here.)

Further, given these statistical assumptions, we can test hypotheses about the coefficients. The coefficients produced by a multiple regression are estimates of the true values of b. The regression also produces a *standard error* for each estimated coefficient. There is a two out of three chance that the true coefficient lies in a band from one standard error below the estimated coefficient to one standard error above the estimated coefficient. Chances are about 19 out of 20 that the true coefficient lies in a band of plus or minus two standard errors around the estimated coefficient.

Suppose the true coefficient b_i is zero. This is equivalent to saying that the variable x_i has nothing do to with explaining y. If the estimated coefficient is far away from zero, in the sense of being many standard errors away, then it's unlikely that the true coefficient is zero. The ratio of an estimated coefficient to it's standard error is sometimes called the *t-statistic.* If the t-statistic of b_i is greater, in absolute value, than 2, there is only 1 chance in 20 that the variable x_i has nothing to do with explaining the variable y.

(All of the statements above are predicated on what are sometimes called the "Gauss-Markov" assumptions. See any good statistics or econometrics text for a thorough discussion of the role of various mathematical assumptions.)

The mathematics of regression is also known as *ordinary least squares.* We can regard the problem of estimating the coefficients in the preceding equation as a question of fitting the equation to the data, without regard to any statistical assumptions. The difference between the value of y and the value predicted by applying our estimated coefficients to the data x is called a *residual.* Ordinary least squares pick values for the coefficients that minimize the sum of the squared residuals.

In addition to the estimated coefficients, their associated standard errors and t-statistics, a multiple regression results in several auxiliary statistics. The R-squared is a "goodness of fit measure." The R-squared is the percentage of variation of y explained by the variables x. R-squared equals 1.0 for a perfect fit and 0.0 in the absence of any fit.

The standard error of the regression estimates the standard deviation of the error terms, u. The sum of squared residuals—which is just what it sounds like—is used in making various statistical tests.

We wrote b_0 above without any associated x variable. A constant term b_0 is equivalent to the coefficient on an x variable made up of all ones, which is how we calculate it in the program below. A regression should almost always have a constant term in it, but our program lets the user decide whether or not to include one.

Regression Formulas

Computation of a multiple regression is easily specified in matrix notation. Let y be a vector containing the values of y and X be a matrix where each column i is the values for x_i. If b is the vector of estimated coefficients then:

$$b = (X'X)^{-1}X'y$$

Remember from Chapter 8 that X' means the transpose of X.

Let SSR stand for the sum of squared residuals, s^2 for the square of the standard error of the regression, and R^2 for R squared. If there are n data points and k right-hand side variables (the constant counts as one of the k), we have

$$SSR = y'y - y'Xb$$
$$s^2 = SSR/(n-k)$$
$$R^2 = 1 - SSR/(y'y)$$

Algorithms for Computing Least Squares

You can see that the formula to compute the least squares coefficients simply requires a few matrix multiplications and one matrix inversion. It turns out that least squares is one of those problems in which the mathematical solution is straightforward, but accurate numerical computation is often difficult. We use the routines from Chapters 8 and 9 to do all the hard work, in particular INV to take care of the matrix inversion. These procedures are completely satisfactory in most cases. However, there are algorithms, specifically tailored to calculating least squares coefficients, which are sometimes far more accurate than and equally efficient as the general purpose routines we use. Discussion of these algorithms would carry us too far afield from the use of the 8087, but the references given in Chapter 9 will point you in the right direction. Chapter 5 of Stewart's *Introduction to Matrix Computations* is especially recommended. Be warned, the material is fairly advanced.

Canned Programs

If you flip to the end of this chapter, you'll find a complete listing of our "8087 Statistical Analysis Program." You may be struck immediately by the fact that the program is several hundred lines long. The code is lengthy despite the fact that this is a "plain vanilla" program, and despite the fact that all the important mathematics can be specified in only a few lines. (The source code for a commercial, mainframe statistics package would be anywhere from 10,000 to a few hundred thousand lines long.)

Computer scientists use the name "modular programming" to describe the technique of breaking up a large problem into several smaller ones, each of which can be dealt with independently. Our canned program is composed of 19 "modules." The modules are classified according to whether they provide a user service, such as regression; a user utility, such as data entry; or a system service, such as program initialization. Because the program is broken up into small parts in this way, a new service could be added for the user with little or no modification to the existing modules. The modules in the program listing are:

User service:

Descriptive statistics—Module 9

Correlation—Module 10

Multiple Regression—Module 11

User utilities:

Catalog data in memory—Module 3

Display data—Module 4

Enter data—Module 5

Edit data—Module 6

Save data to disk—Module 7

Retrieve data from disk—Module 8

System service:

Menu display and command choice—Module 2

Begin program execution—Module 1

Storage allocation and program initialization—Module 12

Program restart—Module 13

Exit—Module 14

Place variable name in symbol table—Module 15

Form list of names—Module 16

Collect product-moment matrix—Module 17

Error-handling—Module 18

Screen-handling—Module 19

Data Storage

A program can be regarded as a group of procedures acting on a set of data. The program modules can be regarded as communicating with one another through the changes they make in the program's data base. In this case the data base begins with the data observed by the program user. Suppose the user has n observations on each of k different variables. We'll store the data internally in an n by k matrix called X. Observations on variable i are stored as the ith column of matrix X. As it is frequently convenient to have a constant vector, the program will automatically set column zero of X to equal 1.

People think in names, not column numbers. Rather than require the user to number variables, we store the names of the variables, in a string array NAMES$, and let the computer make the connection between the user specified variable name and the numerical index for the appropriate column of X. NAMES$ can be thought of as a very simple symbol table. The first variable in the symbol table, "(CONST)", will always point to the ones in column zero.

Several other variable definitions are also useful. TRUE% and FALSE% are set to −1 and 0 respectively. NUMVAR is the number of variables the user has defined. MAXVAR is the maximum number of variables the system can hold, a number which depends on the available memory. NUMOBS is the number of observations on a variable. (Each variable must have the same number of observations.) A number of modules communicate through the array LISTV, which contains a list of the column numbers corresponding to a user specified list of variables. LISTLEN is the number of elements in LISTV. Finally, we adopt the convention that all BASIC variables beginning with a letter between I and N will be integer variables. All other variables are single precision unless a "%" "#", or "$" is appended to indicate integer, double precision, or string, respectively.

Module By Module

We undertake here a detailed, module-by-module explanation of the statistical analysis program. (Since each module is short, this isn't too difficult.) Along the way, we point out some places where the program could be made more flexible or more "idiot-proof," albeit at the expense of a lot more code. If you read through the code and the explanations here, you should find it easy to make your own additions or changes to the program.

We'll "walk through" the program modules in the order which makes it easiest to understand, rather than the order in which they appear in the code.

Menu Display—Module 2—Line 2000

This module displays the available commands and asks for the user's choice. The response must be an integer between 1 and 11. Given any other response, the program prompts for a new answer. Notice the simple trick to check whether a number is an integer. The program accepts any characters as ANSWER$. The VAL function sets ANSWER to zero if the response is not a number. We then set ANSW% = ANSWER. Since ANSW% must be an integer, the two will only be equal if ANSWER was an integer.

Once ANSW% is in hand, the routine does an ON ANSW% GOSUB to the appropriate module. After the program returns, the menu display module starts all over again. To add another command to the program, we need only add a PRINT line to the menu display, add a line number to the GOSUB list, and change the valid answer range from 1 through 11 to 1 through 12.

Catalog Data in Memory—Module 3—Line 3000

This module allows the user to catalog the system's internal data base. The module first prints out the number of observations per variable, the number of variables already defined, and the number remaining still open for definition.

After displaying the catalog, module 3 calls module 19, which asks the user to hit a key to return to the command menu. If the program didn't do this, the display would vanish from the screen without giving the user time to think.

Display Data—Module 4—Line 4000

This module displays the data in one or more user selected variables. Module 16 is called to collect the variable names from the user. Module 16 expects certain information. MAXNAMES is the maximum number of names the user is permitted to enter. In this case, the user can enter as many as have been defined. NEWNAMES = FALSE% tells module 16 not to enter the names in the symbol table. FORCE0% = FALSE% tells module 16 that it should not automatically include "(CONST)" in the list. On return from module 16, LISTV(0) through LISTV(LISTLEN − 1) has the column numbers of the matrix X holding the desired data. (If NAMEERR is true, then module 16 found an error it couldn't handle.)

The data display module prints up to five variables to a line, up to 20 lines to a screen. It then pauses (using module 19) to let the user look at the data. The program could be fancier here in several ways. We might want to display the data differently according to whether the screen displays 40 or 80 columns across. We might also want to allow the user to direct output to the printer rather than the screen. Finally, we could pretty up the display by using more graphics.

Enter Data—Module 5—Line 5000

This module allows the user to enter the data for a single variable. We again use module 16, though this time we only allow one name to be specified and we ask module 16 to place the name as a new entry in the symbol table. Once the variable name is entered, the user is prompted for the data sequentially. Notice that there is no way for the user to "get out" of the data entry sequence except to follow it through to the end.

Edit Data—Module 6—Line 6000

Even a "plain vanilla" program must allow the user some way to correct mistakes. First, we use module 16 to ask the user which variable he or she wishes. Once we know the variable, we ask for an observation number. After displaying the current value, the program asks the user to specify a new value. Then the program displays both the new and old value for the user. The program keeps prompting for new observation numbers until the user responds with the ENTER key alone.

Save Data to Disk—Module 7—Line 7000

Serious statistical work is rarely completed in a single sitting. Module 7 allows the user to dump the system's database to disk for later retrieval. (The user also gets some protection against lost time due to power failure in this way.) The disk storage format is chosen for simplicity rather than efficiency. On the first line we dump out MAXVAR, NUMVAR, and NUMOBS. The next NUMVAR lines contain the contents of NAMES$. Finally, we dump the first NUMVAR columns of X. This simple format makes it possible to access the saved data from another program or to use another program to create data which can be read into our Statistical Analysis Program.

What happens if the user specifies a file name that already exists? BASIC will merrily write over an existing file, but it would be better to provide the user with at least some degree of protection against inadvertently wiping out important data. We use the following program trick to provide some protection. Before OPENing the output file, the program tries "NAME FILENAME$ AS FILENAME$". This command gives a BASIC error message "File already exists" if FILENAME$ is on the disk and "File not found" if FILENAME$ is a new file. The error trapping module, 18, checks to see if either of these errors occurred. In case of "File not found," module 18 RESUMEs execution as if nothing had happened. If this is a duplicate file, then module 18 asks the user for confirmation before allowing execution to proceed.

After storing the data on disk, the program closes the file and prints a message to the user before returning to the command menu.

Retrieve Data From Disk—Module 8—Line 8000

The disk retrieval module complements the disk storage module. This module retrieves a data base that had previously been stored on a disk file. The module first OPENs for input the user specified disk file. (The error-handling module swings into operation if a non-existent file is specified, so that the program won't bomb.) Once MAXVAR, NUMVAR, and NUMOBS are known, module 12 is called to reinitialize the program and allocate storage. (A more complicated program might add the contents of the disk file to the existing database rather than reinitializing the program.) Setting the flag DISKFILE% =TRUE% lets module 12 know that it needn't prompt the user for NUMOBS.

Restart Program—Module 13—Line 13000

Restarting the program is easy. Module 13 sets appropriate flags and calls module 12, which does all the work.

Exit Program—Module 14—Line 14000

One can always let the user hit a Ctrl-Break to end a BASIC program, but it's a lot more graceful to provide a specific command. Module 14 checks with the user to be sure an exit is intended, thus preventing accidental loss of valuable information. Use of the END statement also ensures that all files have been closed properly.

Descriptive Statistics—Module 9—Line 9000

Modules 9, 10, and 11 actually do some "productive" work for the user. Module 9 requests a list of variable names, using module 16, and then prints the mean, standard deviation, and variance of each of the listed variables. The 8087 procedure SUM is used to collect the sum of each variable and the 8087 routine INPROD collects the sum of the squared observations for each variable. Using 8087 routines for these procedures is almost as efficient as writing the entire module in assembly language, since these are the only parts of the module whose execution time is proportional to the number of observations.

Correlation—Module 10—Line 10000

The correlation module accepts a list of variable names (via module 16 again) and calculates the correlation coefficient between every pair of names on the list. This requires the sum of X_i times X_j, for each pair, plus the sum of each variable. The easiest, though slightly inefficient, way to get the sum of a variable is to take an inner product with a vector of ones. Module 10 accomplishes this by setting FORCE0% = TRUE% in order to guarantee that "(CONST)" is the first variable in LISTV. Module 17 is called to collect the "product-moment matrix" (the name given to the matrix of inner products of variable i with variable j). Once all the hard work is done in module 17, the correlation module prints out the correlation coefficients, checking as it goes along to avoid a "Division by zero" error.

Multiple Regression—Module 11—Line 11000

The multiple regression module uses module 16 twice, first to get the number of the dependent variable and second to get a list of numbers of the independent variables. The matrix X'y and the sum of y^2 are formed using INPROD. (Note that "X" refers here to only those columns of the database specified by the user in the list of independent variables.) Module 17 is called to form the matrix X'X. Module 17 only fills in the upper triangle of X'X, since the matrix is symmetric. We copy the upper half into the lower half since the matrix inversion subroutine expects to see the entire matrix. The 8087 routine INV is called to invert X'X. REALERR is used to check that the inversion routine only produced normal numbers. Finally GINPROD is used to multiply $(X'X)^{-1}$ by X'y and to form several auxiliary statistics. Results are then printed. As with the correlation module, all the hard number crunching is done by module 17.

Begin Program Execution—Module 1—Line 1000

Module 1 is quite simple. Module 12 is called after flag FIRSTTIME% is set to indicate that this is the first time through the program and flag DISKFILE% is set to indicate that this is not a call from module 8. The latter flag is logically redundant, but keeps the call to module 12 consistent with other parts of the program. By and large, when programming, consistency is worth a little redundancy.

Allocation and Program Initialization—Module 12—Line 12000

The program offers the user the option of loading data from disk. If the user invokes this option, module 8 is called. Note that module 8 calls back to module 12, which is perfectly legal in BASIC, though it is not allowed in many other programming languages. If the user does not choose to load data from disk, the program asks for the number of observations in the data.

Next the module determines how many variables will fit in memory. Since the data is stored in single precision, the data itself will require 4*n*k bytes. Space must also be set aside for the regression and correlation modules, and for LISTV. The amount of storage needed for NAMES$ will vary according to the length of variable names chosen by the user. Our module figures out the amount of free space by using the FRE function. It then figures out the maximum number of variables that will fit in the available space, leaving some spare room as a "fudge factor," and allocates storage.

If this is not the first time through the initialization routine, then module 12 must take one of two actions, depending on whether it is acting as a service routine for module 8. If we are loading data from the disk, then NUMOBS, and so forth, is already known. Module 12 need only erase the old database and dimension storage afresh. If we are not loading data, then the job is almost the same as if this were the first time through the program, except that we can begin directly with asking the user for the number of observations.

Insert Name in Symbol Table—Module 15—Line 15000

Module 15 attempts to place the name in NAMEIS$ in the symbol table and return its symbol table location in NAMELOC. Two possibilities might prevent completion of this task. First, the symbol table might be full, indicating that there is no more room in the database. Second, the name might already be defined. In either of these cases, module 15 prints an error message, sets the flag NAMEERR to TRUE%, and returns. If neither error arises, the module places NAMEIS$ in the first open location in NAMES$, adds one to the variable count in NUMVAR, and returns the proper value in NAMELOC.

Collect Names From User—Module 16—Line 16000

We've called this module from many other modules. Essentially, its job is to collect a series of names from the user and return their symbol table locations in LISTV. Module 16 treats collecting one variable and more than one variable as different cases, mostly so that we can give the user more intelligent prompts.

In the first case, MAXNAMES equals 1. We ask the user for a name, and call module 15 if NEWNAMES is TRUE%. If an undefined name is entered improperly, the user is given the opportunity to re-enter the name or to give a null response. A null response, or an error, causes the module to return with NAMEERR set to TRUE%. When a correct name is given, LISTV(0) is set to the location of the name and module 16 returns with NAMEERR set to FALSE%.

The problem of module 16 is considerably more complicated when a series of names is called for. We could prompt the user for one name at a time. It's friendlier to allow the user to enter a series of names separated by spaces. (As a side issue, the module must set LISTV(0) = 0 if FORCE0% requires us to include the constant term.) We accept a "variable list" from the user in ANSWER$. The module scans ANSWER$ looking for a space. The substring from the beginning of the scan to the space is taken as a variable name. We start scanning for the next name after the space. The scanning process is complete when the end of the string is reached. We check the names one at a time either by running through NAMES$ or by using module 15, depending on the value of NEWNAMES. (Notice that in this way an entire list of variables can be entered into the symbol table at once, even though the program does not use this feature.) If an error is found in processing the list of names, the user is asked to reenter the entire list.

Notice that the error message for an undefined name displays the offending string within quotes. This is more than a nicety. Suppose the user enters variables named "X" and "Y" and later tries to retrieve "X <non-printing character>Y". The string "X'space' " doesn't match the string "X". By placing the string in quotes we increase the chances that the user will notice the presence of a nondisplaying character.

Module 16 could be usefully modified by putting some restrictions on the legal variable names. Since some other modules only print variable names of limited length, we might want to restrict name length at the time of definition. We also might want to modify this module to accept upper and lower case characters without distinguishing between them. Finally, notice that the user might well enter a string that "wraps around" the end of the line, which is perfectly acceptable, or a string that is longer than 255 characters, which will cause an error that is trapped by the error-handling module.

Collect Product-Moment Matrix—Module 17—Line 17000

Almost the entire computational time of the program is spent in this module. The module creates a double precision matrix named XPX#. Element i,j, in the upper triangle of XPX#, is set to the inner product of the ith and jth variables in LISTV. The 8087 routine INPROD really does all the work.

Error-handling—Module 18—Line 18000

Nothing is worse in a canned program, even a simple one like this, than getting a BASIC error message. The whole point of a program being "canned" is that the user needn't understand its innards. Our program doesn't offer quite this level of protection, but it does catch a few possible errors. For example, if the user enters too many characters in response to the name prompt in module 16, we'd like to allow him or her another shot rather than have the program die. In addition, this routine handles a couple of places where we induce deliberate "errors," such as in the specification of file names.

Notice that we are quite careful to check the line number on which the error occurred before handling the error. In this way, we avoid "fixing" an error the program isn't prepared to handle.

Screen-handling—Module 19—Line 19000

Since the computer can display text faster than we can read, it's very convenient to have a way to make the screen stand still. Module 19 accomplishes this by going round in circles until the user hits a key.

A Little More on Programming Strategy

Our "8087 Statistical Analysis Program" is a very heavy number cruncher. Did you notice that of the several hundred lines of code, 8087 routines are referenced only nine times!?! Such a ratio is not in the least unusual for a general purpose program. However, these few references are responsible for almost all the speed and accuracy advantage of using the 8087.

Our Statistical Analysis Program has been rewritten for this edition for QuickBASIC (4.0 or later). Wherever statement labels are needed, we've retained the line numbers from earlier editions. The program can be compiled, linked, and run with the commands:

```
        BC /E /X /O STAT87;
        LINK
    STAT87+SUM+INPROD+GINPROD+REALERR+INV+STACKERR+XINPROD+
    SOLVE+REDUCE+PIVOT;
        STAT87
```

Notice that we do *not* use the /R switch to have QuickBASIC store matrices by rows. It's the normal statistical convention to treat a data variable as a column. By storing matrices by column, we can use routines such as SUM and INPROD to operate on data variables. Ah! (You ask.) How does INV work? Doesn't it require matrices to be stored in rows? Yes, it does—but, the only matrix that needs to be inverted is symmetric, so rows and columns are interchangeable.

```
'  PROGRAM FOR STATISTICAL ANALYSIS
'  THE PRINCIPLE SECTIONS OF THIS PROGRAM BEGIN AT LINES:
'  1000  PROGRAM EXECUTION BEGINS
'  2000  MENU DISPLAY
'  3000  DATA CATALOG
'  4000  DATA DISPLAY
'  5000  DATA INPUT
```

```
'  6000  DATA EDITING
'  7000  SAVE DATA
'  8000  RETRIEVE DATA
'  9000  DESCRIPTIVE STATISTICS
'  10000 CORRELATION
'  11000 MULTIPLE REGRESSION
'  12000 ALLOCATE STORAGE AND INITIALIZE PROGRAM
'  13000 RESTART PROGRAM
'  14000 EXIT PROGRAM
'  15000 INSERT NAME IN SYMBOL TABLE
'  16000 ASK USER FOR LIST OF NAMES
'  17000 COLLECT PRODUCT MOMENT MATRIX
'  18000 HANDLE ERRORS
'  19000 HOLD SCREEN SCROLLING
'
'
DEFINT I-N
DECLARE SUB SUM (SEG X AS SINGLE, SEG N AS INTEGER, SEG DSUM AS DOUBLE)
DECLARE SUB INPROD (SEG X1 AS SINGLE, SEG X2 AS SINGLE, SEG DSUM AS DOUBLE,
            SEG N AS INTEGER)
DECLARE SUB GINPROD (SEG X1 AS ANY, SEG X2 AS ANY,SEG DSUM AS DOUBLE,SEG
            TYPEX1 AS INTEGER,SEG TYPEX2 AS INTEGER,SEG SKIPX1 AS INTEGER,SEG
            SKIPX2 AS INTEGER,SEG N AS INTEGER)
DECLARE SUB REALERR (SEG X AS ANY, SEG TYPEX AS INTEGER,SEG N AS INTEGER,SEG
            IFDEN AS INTEGER,SEG IFINF AS INTEGER,SEG IFNAN AS INTEGER,SEG
            ELEMENT AS INTEGER)
DECLARE SUB INV (SEG X AS ANY,SEG XINV AS ANY,SEG SCRATCH AS SINGLE,SEG INDEX
            AS INTEGER,SEG IER AS INTEGER,SEG TYPEX AS INTEGER, SEG N AS
            INTEGER)
' DECLARE ARRAYS WITH DUMMY DIMENSIONS, THESE ARE REDIMENSIONED BEFORE USE
'$DYNAMIC
DIM XPY#(1), XPXINV#(1,1), BETA#(1), SCRATCH(1), INDEX(1)
DIM XPX#(1,1)
DIM NAMES$(1), X(1,1),LISTV(1)

1000 'PROGRAM EXECUTION BEGINS
FIRSTIME% = -1'FLAG FIRST TIME THROUGH PROGRAM AS TRUE
DISKFILE% = 0'NOT LOADING A DISKFILE
GOSUB 12000

2000 'MENU DISPLAY
CLS
PRINT "COMMANDS OF THE 8087 STATISTICAL ANALYSIS PROGRAM"
PRINT "1   CATALOG DATA IN MEMORY"
PRINT "2   DISPLAY DATA"
PRINT "3   ENTER DATA"
```

```
PRINT "4   EDIT DATA"
PRINT "5   SAVE DATA TO DISK"
PRINT "6   RETRIEVE DATA FROM DISK"
PRINT "7   MEANS, STANDARD DEVIATIONS, AND VARIANCES"
PRINT "8   CORRELATIONS BETWEEN VARIABLES"
PRINT "9   MULTIPLE REGRESSION"
PRINT "10  RESTART PROGRAM"
PRINT "11  EXIT PROGRAM TO BASIC"
PRINT
INPUT "ENTER DESIRED SERVICE (1-11) >"; ANSWER
ANSW% = ANSWER
IF ANSW% = ANSWER AND ANSW% >= 1 AND ANSW% <= 11 THEN 2200
PRINT "RESPONSE REQUIRES AN INTEGER BETWEEN 1 AND 11"
GOSUB 19030: GOTO 2000
2200 ON ANSW% GOSUB 3000, 4000, 5000, 6000, 7000, 8000, 9000, 10000, 11000,
            13000, 14000
' RETURN HERE AFTER PERFORMING SERVICE
GOTO 2000


3000 ' DATA CATALOG
CLS
PRINT "NUMBER OF OBSERVATIONS PER VARIABLE: "; NUMOBS
PRINT "NUMBER OF DEFINED VARIABLES: "; NUMVAR
PRINT "NUMBER OF REMAINING VARIABLES: "; MAXVAR - NUMVAR
PRINT "DEFINED VARIABLES ARE:"
FOR I = 0 TO NUMVAR - 1: PRINT NAMES$(I): NEXT I
GOSUB 19000
RETURN


4000 ' DATA DISPLAY
CLS
PRINT "DATA IN ONE OR MORE VARIABLES MAY BE DISPLAYED"
MAXNAMES = NUMVAR: NEWNAMES = FALSE%: FORCE0% = FALSE
GOSUB 16000: IF NAMEERR THEN RETURN
' VARIABLE NUMBERS ARE IN LISTV 0 THROUGH LISTLEN-1
' PRINT 4 VARIABLES ON A LINE, 20 OBSERVATIONS PER SCREEN
IF LISTLEN = 0 THEN RETURN
FIRSTVAR = 0: LASTVAR = 3: FIRSTOB = 0: LASTOB = 19
4090 IF LASTVAR > LISTLEN - 1 THEN LASTVAR = LISTLEN - 1
4100 IF LASTOB > NUMOBS - 1 THEN LASTOB = NUMOBS - 1
CLS
PRINT "OBSERVATION   ";
  FOR I = FIRSTVAR TO LASTVAR
  PRINT USING "\             \"; NAMES$(LISTV(I));
  NEXT I
PRINT
```

```
FOR I = FIRSTOB TO LASTOB
  PRINT I,
    FOR J = FIRSTVAR TO LASTVAR
    PRINT X(I, LISTV(J)),
    NEXT J
  PRINT
NEXT I
' ONE SCREENFUL IS PRINTED
GOSUB 19030
IF LASTVAR = LISTLEN - 1 AND LASTOB = NUMOBS - 1 THEN
RETURN
IF LASTOB <> NUMOBS - 1 THEN
  FIRSTOB = LASTOB + 1: LASTOB = FIRSTOB + 19: GOTO 4100
ELSE ' NEXT SET OF VARIABLES
  FIRSTVAR = LASTVAR + 1: LASTVAR = FIRSTVAR + 3
  FIRSTOB = 0: LASTOB = 19
  GOTO 4090
END IF


5000 ' ENTER DATA
CLS
PRINT "ENTER NEW VARIABLE NAME"
MAXNAMES = 1: NEWNAMES = TRUE%: FORCE0% = FALSE%
GOSUB 16000: IF NAMEERR THEN RETURN
' VARIABLE IN LISTV(0)
PRINT "ENTER DATA - (<ENTER> ALONE MEANS 0)"
  FOR I = 0 TO NUMOBS - 1
  PRINT NAMES$(LISTV(0)); "("; I; ") >";
  INPUT "", X(I, LISTV(0))
  NEXT I
RETURN


6000 ' EDIT DATA
CLS
PRINT "ENTER NAME OF VARIABLE TO BE EDITED"
MAXNAMES = 1:
NEWNAMES = FALSE%: FORCE0% = FALSE%
GOSUB 16000: IF NAMEERR THEN RETURN
' VARIABLE IN LISTV(0)
LVAR = LISTV(0)
CLS
6090 PRINT "OBSERVATION NUMBER TO BE CHANGED";
INPUT " <ENTER> ALONE RETURNS TO MAIN MENU >"; ANSWER$
IF ANSWER$ = "" THEN RETURN
ANSWER = VAL(ANSWER$): ANSW% = ANSWER
IF ANSWER = ANSW% AND ANSW% >= 0 AND ANSW% < NUMOBS THEN 6160
```

```
PRINT "OBSERVATION MUST BE INTEGER BETWEEN 0 AND "; NUMOBS - 1
GOTO 6090
6160 PRINT NAMES$(LVAR); "( "; ANSWER; ") = "; X(ANSW%, LVAR);
INPUT "NEW VALUE?>", ANSWER
PRINT NAMES$(LVAR); "( "; ANSW%; ") WAS "; X(ANSW%, LVAR);
6190 PRINT " IS NOW "; ANSWER
X(ANSW%, LVAR) = ANSWER
GOTO 6090

7000 ' SAVE DATA ON DISK FILE
' FIRST LINE HAS MAXVAR,NUMVAR,NUMOBS
' THEN THE VARIABLE NAMES IN ORDER
' THEN THE DATA IN EACH VARIABLE IN ORDER
7060 CLS
INPUT "ENTER DISK FILE NAME> ", FILENAME$
7065 NAME FILENAME$ AS FILENAME$
OPEN FILENAME$ FOR OUTPUT AS #1
WRITE #1, MAXVAR, NUMVAR, NUMOBS
FOR I = 0 TO NUMVAR - 1: WRITE #1, NAMES$(I): NEXT I
  FOR I = 0 TO NUMVAR - 1
    FOR J = 0 TO NUMOBS - 1
    WRITE #1, X(J, I)
  NEXT J, I
CLOSE #1
PRINT "DATA FILED IN "; FILENAME$
GOSUB 19000: RETURN

8000 '' RETRIEVE DATA FROM DISK FILE
CLS
8030 INPUT "ENTER DISK FILE NAME> ", FILENAME$
8040 OPEN FILENAME$ FOR INPUT AS #1
INPUT #1, MAXVAR, NUMVAR, NUMOBS
DISKFILE% = TRUE%
GOSUB 12000
FOR I = 0 TO NUMVAR - 1: INPUT #1, NAMES$(I): NEXT I
  FOR I = 0 TO NUMVAR - 1
    FOR J = 0 TO NUMOBS - 1
    INPUT #1, X(J, I)
  NEXT J, I
CLOSE #1
PRINT "DATA RETRI
EVED FROM "; FILENAME$
8170 GOSUB 19000: RETURN

9000 ' PRINT MEANS, STANDARD DEVIATIONS, VARIANCES
CLS
```

```
MAXNAMES = NUMVAR: NEWNAMES = FALSE%: FORCE0% = FALSE%
GOSUB 16000: IF NAMEERR THEN RETURN
' VARIABLE NUMBERS ARE IN LISTV 0 THROUGH LISTLEN-1
PRINT "VARIABLE", " MEAN   ", "STANDARD DEVIATION"; "  VARIANCE"
' COLLECT SUM OF EACH VARIABLE IN DSUM#
' COLLECT SUM-SQUARE OF EACH VARIABLE IN SUMSQ#
 FOR I = 0 TO LISTLEN - 1
 LI = LISTV(I)
 CALL SUM(X(0, LI), NUMOBS, DSUM#)
 CALL INPROD(X(0, LI),
 X(0, LI), SUMSQ#, NUMOBS)
 AVERAGE# = DSUM# / NUMOBS
 VARIANCE# = (SUMSQ# - DSUM# * DSUM# / NUMOBS) / (NUMOBS - 1)
 PRINT NAMES$(LI), CSNG(AVERAGE#), CSNG(SQR(VARIANCE#)),"
           ";CSNG(VARIANCE#)
 NEXT I
 GOSUB 19000
 RETURN

10000 ' PRINT CORRELATIONS
CLS
MAXNAMES = NUMVAR: NEWNAMES = FALSE%: FORCE0% = TRUE%
GOSUB 16000: IF NAMEERR THEN RETURN
' VARIABLE NUMBERS ARE IN LISTV 0 THROUGH LISTLEN-1
CORRERR$ = "\        \ \        \ WHOOPS CONSTANT VARIABLE"
PRINT "VARIABLE-1 VARIABLE-2    CORRELATION COEFFICIENT"
' HAVE PRODUCT-MOMENT MATRIX COLLECTED IN XPX#
GOSUB 17000
  FOR I = 1 TO LISTLEN - 1
  NM1$ = NAMES$(LISTV(I))
    FOR J = I TO LISTLEN - 1
    NM2$ = NAMES$(LISTV(J))
    COV# = NUMOBS * XPX#(I, J) - XPX#(0, I) * XPX#(0, J)
    V1# = NUMOBS * XPX#(I, I) - XPX#(0, I) * XPX#(0, I)
    V2# = NUMOBS * XPX#(J, J) - XPX#(0, J) * XPX#(0, J)
    IF (V1# * V2#) = 0 THEN
     PRINT USING CORRERR$; NM1$, NM2$
    ELSE
     PRINT NM1$, NM2$, COV# / SQR(V1# * V2#)
    END IF
  NEXT J, I
GOSUB 19000
RETURN

11000 ' MULTIPLE REGRESSION SECTION
' FIRST GET DEPENDENT VARIABLE
```

```
' THEN INDEPENDENT VARIABLES
' THEN GO TO WORK
CLS
PRINT "MULTIPLE REGRESSION"
PRINT "ENTER DEPENDENT VARIABLE"
MAXNAMES = 1: NEWNAMES = FALSE%: FORCE0% = FALSE%
GOSUB 16000: IF NAMEERR THEN RETURN
' DEPENDENT VARIABLE IN LISTV(0)
DEPVAR% = LISTV(0)
PRINT "ENTER INDEPENDENT VARIABLES"
MAXNAMES = NUMVAR: NEWNAMES = FALSE%: FORCE0% = FALSE%
GOSUB 16000: IF NAMEERR THEN RETURN
' VARIABLE NUMBERS ARE IN LISTV 0 THROUGH LISTLEN-1
IF LISTLEN >= NUMOBS THEN 11600
' ALLOCATE REGRESSION STORAGE
11180 L1 = LISTLEN - 1
REDIM XPY#(L1), XPXINV#(L1, L1), BETA#(L1), SCRATCH(L1), INDEX(L1)
' NOW DO THE REGRESSION
CALL INPROD(X(0, DEPVAR%), X(0, DEPVAR%), YSQR#, NUMOBS)
CALL SUM(X(0, DEPVAR%), NUMOBS, SUMY#)
  FOR I = 0 TO LISTLEN - 1
  CALL INPROD(X(0, DEPVAR%), X(0, LISTV(I)), XPY#(I), NUMOBS)
  NEXT I
GOSUB 17000 'COLLECT XPX# - UPPER HALF
  FOR I = 0 TO LISTLEN - 1
    FOR J = I + 1 TO LISTLEN - 1
    XPX#(J, I) = XPX#(I, J)
  NEXT J, I
IER = 0: TYPEX% = 8: L2 = LISTLEN * LISTLEN
CALL INV(XPX#(0, 0), XPXINV#(0, 0), SCRATCH(0), INDEX(0), IER, TYPEX%,
            LISTLEN)
IF IER <> 0 THEN 11700
IFDEN = FALSE%: IFINF = FALSE%: IFNAN = FALSE%: ELEMENT% = 0
CALL REALERR(XPXINV#(0, 0), TYPEX%, L2, IFDEN, IFINF, IFNAN, ELEMENT%)
IF (NOT IFDEN) AND (NOT IFINF) AND (NOT IFNAN) THEN 11300
PRINT "WARNING NUMERICAL RESULTS HIGHLY SUSPECT"
11300 ' NOW FORM XPXINV# TIMES XPY#
IONE = 1
  FOR I = 0 TO LISTLEN - 1
  CALL GINPROD(XPXINV#(I, 0), XPY#(0), BETA#(I), TYPEX%, TYPEX%, LISTLEN,
            IONE, LISTLEN)
  NEXT I
' NOW FORM SUM SQUARE RESIDUALS AS Y'Y-BETA'X'Y
CALL GINPROD(BETA#(0), XPY#(0), TEMP#, TYPEX%, TYPEX%, IONE, IONE, LISTLEN)
SSR# = YSQR# - TEMP#
IF YSQR# = 0 THEN
```

```
 PRINT "ZERO LHS VARIABLE???": GOTO 11510
END IF
CLS
S2# = SSR# / (NUMOBS - LISTLEN)
PRINT "VARIABLE", "COEFFICIENT", "S.E.", "T-STATISTIC"
  FOR I = 0 TO LISTLEN - 1
  SE# = SQR(S2# * XPXINV#(I, I))
  IF SE# <> 0 THEN PRINT NAMES$(LISTV(I)), CSNG(BETA#(I)), CSNG(SE#),
            CSNG(BETA#(I) / SE#) ELSE PRINT NAMES$(LISTV(I)), CSNG(BETA#(I)),
            "-", "-"
  NEXT I
PRINT NUMOBS; " OBSERVATIONS "; LISTLEN; " VARIABLES"
PRINT "STANDARD ERROR OF REGRESSION= "; SQR(S2#)
PRINT "SUM SQUARE RESIDUALS= "; SSR#
PRINT "R-SQUARED= "; 1 - SSR# / (YSQR# - SUMY# * SUMY# / NUMOBS)
11510 GOSUB 19000
RETURN
11600 PRINT "MORE OBSERVATIONS THAN DEPENDENT VARIABLES REQUIRED"
GOSUB 19000: RETURN
11700 PRINT "NUMERICALLY SINGULAR MATRIX"
PRINT "EITHER VARIABLE INCLUDED TWICE OR TOO MUCH ";
PRINT "MULTICOLLINEARITY"
GOSUB 19000: RETURN


12000 ' ALLOCATE STORAGE AND INITIALIZE PROGRAM
IF NOT FIRSTIME% THEN 12420
12040 '
ON ERROR GOTO 18000
TRUE% = -1: FALSE% = 0
FIRSTIME% = FALSE%: WASFIRST% = TRUE%
12095 CLS
12100 PRINT "DO YOU WISH TO LOAD DATA FROM A DISK FILE (Y/N)?>";
INPUT "", ANSWER$
IF ANSWER$ = "Y" OR ANSWER$ = "y" THEN
  GOSUB 8000: GOTO 12410
END IF
12130 INPUT "NUMBER OF OBSERVATIONS>"; ANSWER$
IF ANSWER$ = "" THEN RETURN
ANSWER = VAL(ANSWER$)
ANSW% = ANSWER
IF (ANSW% = ANSWER) AND (ANSW% <> 0) THEN 12210
PRINT "POSITIVE INTEGER REQUIRED";
PRINT "<ENTER> RETURNS TO COMMAND MENU"
GOTO 12100
12210 NUMOBS = ANSW%
' FOR K VARIABLES NEED ABOUT
```

```
'   4NK FOR X
'   16K*K FOR XPX,XPXINV
'  AT LEAST 16K FOR NAMES
'  16K FOR XPY AND BETA
' BETTER LEAVE A LITTLE EXTRA FOR SAFETY, SAY
' USE 2000+K(4N+16K+32)
12285 ERASE X, NAMES$
SPACE = FRE(0) - 2000
K = INT(SPACE / NUMOBS / 4): K1 = SQR(SPACE / 16)
IF K > K1 THEN K = K1'FIRST ESTIMATE FOR K
WHILE (4.0 * K * (NUMOBS + 4 * K + 8)) > SPACE
 K = K - 1
WEND
IF ((1.0*K)*NUMOBS)>=(64.0*1024) THEN K=(64.0*1024)/NUMOBS
MAXVAR = K
IF MAXVAR > 1 THEN 12360
PRINT "TOO MANY OBSERVATIONS"
GOTO 12130
12360 ' NOTE THAT BASIC INITIALIZES EVERYTHING TO ZERO
K1 = K - 1: N1 = NUMOBS - 1: NBYK = NUMOBS * MAXVAR
REDIM NAMES$(K1), X(N1, K1),LISTV(K1)
NAMES$(0) = "(CONST)"
FOR I = 0 TO N1: X(I, 0) = 1!: NEXT I
NUMVAR = 1
12410 IF NOT WASFIRST% THEN RETURN
GOTO 2000 'FAKE RETURN, GOSUB WIPED OUT BY CLEAR
12420 ' NOT THE FIRST TIME INITIALIZED
12430 ERASE X, NAMES$
IF NOT DISKFILE% THEN 12095
K1 = MAXVAR - 1: N1 = NUMOBS - 1: NBYK = NUMOBS * MAXVAR
REDIM NAMES$(K1), X(N1, K1),LISTV(K1)
RETURN

13000 ' RESTART PROGRAM
FIRSTIME% = FALSE%: DISKFILE% = FALSE%
GOSUB 12000
RETURN

14000 ' EXIT PROGRAM
INPUT "ARE YOU SURE YOU WANT TO EXIT (Y/N)>"; ANSWER$
IF ANSWER$ = "y" OR ANSWER$ = "Y" THEN END
RETURN

15000 'INSERT NAME IN SYMBOL TABLE
' NAME TO BE INSERTED IS IN NAMEIS$
' IF SYMBOL TABLE IS FULL, PRINT MESSAGE AND SET NAMEERR
```

```
' IF NOT A NEW NAME, PRINT MESSAGE AND SET NAMEERR
' OTHERWISE PUT NAMEIS$ IN NEXT LOCATION IN NAMES$
' REPORT IT'S POSITION IN NAMELOC
IF NUMVAR >= MAXVAR THEN
  PRINT "SYMBOL TABLE FULL!!!! NO NEW VARIABLES"
  NAMEERR = TRUE%: RETURN
END IF
FOUNDIT% = FALSE%
  FOR I = 0 TO NUMVAR - 1
  IF NAMEIS$ = NAMES$(I) THEN FOUNDIT% = TRUE%
  NEXT I
IF FOUNDIT% THEN
  PRINT CHR$(34); NAMEIS$; CHR$(34); " ALREADY DEFINED - NOT A NEW NAME"
  GOSUB 19000
  NAMEERR = TRUE%: RETURN
END IF
NAMELOC = NUMVAR
NUMVAR = NUMVAR + 1
NAMES$(NAMELOC) = NAMEIS$
RETURN


16000 ' COLLECT A LIST OF NAMES AND RETURN LOCATIONS IN LISTV
' A SINGLE NAME IS A SPECIAL CASE
NAMEERR = FALSE%
IF MAXNAMES > 1 THEN 16500
16050 INPUT "VARIABLE NAME IS?>", NAMEIS$
IF NAMEIS$ = "" THEN NAMEERR = TRUE%: RETURN
IF NOT NEWNAMES THEN 16100
GOSUB 15000
IF NAMEERR THEN RETURN ELSE 16180
16100 NAMELOC = -1
  FOR I = 0 TO NUMVAR - 1
  IF NAMES$(I) = NAMEIS$ THEN NAMELOC = I
  NEXT I
IF NAMELOC <> -1 THEN 16180
PRINT CHR$(34); NAMEIS$; CHR$(34); " NOT DEFINED"
PRINT "RE-ENTER NAME OR <ENTER> TO RETURN TO COMMAND MENU"
GOTO 16050
16180 ' PUT NAMELOC IN LISTV
LISTLEN = 1
LISTV(0) = NAMELOC
RETURN
16500 ' COME HERE TO COLLECT A SERIES OF VARIABLES
' IF FORCE0% THEN INCLUDE CONSTANT AUTOMATICALLY
IF NOT FORCE0% THEN LISTLEN = 0 ELSE LISTV(0) = 0: LISTLEN = 1
INPUT "ENTER VARIABLE NAME(S) SEPARATED BY A SPACE>", ANSWER$
```

```
IF ANSWER$ = "" THEN NAMEERR = TRUE%: RETURN
FOR I = LISTLEN TO MAXNAMES - 1: LISTV(I) = 0: NEXT I
LOOKFROM = 1
' RETRIEVE A VARIABLE NAME
16560 SPACELOC% = INSTR(LOOKFROM, ANSWER$, " ")
IF SPACELOC% = 0 THEN SPACELOC% = LEN(ANSWER$) + 1
NAMEIS$ = MID$(ANSWER$, LOOKFROM, SPACELOC% - LOOKFROM)
NAMELOC = -1
IF NAMEIS$ = "" THEN 16730
IF NEWNAMES THEN
  GOSUB 15000: IF NAMEERR THEN RETURN
END IF
  FOR I = 0 TO NUMVAR - 1
  IF NAMES$(I) = NAMEIS$ THEN NAMELOC = I
  NEXT I
IF NAMELOC <> -1 THEN 16700
PRINT CHR$(34); NAMEIS$; CHR$(34); " NOT DEFINED"
16680 PRINT "RE-ENTER LIST OR <ENTER> TO RETURN TO COMMAND MENU"
GOTO 16500
16700 ' PUT NAMELOC IN LISTV
LISTV(LISTLEN) = NAMELOC
LISTLEN = LISTLEN + 1
16730 LOOKFROM = SPACELOC% + 1
IF LOOKFROM > LEN(ANSWER$) THEN RETURN
IF LISTLEN < MAXNAMES THEN 16560
PRINT "TOO MANY NAMES"
GOTO 16680


17000 ' COLLECT PRODUCT MOMENT MATRIX IN UPPER HALF OF XPX#
L1 = LISTLEN - 1: REDIM XPX#(L1, L1)
  FOR I = 0 TO LISTLEN - 1
    FOR J = I TO LISTLEN - 1
    CALL INPROD(X(0, LISTV(I)), X(0, LISTV(J)), XPX#(I, J), NUMOBS)
  NEXT J, I
RETURN


18000 ' HANDLE A FEW ERRORS HERE
' DID WE RUN OUT OF SPACE?
IF ERR <> 7 AND ERR <> 14 THEN 18070
PRINT "PROGRAM RAN OUT OF MEMORY IN LINE "; ERL
PRINT "SORRY..."
STOP
18070 ' DID WE TRY TO READ FROM A NON-EXISTENT FILE?
IF ERR <> 53 OR ERL <> 8040 THEN 18120
IF FILENAME$ = "" THEN RESUME 8170'BACK TO MENU
PRINT "CAN'T FIND "; FILENAME$
```

```
RESUME 8030 'TRY AGAIN
18120 ' IS THIS A NEW OUTPUT FILE?
IF ERR <> 53 OR ERL <> 7065 THEN 18150
RESUME NEXT
18150 IF ERR <> 58 OR ERL <> 7065 THEN 18200
PRINT "FILE ALREADY EXISTS, ARE YOU SURE? (Y/N)";
INPUT "", ANSWER$
IF ANSWER$ = "y" OR ANSWER$ = "Y" THEN RESUME NEXT
RESUME 7060
18200 IF ERR <> 5 OR (ERL <> 12285 AND ERL <> 12430 AND ERL <> 11180 AND ERL
           <> 17020 AND ERL <> 12460 AND ERL <> 12380) THEN 18220
RESUME NEXT 'OK, WE JUST ERASED SOMETHING THAT WASNT THERE
18220 ON ERROR GOTO 0
END

19000 ' HOLD SCREEN
PRINT "HIT ANY KEY TO RETURN TO COMMAND MENU>";
WHILE INKEY$ = ""
WEND
RETURN
19030 PRINT "HIT ANY KEY TO RETURN TO CONTINUE>";
WHILE INKEY$ = ""
WEND
RETURN
```

13

Commercial Data Processing

The name "numeric data processor" naturally leads people to think of the 8087 as a tool for "scientific" rather than "business" applications. While the 8087's forte is certainly working with numbers, it does have important applications in business and commercial EDP (Electronic Data Processing).

The Cookbook—Chapter 13

Program:	**ADDSTR**
Purpose:	Add array of integer-valued strings.
Call:	CALL ADDSTR(A$(0),SUM,IER,N)
Input:	A$—N element string array. N—integer number of elements of A$.
Output:	SUM—single precision scalar; sum of VAL(A$(I)) IER—integer; − 1 if error, 0 otherwise.
Language:	8087/8088 assembly language.

The 8087 is valuable in any application involving numbers. In the last chapter, we built a small statistical package out of the matrix routines of Chapters 8 and 9. Business people normally don't care about technical aspects of matrix inversion! However, mathematical tools such as regression analysis (which use matrix operations internally) are a regular part of the forecasting and planning function in every large company. The 8087 is an important tool for anyone building software for business people to use.

Typical commercial EDP applications (payroll programs and the like) do relatively little numerical computation. Such programs spend more time converting data from an external "ASCII" format to an internal binary format than they spend manipulating the numbers after the conversion. For this reason, commercial programs often avoid conversion costs by operating directly on data stored in decimal, rather than binary, representation. The 8087 supports such operations through its packed decimal instructions.

Almost all commercial data processing applications are written in highlevel languages. Languages such as COBOL and PL/I allow you to operate on decimal data. The BASIC language offered on personal computers rarely provides a decimal data type. In order to show off the 8087's prowess at decimal operations, we've written a small assembly language routine that replaces part of a BASIC program.

Consider the following BASIC program which creates a string array filled with integers and then totals up the values in the strings.

```
DEFINT I-N
REDIM A$(4999)
N=4999
 REM FILL UP A$ WITH INTEGERS
 FOR I=0 TO N:A$(I)=STR$(I):NEXT I
REM TIME THIS PART
T1$=TIME$
SUM=0
 FOR I=0 TO N
 SUM=SUM+VAL(A$(I))
 NEXT I
T2$=TIME$
PRINT N+1,SUM,T1$,T2$
END
```

Most of the work is in the function "VAL" which converts strings to single precision. (If you change the array of strings, A$, to a single precision array, A, you'll see the program's speed nearly triple.) Assembly language subroutine ADDSTR, below, adds up a vector of strings (representing integers) and returns a single precision sum.

```
DEFINT I-N
REDIM A$(4999),ISPACE(4)
N=4999
 REM FILL UP A$ WITH INTEGERS
```

```
 FOR I=0 TO N:A$(I)=STR$(I):NEXT I
REM TIME THIS PART
T1$=TIME$
SUM=0
IER=0
 CALL ADDSTR(A$(0),ISPACE(0),SUM,IER,N),
T2$=TIME$$
PRINT N+1,SUM,T1$,T2$
END
```

ADDSTR processes each string in three steps. First, it finds the string by untangling the string descriptor provided by BASIC. Second, ADDSTR converts the string's ASCII representation to packed decimal while doing some limited error checking. Third, ADDSTR uses the 8087 packed decimal instructions to add up the converted values.

```
INCLUDE   SUBROUT.MAC
          SUBROUTINE ADDSTR,<A,SUM,IER,N>
;    ASSUMPTIONS:  A - N LONG ARRAY OF STRING DESCRIPTORS
;                      (STRINGS THEMSELVES ARE IN DS)
;                  SUM - SINGLE PRECISION ANSWER
;                  IER - INTEGER, 0 ON RETURN FOR NO ERROR
;                                -1 IF ERROR
;                  N - INTEGER NUMBER OF ELEMENTS OF A
;
;                 ELEMENTS OF A ARE ASSUMED TO BE INTEGERS NO
;                   MORE THAN 18 BYTES LONG.
;
;   ADDSTR ADDS UP VALUES IN A$
;
IFNDEF   QBASIC
%OUT     ADDSTR IS DESIGNED TO WORK WITH QUICKBASIC
%OUT     IT REQUIRES "/DQBASIC" ON THE COMMAND LINE
.ERR
ENDIF
;SET ASIDE 10 BYTES ON STACK FOR WORKAREA
          CHKSTCK   10
          PUSHTEMP  AX
          PUSHTEMP  AX
          PUSHTEMP  AX
          PUSHTEMP  AX
          PUSHTEMP  AX,WORKAREA
          MOV       SI,BP
          ADD       SI,WORKAREA          ;SS:SI=ADDR(WORKAREA)
          LES       BX,[BP].IER          ;ES:BX=ADDR(IER)
          MOV       WORD PTR ES:[BX],0  ;ASSUME NO ERROR
```

```
          LES      BX,[BP].N              ;KEEP COUNT OF ARRAY
          MOV      CX,ES:[BX]             ;IN CX AS USUAL
          FLDZ                            ;CLEAR OUT STACK TOP
          CMP      CX,0
          JG       NOTDONE                ;N=0?
          NEARJMP  DONE
NOTDONE:
          LES      BX,[BP].A              ;ES:BX=ADDR(A$(0))
;NOTICE BX KEEPS TRACK OF THE DESCRIPTORS OF THE STRINGS, NOT THE
;          STRINGS THEMSELVES
GET_DESCRIPTOR:

;THE QUICKBASIC DESCRIPTOR HAS THE STRING LENGTH IN ONE WORD
;    FOLLOWED BY THE STRING ADDRESS IN A SECOND WORD


          MOV      AX,WORD PTR ES:[BX] ;AX=STRING LENGTH
;CLEAR OUT WORKSPACE
          MOV      WORD PTR [BP].WORKAREA,0
          MOV      WORD PTR [BP].WORKAREA+2,0
          MOV      WORD PTR [BP].WORKAREA+4,0
          MOV      WORD PTR [BP].WORKAREA+6,0
          MOV      WORD PTR [BP].WORKAREA+8,0
;
          MOV      DI,WORD PTR ES:[BX]+2 ;DS:DI=ADDR(STRING(I))
;CHECK FIRST CHARACTER FOR MINUS SIGN
          MOV      DL,BYTE PTR [DI]       ;DL IS FIRST CHARACTER
          CMP      DL,45                  ;CHECK FOR MINUS
          JNE      NUMBER                 ;SIGN
;IT'S NEGATIVE
          OR       BYTE PTR [BP].WORKAREA+9,80H ;SET SIGN BIT
          DEC      AX                     ;USED UP ONE BYTE


NUMBER:
;  CHECK STRING LENGTH
          CMP      AX,0                   ;NULL STRING NOT
          JLE      ERROR                  ;ALLOWED
          CMP      AX,18
          JG       ERROR

;NOW START AT RIGHT END OF STRING AND WORK BACKWARD
          ADD      DI,AX                  ;DI POINTS TO
          DEC      DI                     ;LAST BYTE OF STRING
          CMP      DL,45                  ;BUT TEST IF WE HAD
          JNE      L1                     ;ALREADY SUBTRACTED
          INC      DI
L1:
```

```
;WE NEED TO REMEMBER WHETHER TO PLACE DIGIT IN
;LEFT OR RIGHT NIBBLE (HALF OF BYTE)
;KEEP FLAG IN DH, 0 MEANS RIGHT 1 MEANS LEFT
          MOV       DH,0
;NOW TRANSLATE EACH CHARACTER
NEXTNUM:
          MOV       DL,BYTE PTR [DI]    ;GET CHARACTER
          CMP       DL,32               ;IS IT A SPACE?
          JNE       NOT_A_SPACE
          MOV       DL,48               ;IF SO, MAKE IT ZERO
NOT_A_SPACE:
          CMP       DL,48               ;<0?
          JL        ERROR
          CMP       DL,57               ;>9?
          JG        ERROR
          SUB       DL,48               ;MAKE 0-9
          CMP       DH,0                ;RIGHT NIBBLE?
          JNE       LEFT
STOWIT:   OR        BYTE PTR SS:[SI],DL ;STORE DECIMAL
          XOR       DH,1                ;SWITCH NIBBLE
          JMP       NEXTCH
LEFT:     SHL       DL,1                ;GET IT TO LEFT
          SHL       DL,1                ;NIBBLE
          SHL       DL,1
          SHL       DL,1
          OR        BYTE PTR SS:[SI],DL ;STORE DECIMAL
          XOR       DH,1                ;SWITCH NIBBLE
          INC       SI                  ;NEXT BYTE
NEXTCH:
          DEC       DI                  ;NEXT CHARACTER
          DEC       AX                  ;DONE YET
          JG        NEXTNUM             ;MORE?

;NOW WORKAREA HAS A NICE PACKED DECIMAL NUMBER IN IT
          MOV       SI,BP               ;POINT TO WORKAREA
          ADD       SI,WORKAREA         ;AGAIN
          FBLD      SS:[SI]             ;PUSH IT ONTO STACK
          FADDP     ST(1),ST            ;ADD INTO TOTAL
          ADD       BX,4                ;NEXT ARRAY ELEMENT
          LOOP      GOTO_GET_DESCRIPTOR
          JMP       DONE
GOTO_GET_DESCRIPTOR: JMP GET_DESCRIPTOR

ERROR:    LDS       BX,[BP].IER         ;DS:BX=ADDR(IER)
          MOV       WORD PTR [BX],-1    ;ERROR INDICATOR
DONE:     LDS       SI,[BP].SUM         ;DS:SI=ADDR(SUM)
```

```
        FSTP      DWORD PTR [SI]      ;STORE AWAY SUM
        POPTEMP   5
        RETURN    ADDSTR
        END
```

Table 13-1 provides some timing figures with and without ADDSTR.

Routine ADDSTR took over 100 lines of assembly language code to replace three lines of BASIC. In return for the extra work, we got a program that runs and 10 times faster than QuickBASIC. In this example, the speed improvement for a commercial application is the same as we found for scientific applications earlier in the book.

While the 8087 may never become quite so indispensable in commercial work as it is in scientific programming, we can still expect its use to become widespread, especially as 8087-compatible translators for commercial programming languages appear.

Table 13-1. Speed benchmarks for packed decimal instructions (time in seconds).

Program	*Add 2,000 integer strings*
QuickBASIC	3.63
8087 routine	0.33

Postscript

So what has 6 years or so of hardware and software progress brought us? I tend to think of two benchmarks for the progress of numerical computing on personal computing. One comparison is that a program that runs all day and night in interpreted BASIC on an IBM PC takes a minute and a half on a PS/2 model 80 using a modern compiler. A second comparison is that a program that takes all day and night on the PS/2 model 80 would keep a moderate size mainframe busy for most of the working day.

. . . those coprocessors just keep crunching.

Appendix: Instruction Set Reference Data

Table A1-1. Instruction Set Reference Data. Courtesy of Intel Corporation.

FABS

FABS (no operands)
Absolute value

Exceptions: I

Operands	Execution Clocks 8087/287		387	Coding Example
	Typical	Range	Range	
(no operands)	14	10–17	22	FABS

FADD

FADD //source/destination,source
Add real

Exceptions: I, D, O, U, P

Operands	Execution Clocks 8087/287		387	Coding Example
	Typical	Range	Range	
//ST,ST(i)/ST(i),ST	85	70–100	23–31	FADD ST,ST(4)
short-real	105+EA	90–120+EA	24–32	FADD AIR_TEMP [SI]
long-real	110+EA	95–125+EA	29–37	FADD [BX].MEAN

FADDP

FADDP destination,source
Add real and pop

Exceptions: I, D, O, U, P

Operands	Execution Clocks 8087/287		387	Coding Example
	Typical	Range	Range	
ST(i),ST	90	75–105	23–31	FADDP ST(2),ST

FBLD

FBLD source
Packed decimal (BCD) load

Exceptions: I

Operands	Execution Clocks 8087/287		387	Coding Example
	Typical	Range	Range	
packed-decimal	300+EA	290–310+EA	266–275	FBLD YTD_SALES

Table A1-1. Instruction set reference data (continued). Courtesy of Intel Corporation.

FBSTP

FBSTP destination
Packed decimal (BCD) store and pop — **Exceptions:** I

Operands	Execution Clocks 8087/287		387	Coding Example
	Typical	Range	Range	
packed-decimal	530 + EA	520–540 + EA	512–534	FBSTP [BX].FORECAST

FCHS

FCHS (no operands)
Change sign — **Exceptions:** I

Operands	Execution Clocks 8087/287		387	Coding Example
	Typical	Range	Range	
(no operands)	15	10–17	24–25	FCHS

FCLEX/FNCLEX

FCLEX (no operands)
Clear exceptions — **Exceptions:** None

Operands	Execution Clocks 8087/287		387	Coding Example
	Typical	Range	Range	
(no operands)	5	2–8	11	FNCLEX

FCOM

FCOM //source
Compare real — **Exceptions:** I, D

Operands	Execution Clocks 8087/287		387	Coding Example
	Typical	Range	Range	
//ST(i)	45	40–50	24	FCOM ST(1)
short-real	65 + EA	60–70 + EA	26	FCOM [BP].UPPER_LIMIT
long-real	70 + EA	65–76 + EA	31	FCOM WAVELENGTH

FCOMP

FCOMP //source
Compare real and pop — **Exceptions:** I, D

Operands	Execution Clocks 8087/287		387	Coding Example
	Typical	Range	Range	
//ST(i)	47	42–52	26	FCOMP ST(2)
short-real	68 + EA	63–73 + EA	26	FCOMP [BP + 2].N_READINGS
long-real	72 + EA	67–77 + EA	31	FCOMP DENSITY

FCOMPP

FCOMPP (no operands)
Compare real and pop twice — **Exceptions:** I, D

Operands	Execution Clocks 8087/287		387	Coding Example
	Typical	Range	Range	
(no operands)	50	45–55	26	FCOMPP

Table A1-1. Instruction set reference data (continued). Courtesy of Intel Corporation.

FCOS
(387 only)

FCOS (no operands)
Cosine

Exceptions: I, D, U, P

Operands	Execution Clocks 8087/287		387	Coding Example
	Typical	Range	Range	
(no operands)	—	—	123–772	FCOS

FDECSTP

FDECSTP (no operands)
Decrement stack pointer

Exceptions: None

Operands	Execution Clocks 8087/287		387	Coding Example
	Typical	Range	Range	
(no operands)	9	6–12	22	FDECSTP

FDISI/FNDISI

FDISI (no operands)
Disable interrupts

Exceptions: None

Operands	Execution Clocks 8087/287		387	Coding Example
	Typical	Range	Range	
(no operands)	5	2–8	2	FDISI

FDIV

FDIV //source/destination,source
Divide real

Exceptions: I, D, Z, O, U, P

Operands	Execution Clocks 8087/287		387	Coding Example
	Typical	Range	Range	
//ST(i),ST	198	193–203	88	FDIV
short-real	220 + EA	215–225 + EA	89	FDIV DISTANCE
long-real	225 + EA	220–230 + EA	94	FDIV ARC [DI]

FDIVP

FDIVP destination,source
Divide real and pop

Exceptions: I, D, Z, O, U, P

Operands	Execution Clocks 8087/287		387	Coding Example
	Typical	Range	Range	
ST(i),ST	202	197–207	88	FDIVP ST(4),ST

FDIVR

FDIVR //source/destination,source
Divide real reversed

Exceptions: I, D, Z, O. U, P

Operands	Execution Clocks 8087/287		387	Coding Example
	Typical	Range	Range	
//ST,ST(i)/ST(i)ST	199	194–204	89	FDIVR ST(2),ST
short-real	221 + EA	216–266 + EA	90	FDIVR [BX].PULSE_RATE
long-real	226 + EA	221–231 + EA	95	FDIVR RECORDER.FREQUENCY

Table A1-1. Instruction set reference data (continued). Courtesy of Intel Corporation.

FDIVRP	**FDIVRP** destination,source Divide real reversed and pop			**Exceptions:** I, D, Z, O, U, P
Operands	**Execution Clocks 8087/287**		**387**	**Coding Example**
	Typical	**Range**	**Range**	
ST(i),ST	203	198–208	89	FDIVRP ST(1),ST

FENI/FNENI	**FENI** (no operands) Enable interrupts			**Exceptions:** None
Operands	**Execution Clocks 8087/287**		**387**	**Coding Example**
	Typical	**Range**	**Range**	
(no operands)	5	2–8	—	FNENI

FFREE	**FFREE** destination Free register			**Exceptions:** None
Operands	**Execution Clocks 8087/287**		**387**	**Coding Example**
	Typical	**Range**	**Range**	
ST(i)	11	9–16	18	FFREE ST(1)

FIADD	**FIADD** source Integer add			**Exceptions:** I, D, O, P
Operands	**Execution Clocks 8087/287**		**387**	**Coding Example**
	Typical	**Range**	**Range**	
word-integer	120+EA	102–137+EA	71–785	FIADD DISTANCE_TRAVELLED
short-integer	125+EA	108–143+EA	57–72	FIADD PULSE_COUNT [SI]

FICOM	**FICOM** source Integer compare			**Exceptions:** I, D
Operands	**Execution Clocks 8087/287**		**387**	**Coding Example**
	Typical	**Range**	**Range**	
word-integer	80+EA	72–86+EA	71–75	FICOM TOOL.N_PASSES
short-integer	85+EA	78–91+EA	56–63	FICOM [BP+4].PARM_COUNT

FICOMP	**FICOMP** source Integer compare and pop			**Exceptions:** I, D
Operands	**Execution Clocks 8087/287**		**387**	**Coding Example**
	Typical	**Range**	**Range**	
word-integer	82+EA	74–88+EA	71–75	FICOMP [BP].LIMIT [SI]
short-integer	87+EA	80–93+EA	56–63	FICOMP N SAMPLES

Table A1-1. Instruction set reference data (continued). Courtesy of Intel Corporation.

FIDIV

FIDIV source
Integer divide
Exceptions: I, D, Z, O, U, P

Operands	Execution Clocks 8087/287		387	Coding Example
	Typical	Range	Range	
word-integer	230 + EA	224–238 + EA	136–140	FIDIV SURVEY.OBSERVATIONS
short-integer	236 + EA	230–243 + EA	120–127	FIDIV RELATIVE_ANGLE [DI]

FIDIVR

FIDIVR source
Integer divide reversed
Exceptions: I, D, Z, O, U, P

Operands	Execution Clocks 8087/287		387	Coding Example
	Typical	Range	Range	
word-integer	230 + EA	225–239 + EA	135–141	FIDIVR [BP].X_COORD
short-integer	237 + EA	231–245 + EA	121–128	FIDIVR FREQUENCY

FILD

FILD source
Integer load
Exceptions: I

Operands	Execution Clocks 8087/287		387	Coding Example
	Typical	Range	Range	
word-integer	50 + EA	46–54 + EA	61–65	FILD [BX].SEQUENCE
short-integer	56 + EA	52–60 + EA	45–52	FILD STANDOFF [DI]
long-integer	64 + EA	60–68 + EA	56–67	FILD RESPONSE.COUNT

FIMUL

FIMUL source
Integer multiply
Exceptions: I, D, O, P

Operands	Execution Clocks 8087/287		387	Coding Example
	Typical	Range	Range	
word-integer	130 + EA	124–138 + EA	71–83	FIMUL BEARING
short-integer	136 + EA	130–144 + EA	57–82	FIMUL POSITION.Z_AXIS

FINCSTP

FINCSTP (no operands)
Increment stack pointer
Exceptions: None

Operands	Execution Clocks 8087/287		387	Coding Example
	Typical	Range	Range	
(no operands)	9	6–12	21	FINCSTP

FINIT/FININIT

FINIT (no operands)
Initialize processor
Exceptions: None

Operands	Execution Clocks 8087/287		387	Coding Example
	Typical	Range	Range	
(no operands)	5	2–8	33	FINIT

Table A1-1. Instruction set reference data (continued). Courtesy of Intel Corporation.

FIST

FIST destination
Integer store
Exceptions: I, P

Operands	Execution Clocks 8087/287 Typical	Execution Clocks 8087/287 Range	387 Range	Coding Example
word-integer	86 + EA	80–90 + EA	82–95	FIST OBS.COUNT [SI]
short-integer	88 + EA	82–92 + EA	79–93	FIST [BP].FACTORED_PULSES

FISTP

FISTP destination
Integer store and pop
Exceptions: I, P

Operands	Execution Clocks 8087/287 Typical	Execution Clocks 8087/287 Range	387 Range	Coding Example
word-integer	88 + EA	82–92 + EA	82–95	FISTP [BX].ALPHA_COUNT [SI]
short-integer	90 + EA	84–94 + EA	79–93	FISTP CORRECTED_TIME
long-integer	100 + EA	94–105 + EA	80–79	FISTP PANEL.N_READINGS

FISUB

FISUB source
Integer subtract
Exceptions: I, D, O, P

Operands	Execution Clocks 8087/287 Typical	Execution Clocks 8087/287 Range	387 Range	Coding Example
word-integer	120 + EA	102–137 + EA	71–83	FISUB BASE_FREQUENCY
short-integer	125 + EA	108–143 + EA	57–82	FISUB TRAIN_SIZE [DI]

FISUBR

FISUBR source
Integer subtract reversed
Exceptions: I, D, O, P

Operands	Execution Clocks 8087/287 Typical	Execution Clocks 8087/287 Range	387 Range	Coding Example
word-integer	120 + EA	103–139 + EA	72–84	FISUBR FLOOR [BX] [SI]
short-integer	125 + EA	109–144 + EA	58–83	FISUBR BALANCE

FLD

FLD source
Load real
Exceptions: I, D

Operands	Execution Clocks 8087/287 Typical	Execution Clocks 8087/287 Range	387 Range	Coding Example
ST(i)	20	17–22	14	FLD ST(0)
short-real	43 + EA	38–56 + EA	20	FLD READING [SI].PRESSURE
long-real	46 + EA	40–60 + EA	25	FLD [BP].TEMPERATURE
temp-real	57 + EA	53–65 + EA	44	FLD SAVEREADING

Table A1-1. Instruction set reference data (continued). Courtesy of Intel Corporation.

FLDCW	**FLDCW** source Load control word			**Exceptions:** None
Operands	**Execution Clocks 8087/287**		**387**	**Coding Example**
	Typical	**Range**	**Range**	
2-bytes	10 + EA	7–14 + EA	19	FLDCW CONTROL_WORD

FLDENV	**FLDENV** source Load environment			**Exceptions:** None
Operands	**Execution Clocks 8087/287**		**387**	**Coding Example**
	Typical	**Range**	**Range**	
14-bytes	40 + EA	35–45 + EA	71	FLDENV [BP + 6]

FLDLG2	**FLDLG2** (no operands) Load $\log_{10}2$			**Exceptions:** I
Operands	**Execution Clocks 8087/287**		**387**	**Coding Example**
	Typical	**Range**	**Range**	
(no operands)	21	18–24	41	FLDLG2

FLDLN2	**FLDLN2** (no operands) Load $\log_e 2$			**Exceptions:** I
Operands	**Execution Clocks 8087/287**		**387**	**Coding Example**
	Typical	**Range**	**Range**	
(no operands)	20	17–23	41	FLDLN2

FLDL2E	**FLDL2E** (no operands) Load $\log_2 e$			**Exceptions:** I
Operands	**Execution Clocks 8087/287**		**387**	**Coding Example**
	Typical	**Range**	**Range**	
(no operands)	18	15–21	40	FLDL2E

FLDL2T	**FLDL2T** (no operands) Load $\log_2 10$			**Exceptions:** I
Operands	**Execution Clocks 8087/287**		**387**	**Coding Example**
	Typical	**Range**	**Range**	
(no operands)	19	16–22	40	FLDL2T

Table A1-1. Instruction set reference data (continued). Courtesy of Intel Corporation.

FLDPI

FLDPI (no operands)
Load
Exceptions: I

Operands	Execution Clocks 8087/287		387	Coding Example
	Typical	Range	Range	
(no operands)	19	16–22	40	FLDPI

FLDZ

FLDZ (no operands)
Load +0.0
Exceptions: I

Operands	Execution Clocks 8087/287		387	Coding Example
	Typical	Range	Range	
(no operands)	14	11–17	20	FLDZ

FLD1

FLD1 (no operands)
Load +1.0
Exceptions: I

Operands	Execution Clocks 8087/287		387	Coding Example
	Typical	Range	Range	
(no operands)	18	15–21	24	FLD1

FMUL

FMUL //source/destination,source
Multiply real
Exceptions: I, D, O, U, P

Operands	Execution Clocks 8087/287		387	Coding Example
	Typical	Range	Range	
//ST(i),ST/ST.ST(i)	97	90–105	29–57	FMUL ST,ST(3)
//ST(i),ST/ST,ST(i)	138	130–145	29–57	FMUL ST,ST(3)
short-real	118+EA	110–125+EA	27–35	FMUL SPEED_FACTOR
long-real	120+EA	112–126+EA	32–57	FMUL [BP].HEIGHT
long-real	161+EA	154–168+EA	32–57	FMUL [BP].HEIGHT

occurs when one or both operands is "short"—it has 40 trailing zeros in its fraction (e.g., it was loaded from a short-real memory operand).

FMULP

FMULP destination.source
Multiply real and pop
Exceptions: I, D, O, U, P

Operands	Execution Clocks 8087/287		387	Coding Example
	Typical	Range	Range	
ST(i),ST	100	94–108	29–57	FMULP ST(1),ST
ST(i),ST	142	134–148	29–57	FMULP ST(1).ST

occurs when one or both operands is "short"—it has 40 trailing zeros in its fraction (e.g., it was loaded from a short-real memory operand).

Table A1-1. Instruction set reference data (continued). Courtesy of Intel Corporation.

FNOP

FNOP (no operands)
No operation
Exceptions: None

Operands	Execution Clocks 8087/287		387	Coding Example
	Typical	Range	Range	
(no operands)	13	10–16	12	FNOP

FPATAN

FPATAN (no operands)
Partial arctangent
Exceptions: U. P
(operands not checked)

Operands	Execution Clocks 8087/287		387	Coding Example
	Typical	Range	Range	
(no operands)	650	250–800	314–487	FPATAN

FPREM

FPREM (no operands)
Partial remainder
Exceptions: I, D, U

Operands	Execution Clocks 8087/287		387	Coding Example
	Typical	Range	Range	
(no operands)	125	15–190	74–155	FPREM

FPREM1
(387 only)

FPREM1 (no operand)
Partial remainder (IEEE)
Exceptions: I, D, U

Operands	Execution Clocks 8087/287		387	Coding Example
	Typical	Range	Range	
(no operands)	—	—	95–185	FPREM1

FPTAN

FPTAN (no operands)
Partial tangent
Exceptions: I, P
(operands not checked)

Operands	Execution Clocks 8087/287		387	Coding Example
	Typical	Range	Range	
(no operands)	450	30–540	191–497	FPTAN

FRNDINT

FRNDINT (no operands)
Round to integer
Exceptions: I, P

Operands	Execution Clocks 8087/287		387	Coding Example
	Typical	Range	Range	
(no operands)	45	16–50	66–80	FRNDINT

Table A1-1. Instruction set reference data (continued). Courtesy of Intel Corporation.

FRSTOR

FRSTOR source
Restore saved state

Exceptions: None

Operands	Execution Clocks 8087/287		387	Coding Example
	Typical	Range	Range	
94-bytes	210+EA	205–215+EA	308	FRSTOR [BP]

FSAVE/FNSAVE

FSAVE destination
Save state

Exceptions: None

Operands	Execution Clocks 8087/287		387	Coding Example
	Typical	Range	Range	
94-bytes	210+EA	205–215+EA	375–376	FSAVE [BP]

FSCALE

FSCALE (no operands)
Scale

Exceptions: I, O, U

Operands	Execution Clocks 8087/287		387	Coding Example
	Typical	Range	Range	
(no operands)	35	32–38	67–86	FSCALE

FSETPM
(287 only)

FSETPM (no operands)
Set Protected Mode

Exceptions: None

Operands	Execution Clocks 8087/287		387	Coding Example
	Typical	Range	Range	
(no operands)	N/A	2–8	—	FSETPM

FSIN
(387 only)

FSIN (no operands)
Sine

Exceptions: I, D, U, P

Operands	Execution Clocks 8087/287		387	Coding Example
	Typical	Range	Range	
(no operands)	—	—	122–771	FSIN

FSINCOS
(387 only)

FSINCOS (no operands)
Sine and Cosine

Exceptions: I, D, U, P

Operands	Execution Clocks 8087/287		387	Coding Example
	Typical	Range	Range	
(no operands)	—	—	194–809	FSINCOS

Table A1-1. Instruction set reference data (continued). Courtesy of Intel Corporation.

FSQRT	**FSQRT** (no operands) Square root			**Exceptions:** I, D, P
Operands	**Execution Clocks 8087/287**		**387**	**Coding Example**
	Typical	**Range**	**Range**	
(no operands)	183	180–186	122–129	FSQRT

FST	**FST** destination Store real			**Exceptions:** I, O, U, P
Operands	**Execution Clocks 8087/287**		**387**	**Coding Example**
	Typical	**Range**	**Range**	
ST(i)	18	15–22	11	FST ST(3)
short-real	87 + EA	84–90 + EA	44	FST CORRELATION [DI]
long-real	100 + EA	96–104 + EA	45	FST MEAN READING

FSTCW/FNSTCW	**FSTCW** destination Store control word			**Exceptions:** None
Operands	**Execution Clocks 8087/287**		**387**	**Coding Example**
	Typical	**Range**	**Range**	
2-bytes	15 + EA	12–18 + EA	15	FSTCW SAVE_CONTROL

FSTENV/FNSTENV	**FSTENV** destination Store environment			**Exceptions:** None
Operands	**Execution Clocks 8087/287**		**387**	**Coding Example**
	Typical	**Range**	**Range**	
14-bytes	45 + EA	40–50 + EA	103–104	FSTENV [BP]

FSTP	**FSTP** destination Store real and pop			**Exceptions:** I, O, U, P
Operands	**Execution Clocks 8087/287**		**387**	**Coding Example**
	Typical	**Range**	**Range**	
ST(i)	20	17–24	18	FSTP ST(2)
short-real	89 + EA	86–92 + EA	44	FSTP [BX].ADJUSTED RPM
long-real	102 + EA	98–106 + EA	45	FSTP TOTAL_DOSAGE
temp-real	55 + EA	52–58 + EA	53	FSTP REG_SAVE [SI]

FSTSW/FNSTSW	**FSTSW** destination Store status word			**Exceptions:** None
Operands	**Execution Clocks 8087/287**		**387**	**Coding Example**
	Typical	**Range**	**Range**	
2-bytes	15 + EA	12–18 + EA	15	FSTSW SAVE_STATUS

Table A1-1. Instruction set reference data (continued). Courtesy of Intel Corporation.

FSUB — **FSUB** //source/destination,source
Subtract real — **Exceptions:** I, D, O, U, P

Operands	Execution Clocks 8087/287		387	Coding Example
	Typical	Range	Range	
//ST,ST(i)/ST(i),ST	85	70–100	26–34	FSUB ST,ST(2)
short-real	105 + EA	90–120 + EA	24–32	FSUB BASE_VALUE
long-real	110 + EA	95–125 + EA	28–36	FSUB COORDINATE.X

FSUBP — **FSUBP** destination,source
Subtract real and pop — **Exceptions:** I, D, O, U, P

Operands	Execution Clocks 8087/287		387	Coding Example
	Typical	Range	Range	
ST(i),ST	90	75–105	26–34	FSUBP ST(2),ST

FSUBR — **FSUBR** //source/destination,source
Subtract real reversed — **Exceptions:** I, D, O, U, P

Operands	Execution Clocks 8087/287		387	Coding Example
	Typical	Range	Range	
//ST,ST(i)/ST(i),ST	87	70–100	27–35	FSUBR ST,ST(1)
short-real	105 + EA	90–120 + EA	25–33	FSUBR VECTOR[SI]
long-real	110 + EA	95–125 + EA	29–37	FSUBR [BX].INDEX

FSUBRP — **FSUBRP** destination,source
Subtract real reversed and pop — **Exceptions:** I, D, O, U, P

Operands	Execution Clocks 8087/287		387	Coding Example
	Typical	Range	Range	
ST(i),ST	90	75–105	27–34	FSUBRP ST(1),ST

FTST — **FTST** (no operands)
Test stack top against +0.0 — **Exceptions:** I, D

Operands	Execution Clocks 8087/287		387	Coding Example
	Typical	Range	Range	
(no operands)	42	38–48	28	FTST

FUCOM (387 only) — **FUCOM** (no operands)
unordered compare — **Exceptions:** I, D

Operands	Execution Clocks 8087/287		387	Coding Example
	Typical	Range	Range	
(no operands)	—	—	24	FUCOM

Table A1-1. Instruction set reference data (continued). Courtesy of Intel Corporation.

FUCOMP (387 only)

FUCOMP (no operands)
unordered compare and pop

Exceptions: I, D

Operands	Execution Clocks 8087/287		387	Coding Example
	Typical	Range	Range	
(no operands)	—	—	26	FUCOMP

FUCOMPP (387 only)

FUCOMPP (no operands)
unordered compare and pop twice

Exceptions: I, D

Operands	Execution Clocks 8087/287		387	Coding Example
	Typical	Range	Range	
(no operands)	—	—	26	FUCOMPP

FWAIT

FWAIT (no operands)
(CPU) Wait while 8087 is busy

Exceptions: None (CPU instruction)

Operands	Execution Clocks 8087/287		387	Coding Example
	Typical	Range	Range	
(no operands)	3+5*	3+5*	6n*	FWAIT

FXAM

FXAM (no operands)
Examine stack top

Exceptions: None

Operands	Execution Clocks 8087/287		387	Coding Example
	Typical	Range	Range	
(no operands)	17	12–23	30–38	FXAM

FXCH

FXCH //destination
Exchange registers

Exceptions: I

Operands	Execution Clocks 8087/287		387	Coding Example
	Typical	Range	Range	
//ST(i)	12	10–15	18	FXCH ST(2)

FXTRACT

FXTRACT (no operands)
Extract exponent and significand

Exceptions: I

Operands	Execution Clocks 8087/287		387	Coding Example
	Typical	Range	Range	
(no operands)	50	27–55	70–76	FXTRACT

Table A1-1. Instruction set reference data (continued). Courtesy of Intel Corporation.

FYL2X

FYL2X (no operands)
Y Log_2X

Exceptions: P (operands not checked)

Operands	Execution Clocks 8087/287		387	Coding Example
	Typical	Range	Range	
(no operands)	950	900–1100	120–538	FYL2X

FYL2XP1

FYL2XP1 (no operands)
Y $log_2(X+1)$

Exceptions: P (operands not checked)

Operands	Execution Clocks 8087/287		387	Coding Example
	Typical	Range	Range	
(no operands)	850	700–1000	257–547	FYL2XP1

F2XM1

F2XM1 (no operands)
2^x-1

Exceptions: U, P (operands not checked)

Operands	Execution Clocks 8087/287		387	Coding Example
	Typical	Range	Range	
(no operands)	500	310–630	211–476	F2XM1

Notes

1. Add approximately 4 clocks for each bus transfer.
2. Where EA is indicated under "Execution Clocks," between 6 and 14 clocks must be added to allow time for computation of the effective address on 8088/8086/188/186 systems. 286 and 386 systems do not generally require this extra time.
3. If a protection fault occurs in protected mode on 286/386 systems, all bets are off in regard to instruction time.

INDEX

About the Author

Richard Startz is Associate Professor of Economics at the University of Washington. Previously, he taught Finance at the Wharton School of the University of Pennsylvania. He has also been a visiting faculty member at Stanford University and the University of California, San Diego. Startz has been programming as a hobbyist and a professional for over 20 years.

The Norton Portfolio

From Brady Books

Inside the IBM PC

Access to Advanced Features and Programming, Revised and Expanded

by Peter Norton

The most widely recognized book about the IBM PC written by the most highly acclaimed IBM PC expert. Covers the IBM PC, XT and AT, every version of DOS from 1.1 to 3.0.

The classic work includes:

- The fundamentals of the 8088 and 80286 microprocessors, DOS and BIOS
- Programming examples to show how the machine works, in BASIC, Pascal, and Assembly Language
- How ROM is allocated
- A detailed look at disk data storage

Your only source for understanding and using the hardware and software that make up your IBM PC system.

ISBN: 0-89303-583-1 • $21.95 (book)
ISBN: 0-13-467325-5 • $39.95
(book/disk, includes 15 programs)

Peter Norton's Assembly Language Book for the IBM PC

by Peter Norton and John Socha

Learn to write efficient, full-scale assembly language programs that double and even triple your programs' speed. To learn techniques and enhance your knowledge, you'll build a program step-by-step.

The book is divided into three parts:

- Part 1 focuses on the mysteries of the 8088 microprocessor
- Part 2 guides you into assemby language
- Part 3 tackles the PC's more advanced features and debugging techniques

The book disk package includes a fully integrated, powerful disk for instant, hands-on experience in assembly language. The disk contains all the examples discussed in the book, and advanced professional version of the program you build.

With the expertise of Peter Norton and John Socha to guide you, you're guaranteed an experience that's both informative and practical.

ISBN: 0-13-661901-0 • $21.95 (book)
ISBN: 0-13-662149-X • $39.95 (book/disk)
Requires: IBM PC, AT, XT or compatible

Peter Norton's DOS Guide

Revised and Expanded

by Peter Norton

Here's tried and true instruction from the true-blue friend of PC users everywhere. Newly updated with coverage of DOS 3.3, this best-seller is distinguished by Norton's easy-to-follow style and honestly factual approach. Includes advice on hard disk management and discussions of batch files for DOS customization.

Topic-by-topic organization make this manual not only a lively tutorial, but also a long-lasting reference.

ISBN: 0-13-662073-6 • $19.95

To Order:
Complete and mail the form following these advertisements

Brady

More From Robert Jourdain

Turbo Pascal Express

250 Ready-to-Run Assembly Language Routines that Make Turbo Pascal Faster, More Powerful and Easier to Use

Learn to substitute lightning-fast assembly language routines for critical parts of your Turbo Pascal programs with this book/disk package.

Programmers know all too well that 20% of a program takes 80% of the run time. Now run time is pushed into fast forward, thanks to this package. Its two disks are chock-full of more than 250 assembly language routines to manipulate data structures; process strings; handle screens; exploit disk operations; and streamline the fundamental routines that chew up valuable compile time.

The book offers extensive documentation, including details on how each routine functions; specifics on coupling each module to existing programs; hints on avoiding potential trouble spots; and abundant examples of the program modules in action.

ISBN: 0-13-535337-8 • $39.95

Requires: IBM PC, XT, AT or compatible, 256K RAM, 2 disk drives and Turbo Pascal v. 3.0

Programmer's Problem Solver

For the IBM PC, XT & AT

The total IBM programming book you absolutely need. Brady's most comprehensive and insightful complete reference guide to the facts, numbers and procedures you need to achieve program control over PC hardware.

- For programmers in BASIC, Pascal, C and other languages—you'll find disk directory access, keyboard macros, scrolling, paging on the monochrome card, advanced video, and sound control.
- For assembly language programmers—it includes overlays, device drivers, error diagnosis and recovery, COM files, DOS access, and real-time operations.
- For everyone—it explores graphics on the EGA, control of serial and parallel ports and modems, proportional spacing and printer graphics, file operation of all kinds, and assessment of what equipment is installed.

Every section begins with a review of the fundamentals and includes cross-referencing. You'll also find helpful appendices for brand-new programmers, a detailed index, all standard data tables, and an advanced-level glossary. This ultimate reference book is an excellent source of ideas, a valuable tutor, and a tremendous time-saver.

ISBN: 0-89303-787-7 • $22.95

To Order:
Complete and mail the form following these advertisements

Brady

Order Form

Indicate the titles and quantities desired below.
Enclose Check or Money order or use your credit card for payment:

☐ Enclosed is a check for $__________

☐ Charge my ☐ MasterCard ☐ VISA

Account # ____________________

Exp. Date ____________________

Signature ______________________________________

Name ____

Address ____

City __________________________ State _______ Zip _______

(New Jersey residents please add applicable sales tax.)
Dept. 3

Return to:

PH Mail Order Billing
Route 59 at Brook Hill Drive
West Nyack, NY 10994

Title	Code	Quantity	Price	Total

Fold along dotted lines and staple

Place
Postage
Here

PH Mail Order Billing
Route 59 at Brook Hill Drive
West Nyack, NY 10994